THE LIBRARY
ST. MARY'S COLLEGE OF MARYLAND
ST. MARY'S CITY, MARYLAND 20686

SIOUX INDIAN RELIGION

SIOUX INDIAN RELIGION
Tradition and Innovation

EDITED AND WITH AN INTRODUCTION BY

Raymond J. DeMallie and Douglas R. Parks

ILLUSTRATIONS BY ARTHUR AMIOTTE

UNIVERSITY OF OKLAHOMA PRESS : NORMAN AND LONDON

EDITED BY RAYMOND J. DEMALLIE

Lakota Belief and Ritual, by James R. Walker (coedited with Elaine A. Jahner) (Lincoln, Nebr., 1980)

Lakota Society, by James R. Walker (Lincoln, Nebr., 1982)

The Sixth Grandfather: Black Elk's Teachings Given to John G. Neihardt (Lincoln, Nebr., 1984)

Sioux Indian Religion: Tradition and Innovation (Norman, 1987)

WRITTEN OR BY DOUGLAS R. PARKS

A Grammar of Pawnee (New York, 1976)

Ceremonies of the Pawnee by James R. Murie (ed.) (Washington, D.C., 1981)

Sioux Indian Religion: Tradition and Innovation (ed.) (Norman, 1987)

Library of Congress Cataloging-in-Publication Data

Sioux Indian religion.

  Bibliography: p.
  Includes index.
  1. Dakota Indians—Religion and mythology—
Congresses. I. DeMallie, Raymond J., 1946–
II. Parks, Douglas R.
E99.D1S5   1987   299′.78   86-40527
ISBN 0-8061-2055-X (alk. paper)

The paper in this book meets the guidelines for permanence and durability of the Committee on Production Guidelines for Book Longevity of the Council on Library Resources, Inc.

Copyright © 1987 by the University of Oklahoma Press, Norman, Publishing Division of the University. Manufactured in the U.S.A. First edition.

Contents

Acknowledgments

WE wish to acknowledge the North Dakota Humanities Council, which supported the symposium "American Indian Religion in the Dakotas: Historical and Contemporary Perspectives," April 1 and 2, 1982, at Bismarck, North Dakota. Most of the chapters of this book originated from the symposium. Thanks are also extended to the North Dakota Heritage Center and Mary College for providing facilities for the sessions. Wilbur Red Tomahawk and other student members of the Sacred Hoop Indian Club at Mary College handled many practical details, including the registration of those who attended the symposium. David Reed Miller kindly oversaw the tape-recording of the talks.

We have received aid and encouragement from many individuals in the process of preparing this volume for publication. Special thanks are extended to Father Peter John Powell and Professor Omer C. Stewart for their careful reading of the manuscript. Maria LaVigna and the staff of Fort Belknap College in Montana helped to prepare the manuscript copy. Final editing and preparation of this collection for publication was accomplished at the American Indian Studies Research Institute, Indiana University.

Arthur Amiotte generously allowed us to reproduce some of the paintings in his series "Work from the Shamanic Tradition" as illustrations in this volume. Combining deep knowledge of tribal traditions with artistic accomplishment, his canvases are powerful expressions of the attitudes and cultural directions of Native Americans today.

Our greatest debt, of course, is to the participants and the audience who made the symposium a truly religious event in the universal sense of the term. We hope that that spirit is reflected in the pages of this book.

Bloomington, Indiana   RAYMOND J. DeMALLIE
Bloomington, Indiana   DOUGLAS R. PARKS

SIOUX INDIAN RELIGION

Introduction

BY RAYMOND J. DeMALLIE AND DOUGLAS R. PARKS

A TEMPORARY VILLAGE of tents and trailers was circled on the level prairie along the Moreau River at the community of Green Grass, South Dakota, on Cheyenne River Reservation. As we drove down the hill into the valley on August 24, 1980, the bustle of activity was striking. A circular dance arbor had been erected, roofed with now dry cottonwood boughs, their leaves rustling in the hot wind. The sky was cloudless blue. Near the arbor men and women came and went from their separate purification lodges, preparing themselves in the cleansing steam of the sweat bath for the sacred work to follow. A short distance down the dusty road, part way up a hill overlooking the river, a small group of the main participants waited expectantly under a sunshade at the home of Stanley and Celia Looking Horse, the parents of Arval Looking Horse, keeper of the Buffalo Calf Pipe, the most sacred possession of the Lakota people and the very soul of their religious life.

The occasion for this gathering was a ceremony with the Sacred Pipe bundle, in which the Buffalo Calf Pipe is contained. Following instructions from the spirits and fearful of the disrespect they sensed among many who professed themselves believers in the old religion, the keeper and his family had determined to put the Pipe away for seven years, giving the people time to reflect and reorganize and once again be worthy of the blessings that flow from the Pipe. Those who had assembled for this occasion were perhaps two or three hundred individuals. Most of them were Sioux; a few were whites. Many of the Indian people came from cities as far away as Los Angeles, and had borne the financial sacrifices necessary for the long trip because of the special sacredness of this historic occasion. Some of the people had come to the camp for political reasons, to attend a meeting of the Lakota Treaty Council held during the preceding week. Their intention was to help in the struggle for the return of lands, particularly the Black Hills, and to obtain other treaty rights. Most stayed for the Pipe ceremony. Although some individuals resented the presence of non-Indians on this occasion, and said so openly, others expressed satisfaction that the power of the Sacred Pipe had attracted many diverse people, and they prayed that it would bring us all together. In the end the harmony engendered by this sacred event transcended jealousies and suspicions.

When the time was right, the people, carrying sage in their hands to dispel evil, walked barefoot up the hill behind the pipe keeper's home to the small structure where the Sacred Pipe is kept. As we passed one by one through a narrow gateway formed by placing two cottonwood saplings in the earth, we were blessed by attendants waving burning sweetgrass and an eagle-wing fan. As individuals stepped through the entryway into the sacred space, they turned about clockwise, presenting themselves to all the universe.

The door of the red-painted metal building in which the Sacred Pipe is kept was opened, and a large drum was brought out. A group of men sat on the ground around the drum and sang ritual songs. Meanwhile, a wooden tripod was set up in the middle of an altar defined by four cottonwood saplings, from which cloth banners of the sacred colors of the six directions were tied: black on the west, red on the north, yellow on the east, white on the south; a green banner on the east representing the earth, and a blue banner on the west representing the sky. The pipe keeper brought out the Calf Pipe bundle and rested it on the tripod. After the holy men who directed the ceremony had prayed with the bundle, touching their hands to it reverently, the Indian participants filed in, walking clockwise around the bundle, stopping to pray and touch it. Some burst into tears, overcome by the sacredness of the act. All those who owned pipes of their own carried them in their arms, the long fringes of the decorated tobacco pouches dangling in front of them. At the conclusion of the ceremony all the pipe carriers filled their pipes simultaneously with a mixture of tobacco and red willow bark, and all were lighted at once and offered to the six directions and to the pipe bundle, bringing power from the Calf Pipe itself to these individual pipes. They became like the branches of the Sacred Pipe, the pipe keeper said, sharing in its sacred power.

After the ceremony was concluded, and the Calf Pipe bundle was returned to its enclosure, together with an offering of a painted buffalo robe given by one of the participants in fulfillment of a vow, all the people joined in a feast of boiled buffalo meat, chokecherry pudding, fried bread, and coffee. While we were eating, an elder woman harangued the group, reminding us that this was the last time for seven years that we would see the Sacred Pipe bundle, that this was the fault of those who had strayed from their Indian ways, that the people must have proper respect and honor for the old traditions if they expect to live as Lakotas and maintain their dignity and integrity in the whites' world. We watched as many of the younger people, heads turned away, appeared to be paying no attention; but their respectful attitude revealed that the woman's talk was being heard.

Among the people who had gathered at Green Grass on this occasion were at least six individuals—some Indian, some white—who identify themselves with the academic discipline of anthropology. All had come out of respect for the occasion, to participate in the event rather than to study it. The good feeling of sharing and care that grew out of the ceremony brought home forcefully to our minds the dichotomy that seems inevitably to exist between those who study religious traditions and those who live them on a daily basis. If a way could be found to bring scholars and religious leaders together and bridge the gap, the harmony of this ritual occasion might be generalized into mutual appreciation and understanding.

At home in Bismarck, North Dakota, we spoke frequently during the following year of how to bring about such an event—a ritual in itself—that might serve to smooth over misunderstandings and mistrust and bring together scholars and believers to explore American Indian religion today. In talking with Indian students at Mary College we found great interest in sponsoring such an event. Since 1976 the Mary College Indian student association, the Sacred Hoop Indian Club, had hosted an annual spring celebration consisting of a powwow and some associated activity of general interest to Indians on campus. The club, and especially Wilbur Red Tomahawk, the club president, urged the development of a program centering around the general topic of the past and present religious life of American Indian people in the Dakotas.

To bring this about, we drew up a proposal for a two-day symposium. First we decided that it would be most effective to narrow the topic. Instead of attempting to deal with the religious experience of all the tribal groups in North and South Dakota, we decided to limit consideration to the Sioux. There were many reasons for this. Above all, there is a large body of historical scholarship on Sioux religious life from which to draw. There are many people, both Indian and white, currently involved in such studies. And Sioux religious life today is varied and rich.

Historically the Sioux comprised a large number of bands, joined together in political units at a tribal level. During the midnineteenth century three broad geographical groups were identified. The eastern Sioux (sometimes called the Santees) lived in the forested area from the upper Mississippi and Minnesota rivers westward onto the prairies of Minnesota and North and South Dakota. The western or Teton Sioux lived on the prairies and plains of North and South Dakota, moving mostly west of the Missouri River by the midnineteenth century. Geographically intermediate were the Yankton and

Yanktonai Sioux who lived on the prairies of Minnesota and the eastern portion of North and South Dakota. These groups are frequently called by their self-designation: *Dakota* in the Santee, Yankton, and Yanktonai dialects, and *Lakota* in the Teton dialect. (The Yanktons and Yanktonais are frequently characterized in the literature as *Nakota*, although there is no historical evidence that these people ever used an initial *n* in their name; throughout recorded history they have called themselves *Dakota*. The closely related Assiniboines of Montana and the prairie provinces of Canada, however, do call themselves *Nakota*.) (For discussion of Sioux social organization see "The Structure of Society" in Walker 1982:3–67.)

Today the Sioux people in the United States and Canada number over fifty thousand, somewhat less than half of whom live on reservations and reserves. The locus for contemporary religious revitalization is among the Teton peoples living in South Dakota: the Oglalas at Pine Ridge Reservation; the Brules at Rosebud Reservation; the Lower Brules at Lower Brule Reservation; the Minneconjous, Sans Arcs, and Two Kettles at Cheyenne River Reservation; and the Hunkpapas and Blackfoot Sioux at Standing Rock Reservation. Ritual leaders from these reservations have stimulated religious revival elsewhere, including the Sioux reservations in Nebraska, Minnesota, North Dakota, and Montana, as well as the Sioux reserves in Manitoba and Saskatchewan. (For maps and a presentation of contemporary Sioux political groupings see Nurge 1970:299–304.)

The diversity of religious practices on the Sioux reservations reflects the historical interaction of two main traditions, indigenous religion and Christianity. The Sioux people have had contact with Christian missionaries for over three centuries. Among some Sioux groups traditional and Christian practices have become amalgamated; among others they are kept strictly separate. Christian influences on the Sioux represent a wide variety of denominations, each of which has distinctively colored the varieties of Christianity practiced by the Sioux. Nor is traditional religion itself to be seen as a monolithic system, for it reflects the blending of many strains of ideas over the past centuries.

Using the perspective of comparative religion, it is possible to suggest several historical developments in Sioux religion that occurred before the start of the nineteenth century. These would include a fundamental system of belief, articulated in myth, widely shared by related groups of Indian peoples on the plains and prairies; the Pipe complex; the development of the Sun Dance as the focus of religious ritual; and *wakan* (power, the sacred) as the basis of the Lakotas' culturally distinctive theory of existence. Although such a historical approach does little to explicate the Lakota peoples' own religious perspectives, it helps us to appreciate the continuous development in form and content of their religious tradition. (See, for example, Hultkrantz 1979, 1980.)

In 1889 news of a world-renewal rite, the Ghost Dance religion, founded by the Paiute prophet Wovoka, spread from Nevada to the Sioux in South Dakota. By 1890 a considerable portion of the Sioux population had joined in the dances, temporarily setting aside older rituals in favor of the new. The Ghost Dances in South Dakota seemed to come to an abrupt end on December 29, 1890, with the massacre of about two hundred Lakotas by the U.S. Army at Wounded Knee. Afterward, a few ceremonial leaders continued to proselytize for the Ghost Dance, and in 1891 the dance spread to the Yanktonai Sioux at Cannon Ball, North Dakota, on Standing Rock Reservation. From there it spread to the Sioux in Canada, where some features of Ghost Dance belief and ritual became routinized and incorporated into the traditional religious structure. Vestiges survive even today (see Howard 1984:173–79). Sioux people have made occasional attempts to revive the dance, most recently in conjunction with the 1973 American Indian Movement takeover of the village of Wounded Knee. Although little substantive belief or ritual remains from the Ghost Dance, some old people still recall the poignant songs of the ceremony; and the massacre at Wounded Knee Creek still stands as a symbol of white oppression and intolerance of Indian religion.

The peyote religion began to be introduced to the southernmost Sioux reservations (Yankton, Rosebud, and Pine Ridge) during the early years of the twentieth century. Never strong, the Native American Church is nonetheless visible and important for the Sioux today. Many Sioux people, both members and nonmembers of the Native American Church, sense an antagonism between the use of peyote and the use of the pipe as means of prayer. Others find them compatible. Among the Sioux one Cross Fire group of Native American Church members more fully integrates the Bible and adds a greater number of Christian teachings to their services; under the name of the Native American Church of Jesus Christ, led by Emerson Spider, Sr., they seek to make the peyote religion a Christian sect. The more traditionally oriented Cross Fire groups, as well as the Half Moon groups, identify themselves as members of a traditional Native American religion and reject formal connections with Christianity. The peyote religion has not become integrated into the fabric of Lakota traditionalism, but it has had an undoubted effect in relating Sioux individuals through the Native American Church to pan-Indian movements in Oklahoma and throughout the country.

The history of Sioux contact with Christianity is, of course, well documented in the written record. The earliest contacts between the Sioux and Christian missionaries occurred in the area of Wisconsin and Minnesota, where the Jesuit missionary explorers Claude Allouez and Jacques Marquette first met the eastern Sioux about 1665. Sporadic visits from Roman Catholic missionaries continued throughout the seventeenth and eighteenth centuries. Between 1841 and 1846, Father Augustine Ravoux established a mission among the Sioux in Minnesota, and in 1847 he visited the Sioux on the Missouri River at Fort Pierre, but his superiors subsequently reassigned him out of the mission field. Father Pierre Jean De Smet made his first visit to the Sioux in 1839, when he visited the Yanktons to arrange for a peace between them and the Potawatomis; he continued to make periodic visits to the Yanktons and other Sioux along the Missouri River until his death in 1873. During these visits De Smet preached and baptized, but was unable to establish a permanent mission station. (See Duratschek 1947:5–6, 40–41, 56–57.)

The first mission station actually established among the Sioux began in 1834 when the American Board of Commissioners for Foreign Missions authorized T. S. Williamson to found a mission among the Sioux in Minnesota. The next year, Williamson, Jedidiah D. Stevens, and the brothers Gideon and Samuel Pond all arrived among the eastern Sioux and began mission work. In 1837, Stephen Return Riggs also joined the ABCFM mission to the Sioux. These missionaries, together with their children, subsequently dominated the Presbyterian and Congregational mission field among the Sioux. (See Willand 1964:11, 31, 84; Riggs 1887; Barton 1919.)

The Episcopalians entered the Sioux mission field somewhat later. Samuel D. Hinman established a mission and school at Lower Sioux Agency in Minnesota in 1860. The expulsion of the Sioux from Minnesota following the 1862 uprising, however, effectively terminated missionary activity among the Sioux there. (See Church Missions 1914:106–107.)

In the wake of the military campaigns against the Sioux following the uprising, the refugees were gathered together in camps, and those men accused of murder were imprisoned at Davenport, Iowa. Christian missionaries from all denominations visited both the refugees and the prisoners and made many conversions. T. S. Williamson and S. R. Riggs devoted themselves to educating and preaching to the prisoners from 1863 until their release in 1866. John P. Williamson ministered to the refugees, and in 1863 he went with them to Crow Creek Reservation in Dakota, then on to their final home at Santee, Nebraska. In 1869, John P. Williamson moved to the Yankton Reservation to establish the mission that would be his life's work, and Alfred L. Riggs took over at Santee. There he built the first high school, the Santee Normal School,

which became the center at which Sioux children could receive education in their own language. The following year,
S. R. Riggs founded a mission on the Sisseton Reservation in
Dakota Territory. In 1871, Thomas L. Riggs established a mission on Cheyenne River Reservation. This network of missions was expanded during the late 1880s to include all the
Sioux reservations in both of the Dakotas and Montana. The
first general conference of the Sioux mission churches was
held at Flandreau, a colony founded in eastern Dakota by
educated Santees in 1871, and the annual event served to
unite the missions' endeavors and celebrate their successes.
(See Riggs 1887; Duratschek 1947.)

The inauguration of President Grant's Indian peace policy
in 1869 led to the assignment of Indian agencies to the various
Christian churches. Each church was asked to nominate men
to serve as Indian agents to take responsibility for leading the
Indians of the agencies under their supervision to Christian
civilization. By 1872 the Sioux agencies had been divided up
among three churches. The Roman Catholics were assigned to
the Grand River (later Standing Rock) and Devils Lake agencies. The Episcopalians were responsible for Whetstone (later
Rosebud), Upper Missouri (part of which later became Crow
Creek), Cheyenne River, Red Cloud (later Pine Ridge), and
Yankton. The Hicksite Friends, who were never involved in
mission work with the Sioux, were given the Santee Reservation in Nebraska, only because it fell within the jurisdiction of
the Northern Superintendency, which had been assigned
them as a whole. (See Prucha 1984 1:513–19.)

The impetus provided by this system, which remained in
effect until 1881, encouraged churches to establish permanent
mission stations on the Sioux reservations. In 1872 the newly
consecrated bishop of the Missionary District of the Niobrara
in the Episcopal Church, William H. Hare, took up the challenge of Christianizing the Sioux. That year he held the first
convocation at the Santee mission, and he continued to attend
annually until his death in 1909. The convocations are still an
annual event. During Bishop Hare's long tenure he oversaw

the establishment of Episcopal missions on all the Sioux reservations in the Dakotas and Nebraska. He also founded boarding schools to provide children with Christian educations. Bishop Hare's personality and the commitment given to him personally by many Indian priests and deacons were the force behind a very successful program of missionization. (See Church Missions 1914:107–23.)

Although the Roman Catholic Church made initial moves toward establishing missions in 1871, it was not until 1876, when the Benedictine abbot Martin Marty committed himself and his order to the field, that permanent mission stations were established. Beginning at Standing Rock and Devils Lake, the Benedictines extended their work to other Sioux reservations as well. In 1885, Marty invited a group of German Jesuits to take up the work at the Rosebud and Pine Ridge reservations. The missions they founded remain among the most active Christian missions among the Sioux even to the present. Like the other churches, the Catholics eventually established missions on all the Sioux reservations. The first Catholic Indian Congress was held at Standing Rock in 1891, and the congresses have continued annually since. (Duratschek 1947.)

The programs of missionization followed by each of these churches were very similar. Native ministers, deacons, and catechists were trained to serve as agents for converting other Indians and for administering the routine daily needs of the congregations. Schools, aimed at inculcating the white way of life in conjunction with the fundamentals of Christian religion, were important to all the mission endeavors. And annual convocations provided social occasions to renew commitment, assess progress, and enjoy the satisfaction of accomplishments. In the last two decades of the nineteenth century the missionaries observed their Sioux congregations transformed from hunters dressed in Indian garb to would-be farmers wearing the clothes of western civilization. And the training of native clergy gave promise that the mission structure would be superceded by true native churches.

The Christian missions provided the Sioux on their reservations with a focus for organized activity that met with official support from the Indian agents. The Indian ministers, priests, deacons, and catechists formed a kind of local elite dedicated to helping their people through the access to money, influence, and spiritual strength provided by the churches. It is important to recognize the substantial political and economic advantages of church membership as well as exclusively religious motives. An individual's conversion to one of these Christian denominations should not be assumed necessarily to entail the rejection of native Sioux traditional religion.

During the past century there has been a great deal of additional missionary work among the Sioux by a wide variety of Christian churches; the plurality of Christianity among the Sioux reflects that of the rest of American society. Most of these efforts represent outsiders' concerns for bringing Christian belief to the Indian people, but some of them—like the Body of Christ Independent Church at Pine Ridge—have been founded by Sioux people themselves. (See Steinmetz 1980:133–40.)

In recent years fundamentalist Christian sects (such as the Body of Christ Independent Church) have been introduced on the Sioux reservations, reflecting the growing popularity of fundamentalism in the rest of American society. The Church of Jesus Christ of Latter-Day Saints has also proselytized extensively and established a network of church buildings. These denominations actively oppose most expressions of traditional Sioux religion and seek to transcend cultural differences between Indians and non-Indians. Like the Native American Church, these sects are numerically small but vocal and visible in the context of reservation life.

The Sioux today reflect their historically complex religious heritage. Some continuity of traditional religious beliefs and practices has been maintained wherever Sioux people live. Central to this is the pipe as the means of prayer to the Powers of the Universe, *Wakan Tanka*, the Great Mysterious. The offering of the pipe, the physical and spiritual cleansing of the

purification lodge (sweat lodge), the individual sacrifice of
the vision quest, the communal sacrifice of the Sun Dance,
and the healing and conjuring rites of *yuwipi* and *lowanpi*
("sings") have been practiced, to a greater or lesser degree,
without interruption during the past century. These traditional practices seem to have had special continuity at the Pine
Ridge and Rosebud reservations, where religious specialists
have preserved the old ritual knowledge, and today these specialists are sharing that knowledge with younger religious
leaders on other reservations. On all the Sioux reservations
today there is a great reawakening of traditional religious
roots and a re-creation of traditional religious rituals, in which
ever-increasing numbers of Sioux people, young and old, are
participating.

At the same time most Sioux people maintain membership
in, and belief in the efficacy of, some Christian denomination.
Many of the leaders of traditional ceremonies belong to the
Roman Catholic or Episcopal churches. They see no conflict
between traditional beliefs and ceremonies and those of Christianity. For most of the past century they have kept these two
religious modes separate. Some Sioux men entered the ranks
of the clergy and preached against traditional religious practices, but most solved any potential conflict by compartmen-
talizing Christian and traditional activities.

In recent years (since the Second Vatican Council in the
early 1960s directed increased local involvement in church
matters and use of vernacular languages in church rituals) the
Catholic Church has attempted to integrate aspects of traditional Sioux belief and ritual with Church doctrine. Thus the
Pipe, as intermediator between man and God, has become
identified with Christ; the Sun Dance tree, mediating earth
and heaven as the symbol of salvation, has become identified
with the Cross; and White Buffalo Woman, who brought the
pipe to the Sioux people, has become identified with the Virgin Mary. In what has come to be called "fulfillment theology,"
the Catholic Church views these Lakota forms as prefiguring
the coming of Christ—preparing the people to accept the Re-

deemer. Some Indians and whites appreciate this doctrine as providing a new equality, or at least parallelism, between traditional and Christian practices. For others the doctrine amounts only to a restatement of the subordination of traditional beliefs to church doctrine. In either case, the dialogue between traditional Indian religion and Christianity is currently a focus of much religious activity on Sioux reservations.

In order to reflect Sioux religious diversity, we planned the symposium to include a representative cross section and drew up a list of essential topics and potential speakers. It was immediately obvious that such a selection could not exhaust the variety of Sioux religious life. Our goal was to explore the various religious traditions of the Sioux people, viewing them from both historical and contemporary perspectives. Reflecting the religious background of the students at Mary College, which was founded by Benedictine sisters, we focused part of the symposium around Roman Catholic missionization as a case study in the Sioux religious experience with Christianity.

The individuals brought together through the symposium included religious leaders who live Sioux traditions, as well as scholars who study these traditions. Their topics included traditional religion and myth, Christian churches, the Native American Church, and revitalized traditional religions today. The aim was to present many different viewpoints on the religious life of the Sioux, thereby gaining understanding of the entire course of Sioux religious history during the past century. In the process we hoped to learn much about the Sioux, but more broadly, we hoped to gain deeper insights into all of humanity's religious needs, responses, and sentiments—how these are specially expressed by the Sioux people but also how, in spite of outward differences, they are shared by all human beings, no matter their culture.

Entitled "American Indian Religion in the Dakotas: Historical and Contemporary Perspectives," the symposium took place at Mary College and at the North Dakota Heritage Center in Bismarck on April 1 and 2, 1982. Despite inclement weather, there was good attendance by people from through-

out North Dakota and several adjacent states. Many of those
attending were Native Americans from reservations in North
and South Dakota. Talks were scheduled to allow ample time
for personal interaction between the speakers and the audience. The evening before the symposium, Arthur Amiotte,
the Lakota artist, opened a showing of "Current Works From
the Shamanic Tradition" at the North Dakota Heritage Center.
His stark canvases, emblazoned with bold images reflecting
petroglyphs and pictographs, evoke the ancient roots of Lakota
religious traditions. On the first evening of the symposium
Dr. Joseph Epes Brown, professor of religion at the University of Montana, presented a public lecture at the North Dakota Heritage Center, entitled "Perspectives on American Indian Spirituality." Lavishly illustrated with slides, the talk
reinforced the symposium's message of respect and appreciation for the diversity of religious traditions.

The talks presented to the symposium at Mary College
were tape-recorded and transcribed. In order to transform the
oral presentations into written ones, we reorganized material
and edited for clarity. We regularized grammar and attempted
to live up to academic standards of style while we tried to retain the flavor and immediacy of the oral presentations. This
book reflects the structure of the symposium.

Part One is entitled "Foundations of Traditional Sioux Religion." In Chapter 1, "Lakota Belief and Ritual in the Nineteenth Century," Raymond J. DeMallie has attempted to synthesize from the literature written by Lakota people the
traditional foundations of their religion. Utilizing both published and unpublished material, he has summarized the
fundamental beliefs that constitute the common ground for
Lakota religious thought and for the rituals through which
nineteenth-century Lakotas actualized belief in daily life. Although his essay is a description of the past, many of the concepts presented are strongly reflected or continued in contemporary Lakota religious life. Dr. DeMallie is professor of
anthropology and director of the American Indian Studies Research Institute at Indiana University. He has long been inter-

ested in traditional Lakota culture and society. With Elaine A. Jahner he edited the collection of turn-of-the-century documents concerning traditional Lakota religion written and compiled by James R. Walker at Pine Ridge (Walker 1980), and he has edited the interviews of John G. Neihardt with Black Elk, the Oglala holy man (DeMallie 1984).

In Chapter 2, "Lakota Genesis: The Oral Tradition," Elaine A. Jahner complements the first chapter by providing an introduction to basic Lakota mythological beliefs. She outlines the concepts of creation synthesized and written down by James R. Walker from materials he recorded at Pine Ridge between 1896 and 1914. Although they present an outsider's perspective on Lakota sacred traditions, Walker's materials provide the kind of systematic overview of mythic foundations for which many modern Lakota people are searching. Jahner also explains that Walker's synthesis was based on firsthand accounts written in Lakota by George Sword. She makes the important observation that for traditional Lakota people genesis was (and still is) perceived as an ongoing process described clearly in their myths. Dr. Jahner, professor of English and a member of the Native American Studies faculty at Dartmouth College, has edited Walker's manuscripts on Lakota myth (Walker 1983) and has long been a student of Lakota oral literature.

In Chapter 3, "The Sacred Pipe in Modern Life," Arval Looking Horse recounts the origin of the bringing of the sacred Buffalo Pipe to the Lakota people by White Buffalo Woman long ago, the gift that laid the foundation for the Lakota way of life. Mr. Looking Horse's account suggests the important role that the Sacred Pipe plays in daily life for Lakotas today. A member of the Cheyenne River Sioux Tribe, Mr. Looking Horse is hereditary keeper of the Sacred Pipe and resides in Green Grass, South Dakota, on the Cheyenne River Reservation.

In Chapter 4, "The Lakota Sun Dance: Historical and Contemporary Perspectives," Arthur Amiotte emphasizes the countinuity of traditional beliefs and practices in the Sun

Dance as it has been reinstituted on Standing Rock Reservation. He presents a moving account of the preparations for
and performance of the Sun Dance, based on his deep personal involvement in this most sacred of all Sioux religious
ceremonies. Mr. Amiotte, a member of the Oglala Sioux
Tribe, is a professional artist. At the time of the symposium he
was engaged in curriculum research at Standing Rock Community College. He currently resides in Custer, South Dakota, and is completing a master's degree in religious studies
at the University of Montana.

Part Two of this symposium volume is devoted to "Christianity and the Sioux." In Chapter 5, "The Establishment of
Christianity Among the Sioux," Vine V. Deloria, Sr., reflects
on his long life's experience in mission work, both as the son of
an Episcopal priest and as an Episcopal priest himself. Father
Deloria presents an engaging and very personal account of not
only the establishment of Christianity among the Sioux but
also its very real presence among them today. We interviewed
Father Deloria at his home in Pierre, South Dakota, and have
incorporated additional material into his chapter here, particularly the details of his grandfather's traditional religious
life and conversion to Christianity. Father Deloria is a member of the Standing Rock Sioux Tribe. As an archdeacon he has
earned the honorific "Venerable" in the Episcopal Church and
is well known to the Sioux on every reservation.

In Chapter 6, "Catholic Mission and the Sioux: A Crisis in
the Early Paradigm," Harvey Markowitz briefly summarizes
the history of Catholic missionization and reveals some of the
moral and philosophical attitudes of the early missionaries.
He suggests that simplistic notions of conversion to Christianity should be replaced by more dynamic analyses of the
complex ideological and emotional relationship between missionaries and Indian people. Mr. Markowitz has an M.A. in
anthropology and has lived since 1976 at Saint Francis, South
Dakota. He teaches at Sinte Gleska College on Rosebud Reservation and is currently working on a doctorate in missiology
at the Divinity School of the University of Chicago.

In Chapter 7, "Contemporary Catholic Mission Work Among the Sioux," Father Robert Hilbert, S.J., carries some of the themes of the previous chapter into the context of today, revealing the dilemmas of principle and belief that lie at the heart of the mission endeavor. He discusses the wide range of opinion among the Jesuits at Saint Francis Mission concerning the direction and efficacy of their work, and his chapter is a clear reminder how mistaken it is to attribute to missionaries as a group any monolithic ethical or practical stance. Father Hilbert also testifies to the increasing desire among Catholic missionaries today for socially relevant involvement with Indian people, in addition to more traditional spiritual concerns. Father Hilbert is a missionary priest at Saint Francis Mission on Rosebud Reservation.

In Chapter 8, "Christian Life Fellowship Church," Mercy Poor Man expresses the commitment to religious fundamentalism on the Sioux reservations today. Although this topic was not treated at the symposium, we felt that the visibility of fundamentalist churches is such that they should be represented in this book. This chapter is based on an interview tape-recorded in September 1984 by Harvey Markowitz. Mrs. Poor Man, a member of the Rosebud Sioux Tribe, is a minister in the Assembly of God Church on Rosebud Reservation.

Part Three is entitled "Traditional Religion in the Contemporary Context." Chapter 9, "Indian Women and the Renaissance of Traditional Religion," by Beatrice Medicine, is based on personal experiences, including participation in the Sun Dance as the representative of White Buffalo Woman. Of all the contributors to the volume, Dr. Medicine embodies most thoroughly in her own life both the participant in and the student of traditional religion. She particularly emphasizes the involvement of women in the revitalization of the Sun Dance at Standing Rock Reservation. She also stresses the importance of Sioux women's rituals such as the girls' puberty ceremony and suggests the potential value of revitalizing them as well, and the need for complementary understanding of both women's and men's roles in order to gain thorough comprehen-

sion of Lakota culture. Dr. Medicine, a member of the Standing Rock Sioux Tribe, is professor of anthropology and director
of Native American Studies at the University of Calgary, Al-
berta. A lifelong student of and participant in Lakota ways,
she has published many papers on Lakota religion, education,
and women's roles and has edited with Patricia Albers a collection of papers on Plains Indian women (Albers and Medicine 1983).

In Chapter 10, "The Contemporary *Yuwipi*," Thomas H.
Lewis, M.D., describes the religious ritual in which a shaman
communicates with spirits who bring messages and blessings
to the living. Dr. Lewis bases his paper on his personal involvement with the mental-health program on Pine Ridge Reservation and on close associations with several Pine Ridge medicine
men. He particularly emphasizes the role of these ritual leaders and associated religious beliefs in health care. A practicing
psychiatrist currently living in Billings, Montana, Dr. Lewis
has written several papers on Oglala religion and health care.

Chapter 11, "The Native American Church of Jesus Christ,"
by Emerson Spider, Sr., is the story of the historical involvement of Mr. Spider's family with the development of the Native American Church of Jesus Christ, his own conversion to
the faith, and the meaning of the peyote ritual to him. Mr.
Spider emphasizes his wish to merge the Native American
Church with Christian beliefs and expresses the desire that
the legitimacy of his church be recognized by other Christian
denominations. He speaks out of deep personal conviction,
recognizing nonetheless that his point of view is not shared by
all Sioux Native American Church members. Mr. Spider was
unable to attend the symposium as planned, and this chapter
is based on a tape-recorded interview with him in August
1982. Mr. Spider, bishop of the Native American Church of
Jesus Christ, is a member of the Oglala Sioux Tribe and lives
at Porcupine, South Dakota, on Pine Ridge Reservation.

Chapter 12, "Traditional Lakota Religion in Modern Life,"
by Robert Stead, is an account of becoming a medicine man
and the responsibility of guiding traditional spiritual matters

in today's world. Mr. Stead is a member of the Rosebud Sioux
Tribe and lives at Ring Thunder, South Dakota, on Rosebud
Reservation. He is well known for the power of his ceremonies to heal and to bring peace of mind, and he frequently
travels off-reservation to hold ceremonies wherever they may
be requested. Kenneth Oliver, a young Rosebud Sioux man
who has been studying with him as an apprentice, introduced
Mr. Stead at the symposium, and his remarks are printed here.

"Suggestions for Further Reading," a topically arranged
bibliographical essay on Sioux religion compiled by the editors, concludes the volume. It is intended as a guide to the
major published sources and will allow readers to follow up
specific subjects of interest.

Each of these chapters presents a very personal perspective
on Sioux religious traditions. The academicians live up to
scholarly canons and present analytical points of view. The
nonacademic contributors express personal convictions, and
some of their facts and ideas may contradict the academic find-
ings of historians or anthropologists. This volume, like the
symposium from which it results, juxtaposes diverse points of
view. It is intended to provide source material for further discussion, not to stifle debate or articulate consensus. Our hope
is that these essays will stimulate study and demonstrate that
even in so vital an area as religion, the presentation and expli-
cation of a wide spectrum of opinion, from both insiders' and
outsiders' perspectives, can generate mutual understanding.

Many common themes emerge from the chapters. Fore-
most is the continuity of basic ideas permeating virtually all
Lakota religious traditions. For example, there is the firmly
rooted belief that the spirits of the dead are not gone and lost
to mankind but exist here and can be reached for support and
aid. The reverence for traditional Lakota spiritual forms and
concepts, and the pervasive concern with power (*wakan*)—
the sacred—as it is reflected in the workings of this world is a
further unifying thread among the traditions. The sharpest
point of division comes with Christianity, some individuals
finding belief in Christ incompatible with belief in the Sacred

Pipe. Yet the majority of the speakers in the symposium, as well as the majority of the audience who expressed opinions, clearly favored mutual tolerance and acceptance of alternative traditions. Indeed, most Sioux people express themselves as perfectly comfortable embracing more than one such tradition in their own beliefs and practices. This spirit of tolerance and sharing made the entire experience of participating in the symposium and preparing these chapters for publication an especially rich and rewarding one.

PART ONE

FOUNDATIONS OF TRADITIONAL
SIOUX RELIGION

1

Lakota Belief and Ritual in the Nineteenth Century

BY RAYMOND J. DeMALLIE

TRADITIONAL Lakota belief and ritual, as they existed in the last century, have been extensively recorded. We are fortunate that substantial bodies of material, written in the Lakota language by native Lakota people themselves, have been preserved. The writings of George Bushotter (1887–88), George Sword (ca. 1909), Thomas Tyon (ca. 1911), and Ivan Stars (ca. 1915–20)—to name only the most prolific—form a native corpus for understanding traditional culture that is unparalleled for any other Plains tribe. Bushotter and Sword wrote from their own experiences, while Tyon and Stars interviewed other, nonliterate Lakotas to record their stories. The great value of these writings is that they have not been tampered with by outsiders; they present the Lakotas' own viewpoints, expressed in their own words.

In addition to those writings we have been bequeathed an even larger body of material dictated by Lakotas and written down by non-Indians. In this category the outstanding pioneer investigators were James R. Walker (1896–1914), Edward S. Curtis (1905–1908), Frances Densmore (1911–1914), and Aaron McGaffey Beede (ca. 1912–20). From later times we find an ever-increasing quantity of recorded material concerning Lakota culture, of which the most significant part has been the teachings of Nicholas Black Elk, the Oglala holy man, dictated to John G. Neihardt (1931 and 1944) and to

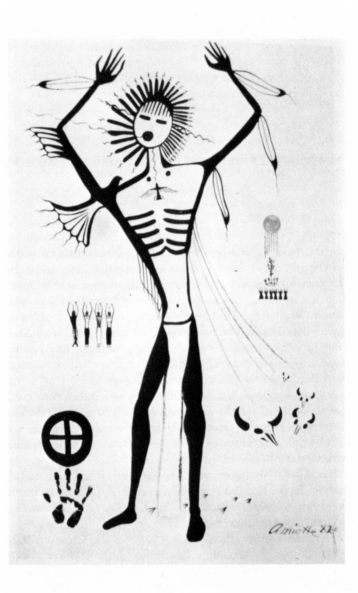

Joseph Epes Brown (1947–49). Also invaluable are the large number of translations of earlier Lakota writings, as well as interviews in Lakota and writings in English, by Ella C. Deloria (ca. 1929–60), herself a Yankton Sioux.

A brief summary of the foundations of nineteenth-century Lakota religion, based on these source materials, will serve as an introduction to the traditional concepts to which religious developments during the past century may be compared. This personal interpretation, developed from my studies as a cultural anthropologist, represents only one of the various perspectives from which nineteenth-century Lakota religion can be understood. Many of the basic concepts of this traditional religious system are still alive among the Lakota people today, who continue to develop them in the context of modern life.

Central to my understanding of Lakota religion is an anthropological concept of culture that focuses on symbols and meanings shared, to a greater or lesser extent, by the individuals who compose a society (see Geertz 1973:3–30). My goal here is to make the implicit meanings that structured nineteenth-century Lakota religion intelligible in terms of the present. To this extent it is an attempt to translate Lakota concepts and to express them in English.

It is essential at the outset to emphasize that traditional Lakota lifeways were not compartmentalized into the distinct institutions that characterize modern America. Religion was not separated out from the rest of social life but was an organic part of the whole. Therefore, a description of nineteenth-century Lakota religion may be phrased in terms of beliefs and rituals that permeated everyday life. And we must understand these beliefs and rituals in the context of the whole of Lakota culture.

Belief

From the perspective of Lakota culture, the world was characterized by its oneness, its unity. Humankind were believed to have been created within the womb of mother earth, just as

were the buffalo, which provided the people with most of
their food. Both human beings and buffalo had emerged upon
the surface of the earth to populate the world as the Lakotas
traditionally knew it. Therefore humans were called *wicaša
akantula*, "men on top." In a very real sense, humankind and
nature were one, just as the natural and supernatural were
one. The distinction between natural and supernatural, so
basic to European thought, was meaningless in Lakota culture. For the Lakotas the important distinction was between
humankind and that which was not human, between the common or ordinary and the extraordinary or incomprehensible.
From the Lakotas' perspective, the quality of incomprehensibility characterized the universe: it was neither to be fully
known nor controlled. Humankind existed not outside nature
but as part of it. Human beings stood in awe and fear of the
universe, venerated it, and dared to manipulate it to the best
of their limited capability. The incomprehensibility of the universe, in which humankind, through ritual, could share, was
called *wakan* (see DeMallie and Lavenda 1977).

Wakan, as Good Seat, an Oglala, told Walker, designated
"anything that was hard to understand" (Walker .1980:70). It
was the animating force of the universe, the common de-
nominator of its oneness. The totality of these life-giving
forces was called *Wakan Tanka*, "great incomprehensibility."
Wakan Tanka was the sum of all that was considered mysterious, powerful, or sacred—equivalent to the basic meaning
of the English word "holy." *Wakan Tanka* never had birth and
so could never die. The *Wakan Tanka* created the universe,
but at the same time they comprised the universe. As Little
Wound told Walker: "The *Wakan Tanka* are those which made
everything. They are *Wakanpi*. *Wakanpi* are all things that are
above mankind. . . . *Wakan Tanka* are many. But they are all
the same as one" (Walker 1980:69–70). Rather than a single
being, *Wakan Tanka* embodied the totality of existence; not
until Christian influences began to affect Lakota belief did
Wakan Tanka become personified. Like the *Taku Wakan*,
which the Lakotas told Densmore referred to the visible

manifestations of *wakan, Wakan Tanka* was an amorphous category most precisely defined by incomprehensibility (Densmore 1918:85, fn. 2).

Among the Lakotas were many *wicaša wakan* ("holy men") who shared to greater or lesser extents in this universal power. Through their personal experiences they sought to impose order and some degree of understanding on *Wanka Tanka*. Sword told Walker that the *Wakan Tanka* were conceptualized as *Tobtob kin*, "the Four times four," a group of sixteen benevolent *wakan*—powers, or as we would say, gods or spirits—many of which were personified as nonhuman beings yet shared human characteristics (Walker 1980:94, 98–99). They included natural phenomena such as Sun, Moon, Wind, Thunder, Earth, and Rock as well as a variety of invisible spirit forms. Outside this classification of *wakan* were yet other *wakan* beings that used their power for evil rather than for good. In Lakota understanding, the *wakan* "power" existed in and was created by these *wakan* beings, each of which was predisposed for either good or evil. Thus *wakan* was not a neutral power, nor did it exist free in the universe; it was bounded and directed.

From the Lakotas' perspective, *wakan* was totally other, entirely outside or beyond the human realm. Little Wound warned Walker that the *wakan* beings ("*Wakanpi*") "have power over everything on earth. They watch mankind all the time. They control everything that mankind does. Mankind should please them in all things. If mankind does not please them, they will do harm to them" (Walker 1980:69). The necessity of pleasing the *wakan* underscored the need to recognize them, but since they were by nature incomprehensible, such understanding as was possible could only be achieved by human beings who shared to some degree in this incomprehensible power. These holy men and women were religious specialists who gained their knowledge through direct contact with the *wakan* beings in dreams or visions, and they became themselves conduits through which this *wakan* power flowed.

For the Lakotas the course of a human life was a clear

reflection of the workings of *Wakan Tanka* in the universe. Finger, an Oglala holy man, explained this to Walker (1917: 154–56). The body of a child was created out of the physical relation between its father and mother, but when the baby was born, its body was animated by *Takuškanškan,* the spirit of movement, who gave it a guardian (*sicun*). This spiritual essence functioned to guard the person against evil spirits; as Walker wrote, "It is an influence that forewarns of danger, admonishes for right against wrong, and controls others of mankind" (1980:73). We might say it was the individual's consciousness or will. For the Lakotas the *sicun* represented the potency of *Wakan Tanka* embodied in a human being. *Takuškanškan* also gave to each baby at birth a ghost (*niya*), which came from the stars, but Finger did not describe its function in life. Each person also possessed a spirit (*nagi*), evidently an immaterial, but immortal, reflection of the body. After death the guardian was believed to escort the spirit to the spirit world beyond the Milky Way (*Wanagi Tacanku,* "Spirit's Trail"); the guardian and the ghost then returned to the places from which they had originally come before the child's birth. The person's body, Finger said, "rots and becomes nothing."

Wakan Tanka, understood as the "power of the universe," was not isolated from the secular world. Lakota culture does not seem to have recognized a sharp distinction between sacred and secular. Since every object was believed to have a spirit, every object was believed to be *wakan.* This spirit was called *tunwan,* a spiritual essence or force that gave power to do *wakan* things. These *tunwan* were not alike or equal; differences in this spiritual essence were reflected in the physical differences among life forms. The *tunwan* might well be considered the material manifestations of phenomena. Such outward forms were not considered to be real but were only physical manifestations of inner power. Thus, according to Sword, "We do not see the real earth and the rock but only their *tonwanpi* [*tunwans*]" (Walker 1917:153).

The unity of *wakan* beings—at least those disposed to do good toward humanity—was expressed in terms of family relationship. Little Wound commented that people should think of the *wakan* beings "as they think of their fathers and their mothers" (Walker 1980:69). This relationship extended throughout the universe, uniting human beings to the rest of creation by bonds of kinship. Black Elk told Brown, "We know that we are related and are one with all things of the heavens and the earth, and we know that all the things that move are a people as we" (1953:97). The Lakotas believed that this relationship had not always existed. In long ago times, for example, the buffalo were said to have been ferocious, continually warring on mankind. Then the White Buffalo Woman, one of the *Wakan Tanka*, brought the Calf Pipe to the people and taught them its rituals. She was sent by the Buffalo People to establish a relationship between them and humankind, so that ever afterward human beings would have food and would increase. The pipe was to be the Lakotas' direct link to *Wakan Tanka*; Finger told Walker that the *Wakan* Woman was herself present in the smoke from the pipe, carrying the people's prayers directly to *Wakan Tanka* (1980:111–12). Significantly, the Lakota word to pray, *wacekiye*, also means to call on for aid, to claim relationship with someone. For the Lakotas the act of prayer was an invocation of relationship, calling on the *wakan* beings to live up to the kindness and generosity expected of good relatives (Deloria 1944:28–29).

Once established, the relationship between humankind, the buffalo, and all the rest of the universe was fixed. Its symbol was the circle, unending and whole. In Lakota culture time was not conceived of as a causal force; history was not directed, nor did it embody that notion of progress and change which is so fundamental to European culture. Instead, the universe was perceived as existing in harmonious balance. As Ella Deloria once put it, "You see, we Indians lived in eternity" (Malan and McCone 1960:13).

When the Lakotas encountered Europeans, the clash of ideas was inevitable. In 1865, U.S. Treaty Commissioners met the Lakotas on the Missouri River and warned them that inasmuch as the buffalo herds were rapidly diminishing and be-

fore long the buffalo would become extinct, the Indians would
have to learn to support themselves by farming. The Lakotas
agreed that the buffalo were decreasing in numbers, but they
did not see this as a process leading to extinction. Instead, the
chiefs told the commissioners that they wanted the whites to
take away the railroads and the steamboats and "return us all
the buffalo as it used to be" (Board of Commissioners 1865:
104). The commissioners were baffled at this reply, treating it
as childish illogic, and they reported to the secretary of the
interior that the Indians "are only too much inclined to regard
us as possessed of supernatural powers" (Commissioner of Indian Affairs 1866:169).

This complete failure to communicate resulted from the
conflict between two divergent systems of belief. For the
whites the irreversability of the process of buffalo extinction
was self-evident. For the Lakotas it was equally self-evident
that *Wakan Tanka* had given the buffalo to the Indians as their
means of life. Moreover, the buffalo and the land were considered as one—buffalo were believed to regenerate themselves by emerging from the womb of mother earth. In fact,
land was insignificant without the buffalo that lived on it.
Asked whether the Lakotas would settle on the Missouri
River, One Horn, the Minneconjou chief, replied: "When the
buffalo come close to the river, we come close to it. When the
buffaloes go off, we go off after them" (Board of Commissioners 1865:34). The Lakota people, the buffalo, and the land
were one; while the people lived and the land existed, talk of
extinction of the buffalo was meaningless to the Lakotas.

In the nineteenth-century Lakota system of belief, the
unity of *Wakan Tanka* embraced all time and space, together
with the entirety of being, in a universe where the place of
human beings was minor but well-defined. Because this universe was most fundamentally characterized by incomprehensibility, it was beyond humanity's power ever to know it fully,
and perhaps it was this futility that made the quest for understanding of the *wakan* the driving force of Lakota culture.

Ritual

Lakota culture possessed a great wealth of rituals, both public and private, that permeated all aspects of life. Some of these were believed to have been taught by the White Buffalo Woman, while others had their origins in visions. All of them were believed to have been patterned originally according to the instructions of *wakan* beings; none were simply created by human beings on their own initiative. Basic to all rituals was the purification lodge (*ini kagapi*), or sweat lodge, which both cleansed a person's body and spirit and prepared him to participate in other rituals. These rituals included great tribal festivals like the Sun Dance; celebrations of changes in life status like the Buffalo sing (*takanka lowanpi*), the girls' puberty ceremony; and rites of togetherness like the *hunka* sing, in which one person ritually adopted another, bringing two families (or bands, or tribes) together as one. Many rituals were expressive of individuals' dream experiences, including the *heyoka* ceremony for Thunder-being (*Wakinyan*) dreamers and ceremonies for dreamers of the Elk and Buffalo. Some rituals were for healing, notably those of the Bear dreamers, who used their *wakan* knowledge to doctor wounds. Still other rituals, like the *yuwipi* ceremonies of Stone dreamers, could predict the future or locate lost objects. Finally, some rituals were completely personal and secret, like those of the Bone Keepers, who made powerful love medicines.

Belief and ritual are interdependent concepts. Belief forms the intellectual and emotional underpinnings of religion, for a system of knowledge representing humankind and the universe. Belief functions to make people's lives and the world in which they live intelligible and acceptable; belief provides the rationale for right and wrong, good and bad. Ritual provides the means for putting belief into action, for expressing belief. The Lakotas spoke of the purpose of ritual in terms of "pleasing" the *wakan* beings who they believed comprised the entire universe. But ritual was not merely a reflection of belief;

it was also a means to further belief, for through ritual a person came to expand his knowledge.

In Lakota society the quest for knowledge of the *wakan*, what Black Elk called "the other world," was largely a personal enterprise and was primarily a male concern. Each individual man formulated a system of belief by and for himself. There was no standardized theology, no dogmatic body of belief. Basic and fundamental concepts were universally shared, but specific knowledge of the spirits was not shared beyond a small number of holy men. Through individual experience, every man had the opportunity to contribute to and resynthesize the general body of knowledge that constituted Lakota belief. Rituals were more standardized than belief; as public performances they gained general and accepted structure through continual repetition. To come to terms with their vision experiences, novice visionaries sought the aid of older, experienced specialists to help them to integrate their individual experiences into the body of tribal ritual.

From the Lakota perspective the power of rituals made them potentially dangerous. Every ritual was composed of three essential components: the *wakan* actions, the *wakan* speech, and the *wakan* songs (see Walker 1980:136). If any of these were performed incorrectly, the ritual would fail to produce the desired end and might actually result in doing harm. Therefore, instruction in conducting rituals in a proper manner was essential for any novice visionary, and this led to greater uniformity of ritual than of belief.

Essential for every Lakota man to achieve success in any endeavor was the vision quest. According to Black Elk, a woman might also seek visions in this ritual way, although almost nothing has been recorded about women's sacred experiences (Brown 1953:44). Clearly, the sacred power of men was considered to be qualitatively different from that of women, just as in all realms of Lakota life male and female roles were precisely defined and rigidly separated. Young men usually went on the vision quest at puberty, the ritual serving for them as a celebration marking their change in status. Before undertaking the quest, known as *hanbleceyapi*, "crying for a vision," a young man was taken into the sweat lodge by a holy man. Cold water poured on hot rocks released the spirit or breath of the rock in clouds of steam. The ensuing heat caused the man to sweat profusely, purifying his body, as George Sword said, "of all that makes him tired, or all that causes disease, or all that causes him to think wrong" (Walker 1980:83–84).

After this purification the young man went away from the village to a hill where he prayed for his vision in solitude. His body was naked, clothed only in a breechcloth, and he wore a furred buffalo robe around his shoulders; his hair was unbraided; and he cried for the vision, tears streaming down his face. All these outward signs—nakedness, unbraided hair, tears—were symbols of humility. The vision seeker made himself pitiable so that the *wakan* beings would be moved to hear his prayers, that is, to acknowledge their relationship to him. Frequently the vision seeker stood on a bed of sage, a plant sacred to the *wakan* beings, whose fragrance repelled the evil *wakan*. At the four directions poles might be erected with offering cloths representing the quarters of the world. Within this circle of sacred space the vision seeker held fast to his pipe and cried aloud for a revelation.

An account of the ritual by Thomas Tyon depicts graphically the vision seeker's mental state. Although he was defenseless, alone, and isolated from the camp, he was instructed to fear nothing, but to be alert to whatever might befall him. Tyon wrote:

Now the vision quester wraps his robe around himself with the fur side out, and until the sun rises, he stands looking east, pointing with the pipe that he holds, praying as hard as he can. All night long he stands in this way, it is said. At last the dawn seems to be visible, and so he stands, rejoicing greatly, it is said. And then possibly, he becomes very drowsy, so very slowly he lies down flat, they say. And with his arms very properly uplifted in prayer, now as he lies there, he hears something stamp the ground behind him, coming towards him, creeping up stealthily, little by little. He is very excited (*lila cantiyapa*). So perhaps, all of a sudden, he thinks to raise up his head as it goes by, they say. And he looks at the thing that comes stamping the earth. And then it is very little even though he heard the sound of its breath (*taninyan honaran*), it is said. It was only a grasshopper walking although it came stamping the ground, they say. [Walker 1980:151–52]

All the vision quester's senses were alert, waiting for the *wakan* beings to communicate with him. Black Elk told Neihardt that for his vision quest he was instructed to walk from the center of his sacred circle to each of the four directions in turn, west, north, east, and south, and to cry aloud at each of the quarters. "While crying I had to say this: 'O Great Spirit, accept my offerings. O make me understand!'" (DeMallie, ed., 1984:228). Black Elk had experienced a great vision when he was a small boy, and as he approached manhood it was necessary for him to undertake the vision quest in order to understand his vision. As he prayed to the four directions, four different birds came to signal to him, and this recognition from the *wakan* caused him to cry all the harder. As the night wore on he had a vision of butterflies, dragonflies, and a dog—the symbols of a Thunder dreamer—and he understood his obligation to become a *heyoka*. Then a great storm broke, and as Black Elk told Neihardt:

I was crying for fear now. I asked the great grandfathers to pity me and spare me—that I had the clearness of understanding now that I was willing to do it on earth. Now you could feel the wind of the hail storm and I could hear and see the falling of the big hail all around me. Then I did not care whether I got killed or not, that probably I would be better off in the other world anyway. I began to lie down and then offered this pipe. I covered myself with the robe and I could hear the growling of the thunder and the flashes of the lightning and I could hear voices saying this all over the heavens: "Hey-a-a-hey!" I looked for the hail to hit me, but not one of them touched me and I did not even get wet. [DeMallie, ed., 1984:230]

The vision quester understood that he had been selected by one of the *wakan* beings to perform a special duty on earth. In the case of a dream of the Thunder-beings, like Black Elk's, it became a duty the neglect of which was punished by death; the Thunder-beings struck down by lightning anyone they favored who failed to acknowledge his duty before the people. Dreams of the Thunder-beings, causing the vision seeker to become a *heyoka,* were powerful yet awesome. They placed an obligation on the dreamer to perform the *heyoka* ceremony for the benefit of the people, a ceremony of public abasement in which the dreamer dressed in rags and acted and talked "backwards," in a senseless manner, causing the people to laugh at him. For example, Black Elk told of a *heyoka* trying to cross a shallow mud puddle who pretended to determine its depth by laying his long crooked bow down on the surface of the water. Then standing the bow on end, he measured it and found that the puddle was deep, the water high above his head. Diving in, he mired himself in the mud to the general amusement of the onlookers. Black Elk explained the significance of these antics thus:

The heyoka presents the truth of his vision through comic actions, the idea being that the people should be put in a happy, jolly frame of mind before the great truth is presented. When the vision comes from the west, it comes in terror like a thunderstorm, but when the storm of [the] vision has passed the whole world is green and happy as a result. In the ceremony of the heyoka this order is reversed, the creation of the happy frame of mind in the people preceding the presentation of the truth. [DeMallie, ed., 1984:232]

Not all *heyoka* visions were as complex and detailed as Black Elk's. Sword told the story of one as follows:

And so now one of the men related a *heyoka* Thunder-being dream in this manner: "I began to dream. A snowbird came for me from the west. I went forth like lightning and as I arrived at the camp of the Thunder-beings I came to my senses. Men had painted themselves white and on each of their limbs they had painted a zigzag line in red, a finger's width. 'Boy, human being, let your mind be completely clear. These rituals you will take back to your people and you shall reveal them,' they said." So it was. On account of this he will make haste and sponsor a *heyoka* ceremony. [Sword, in preparation]

It is important to note that in visions like this one, the vision seeker was not instructed in any rituals by the vision itself; rather, the vision gave him the directive to perform a ritual that was well known to the people. Thus individuals who dreamed of the same *wakan* being organized together in loose associations (*ošpaye*) or societies (*okolakiciye*) and performed the rituals together, inducting new members whenever someone experienced the appropriate vision.

The vision invested the vision seeker with a supernatural aura, a *wakan* quality that set him apart from others. The gift of the vision was knowledge; the vision seeker was exhorted to be attentive, to focus his mind (*wacinksapa*). This attentiveness must be maintained not only during the vision experience but afterward as well. The power originated with the vision but was developed in a practical sense by subsequent contemplation of its meaning. As Densmore was told, mastery of the vision required "effort and study" (1918:85, fn. 2). Black Elk referred to it as "clarity of understanding" (*waableza*). This special knowledge granted by the vision placed on the visionary a corresponding obligation, a sacred duty to use the powers he had received in order to benefit the people. For some Lakotas, like Black Elk, fulfillment of this duty became the dominating theme of their lives.

Many visions granted the vision seeker power to cure the sick. In his great vision Black Elk was given herbs with which to help his people. One day, after he had performed the *heyoka* ceremony for the first time, a man came to him and asked him to doctor his child who was dying. Black Elk instructed the man to present him with a pipe and an eagle feather by way of formal petition, and then he would honor the request. This was to be his first cure. Black Elk commented to Neihardt: "When the power of the west comes to the four-leggeds it is a rumbling and when it passes it leaves the world green and fresh. . . . And so now I used the drum to make the rumbling sound which represented the power of the west. Of course I had never received any instructions from anyone, but I just fixed a way for my curing" (DeMallie, ed. 1984:236).

Black Elk was only nineteen years old at this time, and was unsure of his power. He prayed to each of the six directions individually and sang a sacred song from his vision. He said to Neihardt:

When I sang this I could feel something queer in my body and I wanted to cry. At first I was in doubt but I was in earnest now. After singing this song I walked toward the west where the cup of water was and I saw the little sick boy looking up and smiling at me. Then I knew that I had the power and that I would cure him. The next thing I made an offering and took a whiff at the pipe. Then I drank part of the water and started toward where the sick boy was and I could feel something moving in my chest and I was sure that it was that little blue man [a spirit that he received in his great vision] and it made a different sound from anything else. Then I stamped the earth four times standing in front of the boy. Then I put my mouth at the pit of the boy's stomach and drew the north wind through him. At the same time the little blue man was also in my mouth, for I could feel him there. I put a piece of white cloth on my mouth and I saw there was blood on it, showing that I had drawn something out of his body. Then I washed my mouth with some of the water of the cup. And I was now sure that I had power. [DeMallie, ed. 1984:238–39]

Black Elk gave us a vivid picture of his first experience learning to trust in and make use of his vision power. Although in this case he was not assisted in the ritual by any other holy men, he nonetheless followed the common procedures which he had seen used by other medicine men and which had been used on him during his illness at the time of his great vision. But each ritual action took on new meaning, charged with the symbols of his own vision.

In the prayers and songs of a ritual it was customary for the holy man to speak in the *wakan* language, the language of the spirits. This was called *hanbloglaka,* "relating visions." To speak in this manner invoked the power of one's vision, and because it was phrased metaphorically and aphoristically, the language was relatively obscure to anyone lacking a knowledge of the vision. An example of this ritual speech was recorded by George Sword in telling about the vision experiences of a Bear dreamer:

In the west there is a lodge as high as the clouds. The lodge is painted red, with white painted stripes; at the bottom of the lodge there are likenesses of bears sitting upright. The door is toward the east. At the honor place [the back of the lodge, the west] is the likeness of the sun and a likeness of the moon is at the doorway. Men painted red sat at the right side of the lodge. At the back of the lodge, men who had whitened themselves by smearing their bodies with clay had been invited to sit. I went in the lodge and went toward the honor place by way of the right. All those men who were painted red said "Wohoho!" And they said, "Human man, you will be wise."

Those who sat at the right were good and just men; since he went there, he will have good success; therefore they rejoiced and said "Wohoho!" Then they showed him what they will give him—all kinds of medicines. A man who has these medicines can cure a wounded man and make him live. And then medicine for war, and hawk wing and owl feathers to wear in battle, all this they tell him about. The name of these is *wotawe*. Those they put on and in battle they will not be wounded, so for that reason they make rules for them. The man who went also had a dream of the sacred whirlwind. He returned to his people with these gifts. [Sword, in preparation]

When the man returned home, he made a lodge like the one he saw in the vision, and he was supposed to restrict his activities in it to the right side only. In order to obtain control over the medicines that he had been given, he must perform the Bear ritual to declare his vision publicly. So he painted his body red all over, painted his face yellow, and drew black lines from the eyebrows down his face. He smeared yellow paint on a bear robe and wore it over his shoulders. The robe was decorated with an eagle feather attached at the head. The dreamer carried a red-painted knife. In this costume he greeted the men who came to help in his ceremony and who wished to share in his sacred power. He spoke as follows: "Bear spirit, attentively take heed! In this manner you gave me your authority and so you spoke. Now today your authority I will see revealed. It will be finished and there will be no tragedy befall the people. On a good day, with a cloudless blue sky, I will reveal it. And the people and your children will live without tragedy and without sickness." (Sword, in preparation)

After singing songs from the vision, the dreamer stepped out of the lodge to enact the Bear ritual. He became possessed by the spirit of the Bear. As he breathed, he blew clouds of red clay from his mouth; bear's canines protruded from his lips. Acting like an angry bear, he chased the people about. From time to time he squatted, pulling up prairie turnips out of the soil. When at last he returned to his lodge his helpers met him with a filled pipe and soothed him. Then they smoked together and the ceremony was at an end. Those men who had assisted him would have success on their next war expedition. Those who wished purchased from him some of his medicines for curing or some of the protective *wotawe* for war. In this way they formed a Bear society and would meet again in the future for ceremonies and for curing.

Before curing, the Bear medicine man (*pejuta wicaša*) related his vision in the *wakan* language as before. He said:

> In the west there is a lodge as high up as the clouds. Inside the lodge I was deeply attentive. Men who were painted red sat in the lodge and they showed me a man with a gaping wound whose mouth was red with blood. Speaking, they put medicines in my hands: "Boy, human man, be keenly attentive! With these sacred medicines you will make those who lie suffering among your people to stand." Those persons who spoke gave these to me.
>
> And so he [the Bear medicine man] said this: "They are called bears—those, they are the ones. So humbly I tell their words. Alas! Without these I am nothing." [Sword, in preparation]

The Bear dreamer treated the wounded man first by cleaning out his wound using the tip of a bear claw. Then he applied medicines and dressed the wound. The doctor remained with the wounded one until his recovery was assured. Later, when the patient was well again, he was inducted into the Bear society and allowed to share in their medicines.

The Bear vision serves as an instructive example of Lakota

visions. On the one hand, it reflected a common pattern—the tipi in the clouds and other symbols of the vision were all frequent motifs. The Bear enactment ceremony and the healing ritual were both carried out in accordance with well-known Lakota traditions. The specific content of the vision, however, the words of the vision and the songs, were unique, reflecting the individual visionary's experience. Because individuals who dreamt of the same power united together in societies, the outward uniformity of the rituals was assured; and by selling the medicines to heal wounds and provide protection in war, the sacred gifts of a vision could be widely shared. Thus the vision was at once individualistic and collectivistic.

Conclusion

Study of nineteenth-century Lakota religion provides insights into the foundations of traditional culture. More and more previously unpublished manuscripts are now being made available in print, allowing everyone access to these original sources for understanding the past. The work of analyzing them has only just begun. In this brief survey, however, I have tried to suggest a few fundamental features:

1. Basic concepts formed the core of Lakota belief. These included the idea of *wakan* as the creative universal force; time as nondirected or nonprogressive; the unity of humankind and nature; the existence of a spiritual force in all forms of creation; the essential incomprehensibility of the universe; and the importance of ritual to imbue human beings with spiritual power. These commonly accepted, shared understandings were the cultural building blocks of Lakota religion.

2. Classification of the *wakan* beings, and detailed understandings of each of them, were largely individual concerns, dependent upon each person's visions and religious experiences.

3. Prayer was the act of humbling oneself before the *wakan* beings, making oneself pitiable in order to beseech the spirits to activate the kin relationships that bound them to humanity.

4. Spiritual gifts were the possessions of individuals, but they obliged their owners to use these gifts for the welfare of society. In some instances this required sharing or selling of certain powers.

5. Rituals were culturally conservative, following a small number of set patterns; beliefs were less conservative and involved wide variation among holy men.

6. The content of both religious beliefs and rituals was not conceived of as static, but rather as continually changing, infused with new revelations from visions that might modify older forms.

The large body of information on nineteenth-century Lakota religion is a priceless legacy. Most of it was recorded at a time when the Lakota people felt that their traditional religion must pass away. The men who left these records of the old beliefs and rituals were by and large practicing Christians. George Sword, for example, was a deacon in the Episcopal Church, and Black Elk was a Roman Catholic catechist. Yet they believed that there was truth and goodness in their traditional religion, and they wanted to preserve it for the benefit of future generations. They recorded these sacred things, as Sword said, that "the Gods of the Oglalas would be more pleased if the holy men told of them so that they might be kept in remembrance and that all the world might know of them" (Walker 1980:47). However, history did not decree that Lakota religion should pass away. Surely, the old holy men would be pleased by our efforts to understand their sacred traditions; just as surely, they are with us in spirit.

2

Lakota Genesis: The Oral Tradition

BY ELAINE A. JAHNER

THE DESIRE people have for knowledge about myths of origin is always shaped, in some measure, by the historical realities of the age in which they live; and our scientific era has intensified interest in cosmological myths beyond the expected scholarly concern with gathering data about various belief systems. Today many people are studying the poetry of myth as a framework for articulating fundamental, visceral questions imposed by the insecurities of a nuclear age; and within myths they are finding images that teach about life at the threshold of a new but still endangered world, one with moral dilemmas comparable to those we face as technology creates new worlds for our society. Some people are also seeking to understand their own ethnic history and traditions; they have additional motivation for meditating on the narratives most closely linked to the basic energies of their own cultures. Whatever the predominant reason for the search, people find that narratives on Lakota genesis themes are both compelling and in distinct contrast to the creation myths of many other cultures, both Indian and non-Indian.

When contemporary scholars discuss Lakota beliefs about cosmic beginnings, they generally refer to information James R. Walker recorded at Pine Ridge Reservation between 1896 and 1914; and they do so with good reason. Walker's collected manuscripts include several different kinds of material that together form as complete and poetic a description of Lakota cosmology and cosmography as can be found anywhere. There are fundamental statements of belief like Good Seat's direct and ever-so-brief consideration of origins: "How the world was made is *Wakan Tanka*. How men used to talk to animals is *Wakan Tanka*" (Walker 1980:70). Direct and explicit acceptance of the mystery of origins characterizes all the statements we have from Lakotas who lived according to tribal beliefs.

But people need narratives that focus their sense of how the world came into existence and how their personal and cultural lives participate in that continued coming into being. Walker, of course, found that the Lakotas had such narratives, but what puzzled him was that they had no single story that compelled belief in the way that the first chapters of Genesis function for Christians. So he continued for years to question the holy men who befriended him, seeking narratives based on beliefs about the creation of the universe and waiting to find that one which would possess the authority he thought the others lacked, which would illustrate the relationships between beliefs about creation and the rituals that permitted people to participate in ongoing sacred processes.

During his years at Pine Ridge, Walker found only speculative fragments of stories, which he finally systematized in his own narrative about the initial creation of the universe. In his preface to the document, he stressed that he had not heard his story as oral tradition, but had formulated it out of all that he had learned from the holy men. Nevertheless, the story reflects fundamental Lakota assumptions, and it does so in ways that help us understand how the stories actually told by the Lakotas functioned in relation to beliefs. Walker's materials help us abstract the principles which governed the way people understood and interpreted other stories.

The beginning of Walker's genesis story presents stone as the primal substance and the need to share as the initial impulse to creation:

Inyan (Rock) had no beginning for he was when there was no other. His spirit was *Wakan Tanka* (The Great Mystery), and he was the first of the superior Gods. Then he was soft and shapeless like a cloud, but he had all the powers and was everywhere. *Han* was then but she is not a being; she is only the black of darkness.

Inyan longed to exercise his powers, but could not do so for there was no other that he might use his powers upon. If there were to be another, he must create it of that which he must take from himself, and he must give to it a spirit and a portion of his blood. [Walker 1983:206–207]

The narrative goes on to describe the progressive differentiation of existence. Each change generates needs which become pleas for further change; and as the powers of *Inyan* expand from their primal, simple origin into the diversity of a cosmos inhabited by beings capable of perceiving need, order is necessary to prevent conflict and chaos. Sky (*Škan*) is appointed judge and arbiter for all that exists. Finally, it is Sky who declares that the initial creation has reached its limits: "Creation is now completed. No further power shall be granted for the creation of any other creature. Each living creature shall propagate its kind and all multiply. Each shall exist for a space and then return to whence it came. Others of its kind shall follow while the world exists" (Walker 1983:245).

Walker's own systematization of countless Lakota beliefs served as an impressive philosophical and ethical prelude to the stories he learned from George Sword, who wrote important narratives for his friend Walker. But Walker did not translate them from Lakota until after Sword was dead. When he discovered the content of these manuscripts, he believed that he had found at last the narratives that explained relationships between aspects of rituals such as the Sun Dance and cosmological beliefs (Walker, 1983:11–16). Sword's tales undoubtedly provide us our most easily accessible narrative view of Lakota beliefs about the formation of the world, because their thematic structures bear so close and so clear a relationship to the structure of Lakota ritual and social life, showing, as they do, that kinship rules governed the intelligible design of all that existed and established an ethical imperative that gained its force from the very nature of being (see Powers 1977:68–86, 166–87).

Sword's stories do not address the details of the original

creation; they are set in the world of the spirits before time
and space were given their current order. The first section of
Sword's narrative Walker entitled "When the People Laughed
at the Moon" (Walker 1917:164–80). It depicts how order was
disrupted among the gods and how the need for justice established all of the world's major patterns of order. *Wazi*, the chief
of the Buffalo People, is married to *Kanka*, woman endowed
with the powers of prophesy. Their beautiful daughter *Ite* has
married *Tate*, the Wind, who is the associate of the Sky, and
she has born him male quadruplets, a sign that the children
are gods. By marrying the Wind, *Ite* has established a link between the Buffalo People and the gods; but that is not enough
for her father, who wants to possess his own godlike powers so
that he can rise above the status of the other Buffalo People.
His wish makes him vulnerable to *Iktomi*, Trickster, who
agrees to give him divine powers in return for aid in schemes
of trickery. Frightened by Trickster, *Wazi* consults his wife.
The story depicts her engaging in some pragmatic and ultimately futile reasoning as she decides to try to deceive the
master deceiver and take what Trickster has to give, only to
renege on promises of aid to him. *Iktomi* grants his powers to
the two Buffalo People, but then manipulates them with
the suggestion that their daughter, the wife of a god, should
have her own place among the gods. *Ite* is only too eager to
take her parents' advice, and she finally sits in the place of the
Moon, who is the Sun's proper wife. Thus a mortal shames the
Moon by usurping the Sun's attention and assuming the wrong
place, and she irrevocably alters the order among the gods.

We learn how *Ite*'s action establishes a new order, since the
Sky dispenses justice that spells out the consequences of each
character's choice. We see how disruption of order among the
gods brings about a new order in new places and requires new
temporal divisions as well. The sentences that the characters
receive extend their roles as mediators, roles that are established and controlled through kinship which transforms oppositions into fruitful relationships.

In the second section of the myth, which is well beloved by

those who know it, Sword told how the order of the world was completed when the Four Winds founded the four directions. Each wind is helped or hindered by his willingness to accept his own special relationship to *Wohpe*, the Beautiful Woman who is a mediator between the human and the divine (Walker 1983:58–89).

Sword's stories make explicit the ethical and the emotional forces that were implicit in the style and structure of more traditional Lakota oral narratives, but Sword achieved this in the way of a storyteller, adding details and controlling the structure of his tales so that they could give the insight that Walker had sought so consistently during his years at Pine Ridge. Since the stories were written, we have reason to believe that they represent considerable thought on the part of Sword. The more closely they are analyzed, the more they can be seen to present a whole range of answers to profound questions that troubled the Lakotas during the last decades of the nineteenth century, the time when they changed from a nomadic hunting people to a forcibly settled nation that faced an injunction to become farmers and to learn the trappings of a mainstream American culture as quickly as possible.

Analyzing the logical structure of Sword's tales reveals a dynamic at work that is especially interesting in light of the historical context. Sword presented oppositions only to show how their development works to create a structure of inclusion within which opposing elements can continue to function. Although the conjoint functioning is not always simple or even positive, such combinations of apparently opposing forces always constitute a dynamic within a cosmic situation where the negative is balanced by the positive, and knowledge of that dynamic permits people to live well within the cosmic setting.

For example, in his stories the moon is always both near and far from the sun. When she is literally near, she must hide her face, thereby becoming figuratively distant. When she is far away, her face is clear for all to see, and seeing is a form of nearness. *Ite,* the Double Face, is both wife and inaccessible woman, both immortal and bound to mortal destiny, celestial and terrestrial, mother of sons who combine divinity and humanity. *Ite's* counterpart, *Wohpe*, presents a whole series of combinations. She is divine but chooses humanity. She is from the sky and chooses earth. She achieves a relationship that alternates between that of a sister and of a lover to the winds, who provide human beings with good weather when they view her as a sister, and bad weather when they view her a potential lover. And, of course, Sword's narratives are both a participation in a mythic system and a departure from it. From our twentieth-century perspective, we can see how they show the terms of adaptation from one way of life to another. To what extent Sword understood this, we will never know, but he was a remarkably intelligent man deeply concerned about his people, knowledgeable about two cultures, and imaginative enough to have understood a great deal about the significance of his narratives.

In one important way, Sword's narratives point toward terms permitting adaptation to changed cultural circumstances as his tales mediate between Lakota and Biblical beliefs, showing possible grounds for syncretisms. Sword's stories are close enough to both sets of beliefs to show how one can be interpreted in relation to the other and how philosophical thought stimulated by the Lakota world view could be carried on within the Christian one. This first of his tales describing the expulsion of beings from the sky world recalls the first chapters of Genesis, which Sword knew well; but his characters, *Kanka* and *Wazi*, do not lack knowledge of good and evil. They have, in fact, an extraordinarily devious view of life that involves awareness of all extremes of behavior. To this is added *Kanka's* ability to foresee the future. All she has to do is work out the means to bring it to be, yet that process defeats her because she fails to understand the nature of what she is up against. No one outwits Trickster, and although *Kanka* foresees that her daughter will displace the Moon, she ought to have known better than to take an active role in such socially disruptive scheming. *Kanka* is not quite an Eve in Paradise. She has never been innocent, merely insensitive to the power structure. Nevertheless, she and *Wazi* end up in a situation not unlike that of Adam and Eve: they have lost a way of life and need to live with the consequences. So did the Sioux. Yet all is not lost. *Tate* remains sufficiently committed to his obligations as a father, to provide the nucleus of social organization in the new world.

Within that world the main imperative is to maintain basic family organization, and the second section of the myth begins with a precise description of each person's place in the tipi, even though eventually the brothers must determine the meaning of time by journeying through space to establish temporal divisions. The main feature of this story is *Yata's* forfeiture of his birthright, another theme absent from traditional lore but clearly present in Biblical sources. It is an intriguing episode that scholars have puzzled over. But we can only speculate why Sword was so attracted to the idea of one brother giving his place to another in a moment of physical and moral weakness only to experience resentment later.

Sword's stories are exceptional in many ways, but one of their important distinctions is that until Walker made them generally available, they were known to only a few Oglala holy men. They definitely did not exist as part of the common, popular traditions about creation (see Ella Deloria's discussion in Walker 1983:16–27). What can we find among the available collections of Sioux materials that will reveal the *popular* Lakota understandings about origins? The available data give us much to enhance our appreciation of the complexity, subtlety, and wisdom of the popular traditions.

There is no doubt that the most significant narrative in Lakota tradition is the story of the gift of the Sacred Pipe. Just as the Pipe ceremony is at the heart of Lakota ritual life, so the story of the Sacred Pipe is at the heart of the narrative tradition. The myth is well known. Two men are out traveling when they meet a most beautiful woman. One of the men lusts after her and is destroyed; the other is sent back to camp with instructions to tell the people to prepare for her coming. When she arrives, she brings with her the Sacred Pipe. According to

Black Elk's version of the myth, she told the people: "With this
Sacred Pipe, you will walk upon the Earth; for the Earth is
your Grandmother and Mother. . . . When you pray with this
pipe, . . . you will be bound to all your relatives. . . . These
seven circles which you see on the stone have much meaning,
for they represent the seven rites in which the pipe will be
used" (Brown 1953:5–7).

This myth narrates what to the Lakota people was the
single most important manifestation of the sacred, the one
that founded the Lakota world and gave the people their orientation in time and space. At least one teller of the story
made explicit his feelings that without the Pipe, the people
lacked all that was most basic to their human condition. Left
Heron, an Oglala, expressed how profoundly he felt about the
changes the Pipe wrought in the lives of the people when he
ascribed all of culture to the effects of the Pipe's presence. He
believed that "there was nothing sacred before the pipe came;
there was no social organization and the people ran around
the prairie like so many wild animals" (Mekeel 1931). For Left
Heron at least, the coming of the Pipe, the symbol of the
unity among people and spirits, meant the beginning of all that
is most distinctively noteworthy about the human enterprise.

The story of the coming of the Sacred Pipe possesses some
features that can lead us to a richer understanding of how all
genesis themes operated in Lakota society. The first and most
important of these is its temporal setting. Even though narrators always say that it happened "long ago" or "many winters
ago," the narrative itself quite clearly shows that "long ago" is
not some mythopoeic era before the world achieved its current form. In terms of cosmic time, the events of the story are
very recent indeed; they are part of the sacred history of the
people; they are moments in that history which brought a
whole new dimension to the cosmic extension of humankind's
social existence. Thus the story reveals the basis for the strong
Lakota preference for narratives depicting relationships between human beings and spirits in *historical* terms. As the
myth about the Sacred Pipe shows, even the rituals have their

origin within a concrete historical setting where the rituals permit regeneration and re-creation. This emphasis on sacred time as it interesects with a definite historical situation can be seen as a leitmotif throughout Lakota oral tradition, which either dramatizes the conditions under which people have access to the sacred or, as in the story of the gift of the Sacred Pipe, dramatizes concern about how sacred beings establish definite relationships to the people and teach them how to comport themselves to use spiritual powers to their advantage. The "Lakota Way" is one of care for the conditions that are most likely to effect an intersection between individual human historical experience and the good spirits able to guide individuals and cultures.

Because of this intense concern with how the sacred manifests itself in real places and in times remembered in definite tribal histories, stories that explain how the world first came into being and then achieved its current form held a less important place than those that tell how a particular, definite relationship between human beings and spirits came about and is perpetuated through ritual. Another way of stating the same thing is to say that the Lakota emphasis was far less on an original genesis than it was on the ongoing genesis which is the basis of sacred history. Creation is never over and done with. There is no clockmaker divinity in this tradition. The sacred intersects with human history, establishing what we might call the relational myth of origin.

The general cultural concern for situating myths in relation to historical time and known places can be noted in No Flesh's story about the origins of the *hunka* ceremony. He situates the ritual's origins in times before the Lakotas had achieved their current form of social organization, but it is significant that he gives the matter such direct and clear emphasis: "Before the Seven Council Fires the Sioux Indians all made their winter camp together." As he tells his story, he includes much precise cultural detail so that hearers can relate the events to life as they know it. For example, the motive causing the chief to seek a vision, which results in his learning the ceremony, is

one most families could easily imagine: the chief had lost two
sons in battle; his grief drove him to seeking help from the
spirit world (Walker 1980:193).

While the tales narrating the origins of the rituals that
maintain the relations between the Lakota people and the
spirits bear the stylistic marks of the Lakota concern for history and realistic detail, many of their references to the initial
creation are highly imagistic and open to interpretation. This
fact confused Walker and kept him seeking for something else.
Yet, once we understand the functioning of the more realistic
narratives, we can go back to the poetic references and see
that there is no real conflict among these fragmentary references to creation. For someone who understood the systems
of associations and connotations functioning in Lakota oral traditions, there was continuity of reference between the historically situated tales and the poetic ones.

One of the most significant of these fragmentary accounts
was recorded by Alice Fletcher:

> Everything as it moves, now and then, here and there, makes
> stops. The bird as it flies stops in one place to make its nest, and in
> another to rest in its flight. A man when he goes forth stops when he
> wills. So the god has stopped. The sun, which is so bright and beau-
> tiful, is one place where he has stopped. The moon, the stars, the
> winds he has been with. The trees, the animals, are all where he has
> stopped, and the Indian thinks of these places and sends his prayers
> there to reach the place where the god has stopped and win help and
> a blessing. [Fletcher 1884:276]

If we return to Sword's stories, we can see that they give us
clues how to think about the material recorded by Fletcher.
Sword showed how cosmic order depends on beings assuming
their rightfully earned places in a system of social movements
governed by kinship laws, and the Fletcher quotation also di-
rects our attention to the same basic themes. Movement, rest,
and the alternation between them are the grand themes of the
ongoing genesis, even though they may be expressed in remarkably different kinds of stories. How these principles
translated into actual experience was suggested by Lone Man's

statements to Frances Densmore. Careful consideration of his comments reveals how beliefs about the nature of the universe were discussed in terms of actual observations of how sacred power works, which in turn required further disciplined search for discernible relationships among all beings:

> When I was a young man I went to a medicine-man for advice concerning my future. The medicine-man said: "I have not much to tell you except to help you understand this earth on which you live. If a man is to succeed on the hunt or the warpath, he must not be governed by his inclination, but by an understanding of the ways of animals and of his natural surroundings, gained through close observation. The earth is large, and on it live many animals. The earth is under protection of something which at times becomes visible to the eye. One would think this would be at the center of the earth, but its representations appear everywhere, in large and small forms—they are the sacred stones. The presence of a sacred stone will protect you from misfortune." He then gave me a sacred stone which he himself had worn. I kept it with me wherever I went and was helped by it. He also told me where I might find one for myself. *Wakan Tanka* tells the sacred stones many things which may happen to people. The medicine-man told me to observe my natural surroundings, and after my talk with him I observed them closely. I watched the changes of the weather, the habits of animals, and all the things by which I might be guided in the future, and I stored this knowledge in my mind. [Densmore 1918:214]

Lone Man's description of the course of his spiritual development demonstrates the psychological implications of the beliefs in continuing creation. Lone Man had to learn to balance personal inclinations with careful observation of how natural law worked. The sacred stone provided protection and powers that Lone Man had to learn to use by observing nature as closely as any contemporary scientist and by remembering exactly what he had seen.

The same precise attention to immediate detail characterized the process whereby people interpreted observations that did not immediately reveal their significance. By thinking about new events in relation to traditional beliefs and tales, the Lakotas maintained an important cultural dynamic. Interpretation could relate present and past in ways that challenged intelligence and imagination. For the Lakotas, reckoning one's place in space meant careful watchfulness over all that existed there or impinged upon existence there; and such attentiveness created habits of intelligence and feeling. Reckoning one's proper relationship to time depended on caring for one's physical environs, since the sacred enters time in specific places; and such entries usually called for careful interpretation so that each new manifestation of the sacred could be integrated into the particular circumstances of each social unit. And so the modes of close observation and memory that formed the basis of intellectual growth were combined with meditation on the network of associations that worked to give ethical force to traditional stories. The combinations constituted a particular approach to the act of interpreting the significance of new events, which, in turn, affected tradition as they became part of the cared-for and remembered history of the people.

Another manuscript source gives us information that explicitly links Sioux genesis themes with Sioux ideas about the human mind and the mind's ability to learn, remember, and concentrate intensely. Among Aaron McGaffey Beede's papers there is a remarkable passage that deserves quotation, in spite of its length. It begins with a general description of human spiritual growth and learning and then moves to an explanation of how human mental effort is an image for the ongoing development of the entire universe. Beede wrote:

The fact is that the western Sioux mythology, so far as they had a mythology, was strictly geocentric and firmly fixed thus. I had heard them talk as follows: "A man's mind (*tawacin*) and soul (*wicanaġi*) is all around the man and reaches a great way off. When a man is intently using his mind for something, he calls to the use nearly all of his mind but still it is extending far away in every direction. When a man is not using his mind, nearly all of it, leaves him and goes away on a far journey so that the man is 'nearly-the-same-as-dead (*t'anuns'e*)' but the mind has not left him. . . . A man cannot stretch himself very much. . . . But the mind (*tawacin*) as the child grows into a man learns to stretch himself far and wide. Thus the mind and soul (*tawacin wicanaġi kici*) may stretch himself far away while the man is asleep or in a vision (*wihanble*) and behold many things; and may even travel to the home of the Great Spirit. The mind and soul grows (*icaġe*) and becomes the ruler as the child grows into a man but it all begins with the child who has its body before it has much mind and soul and the child begins with its mother. . . . In the same way Holy Mother Earth has grown from childhood to maturity. Her mind has grown and stretched himself (this mind of earth is regarded as primarily masculine, though the element of the feminine inheres in it) far and wide in all life forms. . . ." [Beede 1912–20]

Beede went on to discuss creation in terms of the continuous stretching of mother earth. Earth herself stretches; development occurs, and human minds, like the earth's inner powers, stretch out in visions to establish appropriate relationships. This view of continuing creation gives a particular dimension to the meaning of sacred time and space. As Mircea Eliade characterized sacred time, it involves "reactualization of a sacred event that took place in a mythical past 'in the beginning'" (1959:69). We have seen that in Lakota traditions the mythical past can be part of the immediate historical past because sacred time intersects with ordinary duration. "In the beginning" can be any time in which humans and spirits interact in sacred space and move in a sacred manner. It can be any time in which spirits call to human beings as they called to Black Elk saying, "It is time. Now they are calling you" (Neihardt 1932:21).

In what I have just described, I have kept using the words "can be" because I am referring to the privileged and favored genesis themes, but those were not the only ones. Popular stories also exist that are set in a mythopoeic past and describe aspects of creation. These stories, called *ohunkakan*, express beliefs through artistic invention, operating through centuries and across cultures so that the images and themes resonate throughout the entire culture (see Deloria 1932:ix–x). An immense associative network of meanings establishes the terms for interpretation, and as these associations change, so does the meaning of the story. Concepts and connections easily grasped in personal-experience narratives like Lone Man's, or even in the highly poetic description of creation recorded by Alice Fletcher, operate more indirectly and dramatically in the *ohunkakan*. One popular time-honored tale with direct reference to creation themes tells of an encounter between *Iktomi*, the Trickster, and *Iya*, the eating monster who consumes and limits without necessarily destroying or killing.

Ella Deloria placed this story as the first of her Dakota texts, and according to the version she published, *Iktomi* was wandering along one day when he met *Iya*. Frightened but thoroughly in possession of his clever wit, he confronts the problem of how to greet *Iya*, since kinship terms dictate salutations. "Which of us is the elder anyway?" asks *Iktomi*; and *Iya* answers, "Why I was born when this earth and sky were created." *Iktomi* has received exactly the answer he was seeking, and replies: "So? Well, you fool, I made the earth and the sky myself! Oh, of course, now, as I recall it, there was a bit of leavings after I had finished making the earth and sky which I didn't know what to do with; I therefore rolled it into a wad and tossed it aside and you grew from that!"

The story goes on to explain how *Iktomi* tricked *Iya* in order to get people to kill the monster, thereby releasing the tribes living within his body: "They tore open his body; and then, for one entire day, great tribes of people crawled out of *Iya*, moving their camps, and settled by groups in the many pleasant bends of the river; and soon they built their fires for cooking the evening meal, and no matter where one looked, one could see the campfires, sparkling like stars, and it was a beautiful sight. Now if *Iya* had not been destroyed in just that way he would undoubtedly still be eating people up" (Deloria 1932:7–8).

Thus Trickster destroys a fundamental limitation in existence and helps people emerge into new possibilities. Without overinterpreting the episode, we can see how it is easily understood as a drama of the radical vicissitudes of human existence, which involves *Iya*-like barriers to expansion as well as emergences into new ways of life. These same ideas are recapitulated and expanded in another extremely popular story with Stone Boy as hero. It is evidence that the Lakota people have long loved and appreciated the immense possibilities of the Stone Boy story that a version of it shows up in virtually every folktale collection. Often it is the first tale that comes to mind as people try to remember the old *ohunkakan*.

Before commenting on the most popular version of the tale, I want to discuss a version that Bad Wound gave to James R. Walker. It is, as Bad Wound and Walker noted at the time, "widely divergent" from most others, but it deserves notice because it has explicit connections to the narrative about the encounter between *Iktomi* and *Iya* (Walker 1917 : 193–203).

Bad Wound's tale opens with a scene common in Lakota *ohunkakan*. Four brothers are living alone. Then a woman is miraculously born from the toe of one of them. She is the ideal sister, but the brothers go away, one by one, never to return. Left alone, she goes to a hill and mourns. In her sorrow she accidentally swallows a white pebble and then has a vision, in which she learns that the brothers are "kept by a stone and that a stone would find them and bring them back." As a result of swallowing the pebble, she gives birth to a son whose flesh is stone. When he grows up, he determines to find his uncles. At a feast sponsored by his mother he receives powerful items from the guests to help him in his quest. Then he travels westward until he comes to a barren valley where there is nothing but a stone, a tree whose branches are snakes, and a little brown hill from which smoke is rising. As he watches, he sees a bear carrying captured people. The bear holds the people up to the snake tree, which bites and paralyzes them so that the stone can roll them down and flatten them. Soon Stone Boy realizes that the brown hill is really a tipi made of the flattened bodies of people. Then begin Stone Boy's great battles with a coyote larger than a buffalo, the snake tree that can move about, and the living stone that drinks water. Stone Boy destoys them all before confronting the inhabitant of the dwelling made of flattened people. At first that being appears as an old woman who tries to kill him, but after a time Stone Boy learns that the being is *Iya*, the monster who can only be destroyed by living stone.

Stone Boy's final task is to destroy *Iya* in order to restore to life the people whom *Iya* had captured. In his combat with *Iya*, Stone Boy needs all the powers given him by his mother's people. First Stone Boy tramples on *Iya*'s hip, so that great floods of water flow from him causing the earth's bitter alkaline springs and lakes. Then Stone Boy tramples on *Iya*'s stomach, and *Iya* vomits cherrystones which are in reality people whom *Iya* has sucked in. Stone Boy restores the people, feeds them, and sends them back home. "The people spoke many different languages and could not understand each other but the Stone Boy could speak to each one in his own language," said Bad Wound.

When Stone Boy treads on *Iya*'s chest, a great whirlwind buffets the earth, causing tremendous destruction until the Thunderbird stops it. Finally, Stone Boy flattens *Iya* in the same way that the monster had flattened his human victims. The defeated monster can feel heat and cold, hunger and thirst, but never can he gain relief.

This story, like the simpler episode of the meeting between *Iya* and *Iktomi*, dramatizes the dark continuum of radical transition and transformation that is ultimately the image of cosmic progression. For the people are finally brought forth to a new existence. In Bad Wound's version Stone Boy accomplishes the emergence that usually is *Iktomi*'s feat; Stone Boy is something of a trickster himself and very much the creator, the continuing form of the creative principle, born of the living stone. The reality of stone's existence is irreducible, and therefore it is the essential relevant factor in cosmic continuity. Stone Boy is one mythic embodiment of the alternately creative and destructive principles that keep the universe in existence. He is master of these principles, but he has also been formed by them. He has to defeat his father and his grandfather. As he says to *Iya*, "I broke my own father in pieces because he was evil. Do you think I would spare you because you are my grandfather?" (Walker 1983:149).

One observation that is quickly made about Bad Wound's story is that it abounds in dazzling, excessive, visually extraordinary images that appeal to the imagination as they invite interpretation. This is a direct clue to its particular value as a way of teaching people how to live in a society that was always establishing additional relationships with the spirit world to keep itself in existence and continue the creation process. The description of the snake tree is a good example:

> The tree could not walk up the hill so Stone Boy went down into the valley and when he came near the tree, the branches began to strike at him, but he held up the shield the warrior had given him and when one of the branch snakes would strike it, its teeth would break off and its head would be smashed. And so the Stone Boy danced about the tree and sang and shouted until every branch had smashed itself to death on his shield. [Walker 1983:145]

Such imagery makes a strong emotional appeal, helping listeners tap their own resources of instinctual energy. The imagery compels emotional involvement as it teaches about the need to direct both emotional and intellectual resources toward community needs. Stone Boy's observation of his mother's anguish over the loss of her brothers leads him to face dangers far beyond anything existing for listeners to the story. His unquestioning belief that relationship involves a sacred trust drives him to the vastly dangerous realm of the unknown to rescue his uncles and to learn, in the process, about his own ancestry and destiny. As in most Lakota *ohunkakan*, Stone Boy's feats have definite and, in a sense, ordinary consequences for the Sioux people, in that the results of the hero's fantastic encounters are easily observable in daily life. The ordinary has origins in what exceeds human comprehension. "How things came to be is *Wakan Tanka*."

Bad Wound's story does not end the way most versions of the Stone Boy story end. Bad Wound left listeners with a mystery, a puzzle, a riddle. The last actions of his story are the following: "*Iya* could not hurt the Stone Boy but he held the feet very tightly between his teeth and when the Stone Boy drew out one foot, he closed still on the other, so that when that one was dragged out, the moccasin was left in *Iya's* mouth and was invisible and could not be found" (Walker 1983:153).

Stone Boy loses a moccasin to *Iya*, the evil one. He does not quite escape entirely. Part of him remains in the opaque realm of what is beyond culture or clear understanding. That realm of otherness has directly and fundamentally challenged Stone Boy's mastery and had defeated his weaker uncles, flattening them without killing them. What is the message of the missing moccasin? This question can call for answers throughout the ages, and it admits of as many interpretations as human beings have the intelligence to conceive.

The ways in which creation themes operate in the most commonly told versions of the story are less obvious than in Bad Wound's, but a fragmentary record of one of Left Heron's tellings proves that at least some narrators were quite aware of the story's links to genesis themes (Mekeel 1931). Because this version of the Stone Boy story is somewhat closer to the observable realities of Lakota society, interpretation of its relationship to creation themes can suggest some of the reasons for its continued vitality in Lakota culture.

An example of the commonly told version is that given by George Sword (Walker 1983:89–100). The tale begins by presenting four brothers who live alone. There is the nucleus of a band, a basic unit of Lakota society; and the brothers have an organized life where rules and obligations of kinship are observed, but they keenly feel their lack of a sister.

Then a woman comes. The brothers really have only two choices: to risk inviting a woman of unknown character into their tipi or to risk the continuing vulnerability of being a group without a woman. So they decide to give her the role of sister, and they invite her in. Once she crosses the threshold, a whole new phase of their lives is underway.

The arrival of the woman turns out to be disastrous for the brothers. The youngest discovers that she is really a cannibal, so he and his brothers flee from her. She pursues and kills all but the youngest, who uses supernatural aid to defeat her. He then builds a sweat bath to bring his brothers back to life.

The incident of the arrival of an unknown woman is then repeated. Fearfully, the brothers invite the second woman. Happily, she turns out to be a good sister, but one change necessitates another, and the brothers leave to bring her what she needs, only they never return. Finally she is left alone. While mourning, she accidentally swallows a stone, becomes pregnant, and gives birth to Stone Boy, whose first task as an adult is to rescue his uncles from their captivity among the Buffalo People ruled by the tyrannical Crazy Buffalo. With the help of powers given him by women whom he has met along the way, Stone Boy succeeds not only in freeing his uncles but also in getting them Buffalo Women as wives. Then he returns home.

The social unit is now healthy, growing, at peace. Then occurs the episode in the story that has endured beyond all others in the oral tradition. Stone Boy decides to go sledding. He sees four young Buffalo Women sliding happily down a hill and asks if he can join them. They assent. As they slide down the hill, he, with his stone body, rolls right over the top of them, killing them and inciting the revenge of their father. But Stone Boy, in rescuing his uncles, had established the security of his home and now he can celebrate that security by rebuffing the attacks of the buffalo. He builds walls around his family's tipi and sits atop one of them, gleefully watching the buffalo come only to break their horns in their futile attacks. The buffalo leader finally announces that Stone Boy's powers are greater than theirs and the tale ends.

We can best understand this final incident and its significance if we refer to features of the story that Left Heron made explicit in his telling of it. Left Heron gives etiological meaning to events, thus stressing the assumed connections between Stone Boy and aspects of creation:

Jack Rabbit and Eagle came and said, "You are too powerful" and prayed for him to leave the earth. Rock Boy asked his relatives where they wanted to go. The six uncles became the seven sisters star constellation; three were part of the head and one served as the tail making the ten uncles in all [?]. Then he asked his mother and she became the North Star, but Rock Boy decided to stay on earth to help. The Uwipi Wasicun [*yuwipi wašicun*] is used in the Sun Dance and some medicine men use it and they are called upon to make good weather. [Mekeel 1931]

While the four buffalo girls become flowers, Stone Boy's own relatives become stars, and he himself remains as the stone whose movements manifest the sacred among the people.

If we use the insights that Left Heron's version of the story gives us, we can return to Sword's story and see that the same basic themes operate in both the written creation stories that Sword gave to Walker and the Stone Boy story. At first social life is represented by people who have definite places and patterns of movement. Then someone usurps a place not rightfully hers and all must be reorganized in order to maintain order. Such re-creation requires the aid of spiritual beings of extraordinary power such as Stone Boy or *Tate* and his sons, the winds. It also involves women as intermediaries so that oppositions can be changed into fruitful relationships. By sending his relatives to the sky, Stone Boy links earth and sky. By making the buffalo girls into flowers, he links animals and plants. By challenging the buffalo to a test of powers, he establishes relationships of respectful submission between the buffalo and human beings. And finally, by becoming the *yuwipi wašicun*, Stone Boy links myth and history, the vague mythic past and the known historical past, which impinges on the present and calls upon the future through the way it establishes expectations and needs for new contacts with the sacred and new creation.

Thus we come full circle. Ceremonies function in historical time, renewing life and thereby continuing the process of creation. Different kinds of narratives celebrated and taught the meaning of the ritual intersection between the world of the powerful spirits and that of human beings. Those recited with greatest reverence and in closest relation to ritual were the ones showing the concrete operation of the spiritual in human history. People could claim that they knew where and when such incidents had occurred and could give direct assent to such stories, which fulfilled all their demands for credibility. There were also many fascinating artistic constructs recognized as such by the people. These old tales had a less direct link with beliefs than the narratives more directly related to ritual, but because of the rich body of cultural associations that they evoked, they too taught the significance of ongoing creation. Just as Stone Boy recapitulates the cosmic coming into existence through his own rites of passage into adulthood, so does every person participate in continuing creation through ceremony. The old tales admit of a wide range of interpretation, all of it true to the specific realities of Lakota culture; and where that range has been great enough to encompass twentieth-century realities, the tales have remained alive in oral tradition, even if a traditional way of life appears tenuous. Such is the fate of Stone Boy, who seems destined to live as long as Lakota people perform the old ceremonies and re-create their world.

3

The Sacred Pipe in Modern Life

BY ARVAL LOOKING HORSE

I AM a Cheyenne River Sioux, a *Mnikowoju* (Minneconjou) through my father. My name is Arval Looking Horse, but I have an Indian name, too, *Šunka wakan wicaša*, Horse Man. A long time ago names were earned when a person did something great, but my grandmother gave me that name when I was a little boy. Her name was Lucy Looking Horse, and her father's name was Bad Warrior. She was the keeper of the Sacred Pipe of the Sioux people. Just before a keeper of the Sacred Pipe dies, he has a vision of who to give the Pipe to. It is always given to a blood relative, either a man or a woman. Just before my grandmother died, she had a vision and gave the Pipe to me. That was in 1966; I was just twelve years old. My grandmother taught me how to be the keeper of the Pipe, but I was young at that time, so I forgot most of the things she told me. Later, my father taught me the rest. This Sacred Pipe has been handed down through the generations, through blood relations. With it, our religion has been brought down through oral tradition—not written tradition. So I was taught the old way of carrying on the Pipe for the Sioux nation.

The Sacred Pipe was brought down to earth and given to the first keeper, Buffalo Standing Upright, a long time ago. I am the nineteenth generation to serve as Pipe keeper.

A story is told about the Pipe before it was brought to the Sioux people. A man was out scouting and came upon what we now call Devil's Tower, in Wyoming. This is a sacred place, a sacred hill. There used to be a hole through it, straight across from the east to the west. It looked like a big tipi, open both on the east and the west. The man entered, and on the north side of the tipi he saw the Sacred Pipe, and on the south side he saw a sacred bow and arrows. He was going to pick up the Pipe, but instead he chose the bow and arrows and walked out the west side of the tipi. Since then the Cheyennes have had the Sacred Arrows.

Later, the Sacred Pipe was brought to the Sioux. This happened on what is now the Cheyenne River Reservation, near the community of Iron Lightning.

Two warriors were out hunting buffalo. There were hardly any to be found, so they went farther and farther away from camp. As they stood on top of a hill, looking into the distance, they saw something white coming. They went closer to look at it and found a woman walking toward them, carrying a bundle. One of the young men had good thoughts toward the woman. He realized that buffalo were scarce and the people needed some kind of help. But the other young man had bad thoughts. "This woman is pretty," he said, "so I want to have her." The first young man said, "No, *Wakan Tanka* must have sent this woman." But the young man who was thinking evil reached out to touch the woman. Suddenly a cloud came over them. The good young man heard rattlesnakes inside the cloud. When the cloud lifted, the young man saw that his companion was nothing but bones, just a skeleton lying there. Then the woman said to him: "Tomorrow make preparations for me to come to bring the bundle for the Sioux people. With this you will survive on the earth."

The man went back to the village and told the people what he had seen and what had happened. So the people prepared for the woman to come. The next day she arrived and presented them with the Sacred Calf Pipe. The woman taught them how to use the Pipe, how to pray with it, and how to do different things to take care of it. She gave the pipe to Buffalo Standing Upright, a medicine man, one of the leaders. She ex-

plained everything about it, and then she left. She left the
camp circle in a clockwise direction, then headed west. As she
went she changed into four animals. The last was a white
buffalo calf, which disappeared over the horizon.

Ever since then the Sioux have had this Sacred Buffalo Calf
Pipe. From then on it has been our religion. Every distinct
people has its own religion, and this is the Sioux religion. Now
the Pipe is in Green Grass community, on the Cheyenne
River Reservation. When people talk about it in English they
call it the Sacred Pipe, which they get from books, but when
they talk about it in Indian it is always called *Ptehincala hu
cannunpa*, the Buffalo Calf Pipe. It is used for prayer in our
religion; *cannunpa iha wacekiya*, "to pray with the pipe."

Sometime ago we tried to get a permanent building to
house the Sacred Pipe. We founded the Mystic Calf Pipe Association to raise money for this purpose, but finally we gave
up the idea. We realized that if we built such a place it would
only become a tourist attraction, and the Pipe would be dis-
honored. So we disbanded the association.

The Pipe is for all people, all races, as long as a person believes in it. Anyone can have a pipe and keep it within their
family. But only the Sioux can have ceremonies with the Sacred Calf Pipe. The Pipe bundle has always been opened now
and then by the person who is taking care of it at the time.
Different people are chosen to help in this ceremony. The Sacred Pipe is very powerful; it is at the center, and all other
pipes are like its roots or branches. The Sacred Pipe transfers
its power to the other pipes. All pipes have to be blessed,
made sacred (*yuwakan*). Any medicine man has the power to
do this, for a medicine man's pipe is very powerful. But many
people want their pipes blessed by the Sacred Pipe. Every
year they come to Green Grass to pray with the Pipe and have
their own pipes blessed.

In 1974 they had a Sun Dance in Green Grass, and we decided at that time to have a Sacred Calf Pipe ceremony, the
first one since I became the keeper. It is a hardship to have so
many people coming one at a time to pray with the Pipe, so we

thought we would have a big ceremony and let everybody come at one time. On the hill by my father's house we made a big altar (*owanka*) with four poles set in the four directions. Colored cloths symbolizing the four winds are tied to these poles. The altar is in the shape of a square, the four directions. It is supposed to be outlined with small bundles of tied tobacco (*canli wapaȟta*), but because we use this altar over and over, we have outlined it with rocks. The Sacred Pipe is kept nearby in a little house painted red. It is well protected. The Pipe is wrapped in a plain tanned buffalo robe. Other things that go along with the Pipe are also kept in the house, including a drum and various offerings that have been presented to the Pipe.

In the ceremony the Pipe bundle is taken out of its house and placed within the altar. It is not allowed to rest on the ground, but is instead placed on a tripod. All the people can come and pray with it. First they must cleanse themselves in the sweat lodge. Many medicine men help us in these ceremonies. Everybody knows what to do; no one tries to be the leader. During the ceremony the drum is brought out and the singers sing the special sacred songs of the Pipe ceremony. The singers come from all over; they are not medicine men, but are the men who know all of the ceremonial songs. Every year people bring their own pipes to this ceremony to have them blessed or reblessed. A person may have his pipe reblessed whenever he feels that he needs it.

Our people have had all kinds of trouble in recent years, and many have failed to respect the Pipe and our religion. Sometimes even medicine men have acted badly. Many times people have not prepared themselves properly for ceremonies. They have not cleansed themselves in the sweat lodge. In ceremonies the spirits told us that we should put the Sacred Pipe away for seven years, to give the people time to think about their lives and straighten out. The last Pipe ceremony was held in 1980, during the summer. We still have a long time to wait for the seven years to pass. Then we will have the Pipe ceremony again. Some people say that when times are bad, the Pipe grows shorter, but this is not so. It is the same length now as it has always been.

The power of the Pipe is real. Once the Indian agent sent the Indian police to bring the Sacred Pipe to Cheyenne Agency, the reservation headquarters. As soon as they did, the Indian police began to die, one by one. So the agent asked the keeper to come after his Pipe. He went and got it and instead of riding, he walked all the way home to Green Grass. But all the policemen involved in it died off.

Our people used to be probably in the Minnesota area, or eastern South Dakota. Then we came west of the Missouri River and pushed out different tribes that were here. The Sioux were strong; they had many societies, and they were well organized. They taught their children a positive attitude. From the time they were nine or ten years old, children were taught how to use the power of their minds. Then they prepared them to go up on the hill—to go on a vision quest. Before people went on the hill they had to prepare themselves for a long time, keep themselves clean and prepare for a year. They had to learn everything they needed to know before they went on the hill, for it was in this way that individuals got their power.

The sweat lodge was basic to this. It is called *ini kaǧapi,* "purification lodge." The sweat lodge is a world half on top of the earth, half under it. Probably it means day and night, I don't know. The center is the fireplace where the sacred rocks (*inyan wakan*) are placed. They build a fire some distance away to heat the rocks for the sweat lodge. When the fire is lit they use the smoke from burning sage to purify the path from the fire to the sweat lodge. This is the *inyan canku,* "road for the rocks." Once they start the fire, people should not cross this path. The first four heated rocks are placed in the sweat lodge fireplace in the pattern of the four directions. The next three represent up, down, and center. So the first seven rocks represent all seven directions. The other rocks represent different spirits and are placed in any order on top of the first seven. It does not matter how many rocks there are altogether. It depends on the person who is making the sweat lodge.

The sweat lodge is very sacred. It is the mother's womb. They always say when they come out of the sweat lodge, it's like being born again or coming out of the mother's womb. Each person carries some sage with him into the sweat lodge. When the lodge is closed, and the steam is very dense, chewing on the sage helps you breathe.

After being purified in the sweat lodge, a person may go on the hill for a vision quest. There the spirits come to a person and become the person's helpers. These helpers work between the earth and *Tunkašila,* "Grandfather." *Tunkašila Wakan Tanka* is our Great Grandfather, and the spirits work between here and there. A medicine man has to put a person on the hill because the medicine man knows what to do. He must communicate what the person is doing on the hill. Both the person on the hill and the medicine man have to use their minds. By sitting down and thinking about it, a medicine man can feel how the person is doing on the hill. If a medicine man is going to put a person on the hill, he has to know how to go about it. Each person has to have his own vision; he cannot buy a spirit helper. Some people sell medicine rocks—usually for money—but they are really not supposed to do that.

The *yuwipi* and *lowanpi* are different ceremonies that medicine men perform. They are very similar and both use the pipe. These different ceremonies come from the different visions that people have on the hill.

Myself, I am just a normal person like anybody else, living day by day. I always visit with the old people and learn their stories. I put a lot of things together from what they tell me. It is really oral tradition, from my family and from medicine men. Sometimes I have ceremonies. The medicine men call me on the telephone and give me advice, tell me what is going on. That way I keep on top of things. The medicine men do not communicate too much among themselves, but they all try to help me out because I am supposed to use the Sacred

Pipe to help my people. Someday, I will pass the Pipe on as my grandmother did.

Everybody—almost every family—has a pipe. I, too, have my own pipe with which I pray. The pipe is very sacred, for the stem represents a man, and the bowl, which is red, represents a woman. The Sacred Pipe is the center, and all the other pipes are the roots. When the people pray with the pipe, then the spirits come. Sometimes it takes time, but they do come. It is our way. The Sioux people believe in the Sacred Pipe.

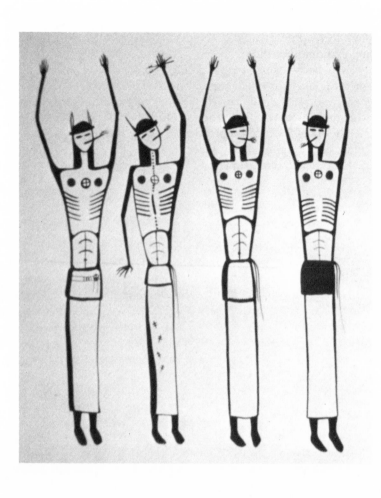

4

The Lakota Sun Dance
Historical and Contemporary Perspectives

BY ARTHUR AMIOTTE

DURING recent years I have affiliated myself with several elderly men who are the active and functionary intercessors of the contemporary Lakota Sun Dance ceremony. I have performed much as their helper, as an apprentice, and so my understanding comes from that relationship. In addition, I have studied the published and unpublished manuscript materials. This is a phenomenon that we will see occurring more and more in the future, as young Native Americans search for a deeper and more profound understanding of their contemporary culture by studying written records. Moreover, these people will bring to those records knowledge gained from actual experience observing and participating in traditional ceremonies.

Contrary to what many people say, or what we may read in the literature, even though the Sun Dance was officially prohibited during the 1880s, it never became extinct. From oral tradition we have evidence of people on numerous Sioux reservations having sneaked off to the badlands or to hidden places in the hills where these formal ceremonies took place in as close to their original form as they could be. Beginning as early as 1924, and developing especially during the 1960s and seventies, we had the revival of the ceremony proper, gradually moving out of its transitional phase where it was part powwow and part Sun Dance and part annual fair. We have seen a renaissance take place recently in which the Sun Dance was returned somewhat to its formal, intensely sacred character, with many of the same restrictions and dimensions that it had in its historical setting.

There are, of course, many things about the technological age in which we live that simply cannot be avoided, so my presentation is going to deal with the contemporary Sun Dance. But I think you will be able to perceive something of the historical element that still persists in today's Sun Dance.

Deep in the heart of winter on any reservation, now at this moment, on this day, there may be people gathered together in a meeting hall. Perhaps there are women cooking pots of soup, getting prepared for an evening meeting, perhaps even this evening. At the appropriate time, when it seems right, the people will arrive at someone's house. There they will select from among their own, or from others afar, he who will be the *wicaša wakan*, the *itancan wakan*, the "sacred man," the "head man" of the sacred camp, he who will be the intercessor, the shaman who will intercede on behalf of the people. It is he who will perform the tasks of sacrifice in order that the world may be recreated and that man be reactivated with the *wakan* force of the universe. Numerous other officials, the assistants to the intercessor, will be selected as well.

The head singer—that person who knows the numerous songs that go with each intricate part of the rite—must be selected. There will be the selection of the sacred woman, she who will become *Pte san win*, White Buffalo Woman, she who will dance with the pipe and endure and sacrifice much the same way as the men do. One lady will be chosen to attend to the ladies in their sweat lodge. Men will be chosen in the capacity of grandfathers to the young men who will be dancing. Young virgins will be selected to perform the tree-chopping ceremony. Those who are to preside over the tree ceremony and those who will carry the tree back to camp will also be selected. There will be chosen from among the people those who will sponsor and sacrifice and feed the people at any other ceremonies that might take place at the same time, such as the *hunka* ceremony or the White Buffalo ceremony for the young ladies in the camp. Perhaps there will be a name-giving ceremony. People will step forth and make pledges, donating thousands of dollars worth of beef and goods to be given away as gifts to visitors and to the dancers from afar. The lodgemaker will be chosen—that man and his family who will construct the sacred lodge as a sacred task. He may have helpers. Attendant with that will be the selection of those priests who will assist in the creation of the sacred place.

Such preliminary meetings did not occur in historical times. Today they are necessary because the people no longer live all in a single place, and coordination of the many activities required for the ceremony has become more complicated.

All of these things must be accomplished before the sacred time comes. The Northern Lakota tradition, that of the Hunkpapa and Sihasapa (Blackfoot Sioux) bands, is to have the Sun Dance take place around the summer solstice, when the juneberries are ripe. When the time has been designated, realizing that there are many hundreds, perhaps thousands, of people coming from hundreds of miles away—in automobiles, not on horses as they did long ago—preparations must be made to select the site. Originally a place was chosen that had not been used by other people, a place where water and cottonwood trees were close and there was an abundance of *peji hota,* the sacred sage, and an abundance of dry wood for the campfires. In modern times such places are comparatively rare, an indication of how life has changed.

As it is, weeks, perhaps even months before the dance, the four priests will have made four journeys on four separate days to look for and examine a particular site that they think will be suitable to take care of the people. Done as committee work, there is perhaps a bit more stress and strain, but once the headman has been chosen he becomes the officer, the person in charge, and the rest of the people yield to his judgment. With his shirt of office, the people hope that he will make wise decisions so that everything will go properly.

Historically, we know that once the Sun Dance camp was formally established, the temporal leadership—the *itancan* or *naca omniciya* (the chiefs or the council)—no longer had power. The power to rule this camp was handed over to the sacred leaders, and the *akicita* societies (men's societies) became the regulators of the sacred camp. Today, people are appointed to some degree to represent the old *akicita* societies, and the period of sacred leadership begins.

Meanwhile, at great distances away—Chicago, Bismarck, Rapid City, Los Angeles, Washington, D.C.—families have already taken pledges, and some are already preparing themselves, abstaining from the mundane affairs of life, perhaps fasting one or two days a week, attempting to hold the sharpness of their tongues, and storing away money to be used for expenses in journeying to the sacred center. Perhaps in their minds they are returning to that mythical time at the beginning of the world, to the sacred lodge of the *Pte oyate* (Buffalo People, the ancestors of the Lakotas) that existed originally underneath the world, to a re-creation of that sacred spot through which the Buffalo People came into this world, and the other beings with them (see Walker 1917:181–82; 1983: 245–89).

The young ladies who have been selected for their offices are not allowed to attend local school dances. They are not allowed to date boys. They, too, are leading a restricted life in preparation for the sacred journey. The old-man-who-counts watches the sunset, cutting notches in his stick, even though with calendars this is no longer necessary. The old man watches until the sun sets on a well-known landmark. When finally it reaches the appropriate place, the time has come to make the sacred lodge.

Following the purification rite, the four priests with their sacred media proceed to the sacred area. There, with their sacred paints and sacred tobacco, they step to the spot where the sacred tree will be planted. They stop four times along the way, joking with one another, replicating the state of chaos that the world is in at this time. The final step becomes one of ultimate seriousness, however, for they have arrived at the potential place that will become the center of the world.

First sanctifying the knife over burning sage to dispel evil, then resanctifying it in the smoke of sweetgrass to bring in the good influence, the earth is cut in a sacred mandala. This is the first of the "mellowed earth altars" that release the potential of the earth. For this is where the axis mundi will be placed, the tree of life, that central connection between the masculine powers of the zenith and the feminine powers of the nadir; that means, that principle, that pipe, that body, that avenue through which the sacredness of the world will be connected, and to which man in awesome sacrifice will be connected so that he, too, may participate in the bringing down and the bringing up and the sharing of that sacred power of the *wakan*. In a cross formation, the lines are cut in the four cardinal directions to reestablish this place as indeed the center of the world. Sacred tobacco and sacred paint are placed in these cuts.

Then the sacred cottonwood stake with a rawhide thong attached is drawn into this center of the world and touched with the sacred pipe, for these are one and the same happening now, which will become one and the same in the future when the tree is brought in. Next the lodgemaker unrolls the cord of life out to the west and marks off the western entrance, then proceeds around the outside edge of the sacred ground and establishes the north, then the east, then the south. Attached to the center by the once-living cord of the bison, that living cord which connects us all to the sacred, he reiterates in his mind the travels of the sons of *Tate* (the Four Winds that are sons of the Wind) as they set out to create the directions when there was no direction. Entrances—not walls—are marked off at each of the four directions. Two tipi stakes are placed on each side of what will be an entrance to the sacred area. Then the entire area is purified with burning sage and resanctified with burning sweetgrass. Finally, the people recede, walking backward to the edge of the space. They return to the sweat lodge, before resuming their mundane tasks until the time of the Sun Dance proper. All is in readiness; the lodge is partially built.

On the appointed day, coming from great distances, their headlights appearing at four or five o'clock in the morning, the people arrive, and all of a sudden the circular camp of the Lakotas appears miraculously—tipis, whitewall tents, brightly colored modern nylon tents. Their vehicles are parked behind or beside—no longer is the favorite horse attached to the tipi, but rather the favorite car. Those who had pledged to provide for the smaller ceremonies immediately begin making preparations, perhaps by the morning of the first day. They may take two or three days to set up the camp. Already at that time small *hocoka* (camp circles) set with flag offerings to the four directions are established before the individual camps. Great quantities of meat and other food are being prepared behind the individual camps.

At the appropriate time the *eyapaha* (crier) travels around the camp in his vehicle, perhaps with a loudspeaker attached, singing a song to the people, inviting them to so-and-so's camp because they are providing a feast for their daughter. Their daughter is one of those who is going to be chopping the tree, so they invite the people to their camp to honor her, for on this day she will be made a Buffalo Maiden. All the people move toward this one camp, bringing their dishes of tin, paper, or plastic. When they arrive, they sit down. Already the sacred altar has been made. Then the whole family comes out of the tent, parading their goods, parading their people into the center for *Lakol wicoȟ'an waštelaka* (for the "love of Lakota tradition"). For the love of tradition, they say, we are going to do this. We are going to sacrifice. We are going to sanctify. We are going to enter a miniature center of the world in preparation for the big one.

The ceremony takes place, the child is sanctified, the people are fed, great quantities of gifts are given away, and about that time it may be ready for the Sun Dance proper to begin. The dancers congregate at the purification lodges, taking with them all the things that they will need for the next day. Some of them begin their fasting and begin purifying themselves in the sweat lodges.

Early the next day the scouts are sent out to survey the countryside to select the sacred tree, that one which is standing at the center of the tree nation, that one we will rely upon, that one which will come back and be the tree of the world. They leave, and in due time they return, proceeding in a zigzag fashion toward the east entrance of the sacred lodge. Meanwhile, standing in the entrance of the sacred lodge, is the *wicaša itancan wakan*, the holy headman, with his helpers and the singers. The singers are singing *akicita olowan*, songs that honor returning warriors. As they come back they march in a zigzag fashion, stopping four times and howling like wolves to indicate their success. As they approach the east entrance, the intercessor asks in sign language, "Have you located the enemy?" And they sign, "Yes, we have."

Everyone in the encampment, dressed in their finest regalia, wearing their Lakota best, rides on their four-wheeled horses in a long procession to where the sacred tree is standing. They may have to walk part of the way, because one sometimes cannot get close to tree people in vehicles. Once they are assembled beneath the sacred tree the rite begins, prayers are said, the pipe is filled. Perhaps by now the' intercessor has hushed away the protector spirit of the tree, which sometimes exists in the form of a snake lying coiled about the bottom of the trunk. The snake must be escorted out of the sacred area without injuring it, telling it, "Your job is done now." (Once, when a huge bull snake was being shooed away, I could have sworn that, as it slithered off, it looked back as if to say, "Well, okay, I'll go then!") The intercessor, with his pipe and his stick, shoos away the snake so that the rite can proceed.

The four maidens are brought before the tree with their aunts or their mothers standing behind them. There they are reminded of their significance and their relationship to the earth. They are told: "You are the pure, you are the good, you are the fecund, you are the new life of the people. Through you, the women, even the bravest of warriors must come into this world. You are the earth, and by helping us to recreate this earth, you will be giving new life to the tribe. On this day you are going to undertake a difficult task." The maidens have their hatchets with them. Their faces are painted red, and each wears something red. Again they are told: "Remember this tradition that you may teach your own children, that it will never be forgotten. Without you this ceremony cannot be completed."

One by one, the maidens are led to the tree, where each strikes it with her hatchet, thereby symbolically killing the enemy. The drum beats, the women make the *li-li-li-li* sound (the tremolo), and the men give the warrior shout, *akiš'a*. Prior to this the uncles of each of these girls have gotten up and told their brave deeds in active service, vicariously transferring their warrior status to their nieces. After the girls are finished, their warrior uncles—the veterans—actually cut down the tree. Meanwhile, the ladies and the men have gathered robes, for the tree cannot land on the ground. All the ladies and the girls who participate lay out their shawls, their robes, their blankets, so that the sacred tree will not touch the ground. As it falls to the south, the direction to which all souls go when they leave this world, it is received by the people. The men carry the tree upon their shoulders, while the ladies walk behind and underneath, holding their robes so that none of the leaves touch the ground. They proceed now to a flatbed truck and place the tree on the rack, all wrapped in the robes so that no part of it touches the ground. No one can go in front of the tree from this time on.

As they proceed back to the sacred circle where the tree is to be planted, the songs for a fallen warrior are sung once again, for this tree being which is to stand at the center has been ritually killed and transformed into something else. Sacrificial transformation (in Latin, *sacer faceri*, "to make sacred," to transform one sacred substance into something other than what we perceive it to be) is a key to just about every aspect of Lakota ceremonial life.

When the tree has arrived at the Sun Dance camp, it is brought through the east entrance of the sacred circle. Four times the men carrying it stop to howl like wolves or coyotes. As the sacred tree is received at the center, a shaman begins to dig a hole to receive it. The dirt itself is removed from the earth, and offerings—*wasna* (pemmican), sacred red paint, buffalo fat—are fed to the earth as gifts. Meanwhile, a man paints the tree in a sacred fashion, using the sacred red paint. He is a very old man, and he weeps as he goes about his work because he realizes the significance of what is to take place.

Offerings are attached to the top of the tree—formerly, a quilled buffalo robe, but in modern times a piece of red cloth. Then the rawhide cutout images of a man and a buffalo are tied at the top to the fork of the tree. The man represents our enemy, the buffalo represents that which we need to support our lives. In modern times life is different, but we still seek to conquer that which stands in the way of true enlightenment, and man is still his own worst enemy. The bison represents the plentitude of the earth, something that we all need today as much as ever. At this time the sacred bundle is also attached to the crutch of the tree. It contains the sacred implements for making life—the *wahintke* (hide-tanning tool), the knife, a piece of *papa* (dried meat) with an arrow stuck through it, a woman's sewing awl, a tent stake for staking out a horse—all those things that mankind needs to construct and preserve life. The very tools that he uses are placed in a rawhide bundle and attached to this tree, as much as to say: "Oh, Ancient Gods, we wish to live! This is how we live. Give us strength to use these tools properly that the people may live."

At the appropriate time the ropes of sacrifice are attached to the tree, and by lifting and pulling the tree in four successive stages, it is raised up and centered into the hole. Whereupon the cry of the people goes up—the women give the tremolo, the men the warrior shout, the drummers beat their drum, the people cheer. At last, after all this time, we have arrived home. Our center is here. This is where we were, this is where we are, this is where temporal time is negated. We have now returned to mythical time. The world is repleat, the world is complete. By doing what we have to do, we can assist in the ongoing creation of this world, for this is the way our grandfathers taught us to do this. This is the way the White Buffalo Woman taught us to do this.

These are the ancient ideas that perhaps existed even before the Pipe was brought to us, but which became formalized as a result of the Pipe, for the Sun Dance is probably the most formal of all learning and teaching experiences. Inherent in the Sun Dance itself is the total epistemology of a people. It tells us of their values, their ideals, their hardships, their sacrifice, their strong and unerring belief in something ancient. In joyous recognition of having arrived home, having conquered the enemy, having conquered time and space, a victory dance is held at which all the people are welcomed to dance here about the center of the world, smashing down the grass, clearing the dance circle of pebbles and twigs that might be in the way of the dancers' feet.

At the conclusion of the dance it is not uncommon to see standing at the east entrance a young mother and father, perhaps an old mother and father, perhaps a grandmother and grandfather, with a tiny child. They come into the center, to the tree, bringing their gifts. Sometimes they have horses, sometimes they do not. The little child is brought in before the sacred tree. The appointed officials bring their little sharp tools and with proper purification, the child's ears are pierced—his spiritual ears, the ears of his *naġi*, his ghost. The child's physical ears are pierced indeed, but more importantly, the ears of his intellect, his mind, are also pierced so hopefully from then on he can hear the voices of the spirits and of the grandfathers. That done, the parents distribute their gifts to the crowd, take up their child and walk away.

Following the victory dance, the purification lodges begin and continue until the next day. At sunrise each day, from the inception of the dance up to the time that it actually takes place, there are morning songs for securing good weather. Perhaps some families have even made offerings to the West.

For this puppies are painted with sacred blue paint, choked, butchered, boiled, and eaten in sacrificial ceremonial feast. These sacrifices are made so that the Powers of the West will be benevolent with their weather, that the sky will be a clear blue color with not too many clouds, and that the nights will be pleasant.

On the morning that begins the first day of the Sun Dance, the dancers arise and prepare themselves with their accoutrements. At this time the sacred paints may be applied to them. In a long procession they walk around the outside of the sacred lodge to stand at the entrance. Then they proceed into the center of the lodge and stand facing the east, waiting for the sun to rise and travel down the eastern road into the Sun Dance lodge. But before this can happen we hear a single man's voice, accompanied by a hand drum, singing the song that White Buffalo Woman is supposed to have sung when she came from the east: "I Walk in the Sacred Manner." We see the sacred woman appearing on the horizon in her white buckskin dress, her face painted red, walking very, very slowly. All the people are gathered facing her. As she comes, she walks around the lodge clockwise, proceeds to the center, presents the pipe to the intercessor, then goes to her sacred place, where the mellowed earth altar will be built.

At this time the pipe is ritually filled with sacred tobacco. Symbolically identified with all things in the universe, the grains of tobacco are carefully placed in the bowl, the bowl itself being the center of the world. This is touched to the sacred tree, and the pipe is then taken and handed to the White Buffalo Woman. She offers it to the Powers and at last the dance begins. The dancers face the sun, looking into it, protected by the wreaths of sage around their ankles, their wrists, their heads. They stare into the sun with upraised arms, beseeching, praying. Some hold their hands open, palms to the sun, honoring the Powers. Others bunch their fingers together in a ritual gesture, calling down mercy and strength from the Powers.

As the dancers begin their sacred dance, the mellowed

earth altar is constructed. It, too, is a center—another center. The maker of the sacred place lies down and weeps to the earth and the sky, asking them to forgive him for what he is about to do, but saying that it is necessary if life is to come into this world again. With the properly incensed and purified instruments he proceeds to cut into the earth for the altar, mellowing it, picking it free of any small twigs or grass, making it nice and clear. Then he places upon it the mandala of the center of the world, filling the design with the sacred tobacco and the sacred paints. He places the meat rack at the back of the altar, near the buffalo skull which has been brought in previously.

A Northern Lakota tradition calls for a visitation to an ancient site where there are petroglyphs, sacred markings on rock. The intercessors leave during one of the breaks in the ceremony and go to the sacred place. There offerings are made to the sacred markings. The designs are memorized, brought back, and replicated on the mellowed earth altar. Oddly enough, it is not unusual to find that a certain kind of transformation does take place even today. Year after year the visitation to the sacred site reveals to us that the marks do change, and in each year they are in turn brought back and replicated on the sacred altar. Following the Sun Dance proper, the shamans gather together in the purification lodge—the sweat lodge—and interpret those markings in terms of the potential message that they might have for the people during the forthcoming year.

Before we can understand the Sun Dance, we need to examine the nature of the Lakota person and how he perceives himself in relation to the world. For the Lakota believes he has not one soul but four. Without understanding this we cannot very well appreciate the significance of the ritual.

The first soul is called the *niya*, a word which comes from *woniya*, "life breath." It is that aspect of an individual that ties his body to his innermost. In the purification lodge (*inipi*) a person not only sweats and releases toxic matter through his pores but also does something to his innermost, just as the process of eating purified food, food cooked in a ritual fashion, takes care of one's physical being. Anyone who has seen a corpse knows that something is missing from that body. It is devoid of movement. The Lakota people would say its *niya* is gone. Now the other three souls just might still be there—which gives rise to the meaning of ritual burial.

The second soul is the *naġi,* which is comparable to the stereotypical ghost—it looks like us, it retains our personality. In the Lakota person it is very capricious. When you consider the range of individual personalities, a *naġi* separated from its body could be malicious or benevolent depending upon the nature of the person it originally belonged to. So in a sense the *naġi* retains something of the personality of the individual.

The third soul, the *naġila,* the "little ghost," is another approach to the concept of *Takuškanškan,* "That Which Moves," or "That Which Causes All Things to Move." Inherent in this concept is a vision of the entire universe as infused with a force of movement. We can think of *Takuškanškan* as that which causes the sun to shine, the stars to twinkle, the earth to move (since science tells us it does move), the sunlight to reach the earth, the water to penetrate the earth, the seed to start regenerating within itself for life to come. *Takuškanškan* is that which from the moment of conception causes those two things that a man and a woman bring to new life to start multiplying, that which causes all things to be in motion and to be alive. The *naġila,* to some degree, is that part of *Takuškanškan* which is in all of us. If there is a prayer in Lakota that adequately expresses this, I think it is *Mitakuye oyas'in,* which means "I am related to all things," "all my relatives," or "I am related to all that is." When you consider that we share the common energy force of *Takuškanškan,* of course, we are related to everything. The Lakota person does not forget this.

The fourth soul, the *sicun,* has to do with that sacred power that can be received by people through the intervention of and intercourse with the supernatural. The man who has a vision of the eagle is himself in a state of *naġi* at the time that it happens. Perhaps it is the *naġi* of that eagle that appears to the man in a sacred-vision questing place and tells him: "*Kola,* you have done this. I wish to give you something of myself, something of my power." It may be an animal part, a song, a prayer, a stone. When that man is purified after the ritual and returns home to his mundane life, he has within his own bundle or medicine object that thing given to him by his spirit helper, imbued with, bursting with, imploding with *sicun.* When he proceeds to utilize it to do fantastic things in curing or as a protective device before he goes into battle, or as a means of honing his intellect in preparation for doing difficult things, with proper ritual he opens his *wotawe* (war medicine) or his *wopiye* (medicine bundle). He puts his ritual paraphernalia about himself and goes back in his mind to the time he received it through the vision experience, in some degree activating it so that its power joins with his own power, thereby transforming him. He is no longer himself. He is his spirit helper; his spirit helper is him. This can be attested to by the change in his voice, the change in the pattern of his movement. He is something else. Those who have the capacity have been able to see shamans in broad daylight as being other than what they are as human beings.

Realizing that each of these four souls needs to be attended to, the role of Lakota ritual is to nurture them all. The *niya* needs to be strengthened, the *naġi* needs to be strengthened, the *naġila* needs to be strengthened, and one can gain *sicun* through proper sacrifice. So in the Sun Dance, when the dancer's flesh is cut and the thongs are attached, the man perceives this not as torture but rather as the embodiment of the profound truth that the entire four parts of him are literally being joined to the sacred power inherent in the sun, the tree, the zenith, and the nadir, all of the forces of the earth that are centered there. Through sacrifice, through being made sacred, through being transformed, his very spirit selves are attached to That Which Is Sacred.

We all know it is dangerous to try to stay in the sacred world for very long, so the teaching is that one must try to release one's self as quickly as possible. Otherwise one might find it so wonderful there that one would want to stay. So those attached to the sacred tree must use every effort to free themselves quickly. Some people mistakenly perceive this as self-torture, and it is exactly because of this misunderstanding that the dance was originally forbidden as a heathen rite. But for the one who understands it, there is a profound realization in the dance, a sacred ecstacy, a transformation whereby he realizes the wholeness and unity of all things. The spiritual, the temporal, the gross, the profane, the common all come together at one time. Through this the individual transcends all that we know of this life and finally arrives at the real world, the real place.

Today we may hear criticisms of the use of tin buckets, kettles, loudspeakers at the Sun Dance. I think we should realize, however, that Lakota culture has never been static; it never has been monolithic. It always has been undergoing a process of change. In fact, the process of life itself is one of transformation. As cultural beings what is important to us is, that despite our having taken on many aspects of modern technology, the sacred intent continues to remain the same. That is the very core of the meaning of sacred Lakota traditions.

PART TWO

CHRISTIANITY AND THE SIOUX

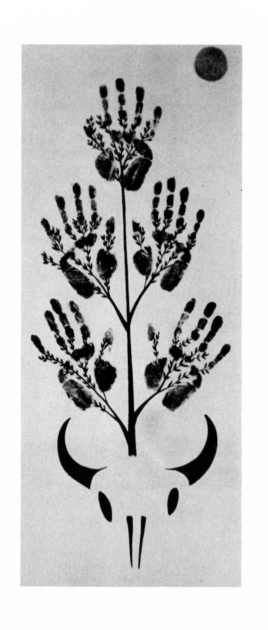

5

The Establishment of Christianity
Among the Sioux

BY VINE V. DELORIA, SR.

MY SUBJECT is the establishment of Christianity among the Sioux. First I want to say that I am not a scholar. What I am going to relate comes from the people from whom I heard it, early missionary workers. My grandfather Francis Deloria was the son of a Frenchman, named Philippe des Lauriers, who was married to a Sioux woman. Grandfather was born about 1816 and died in 1876. He was a leader among the Yankton Sioux, and he was a member of the first generation to put aside the old beliefs and turn to Christian teachings. His son Philip, born in 1854, was my father, and he told me about Francis Deloria's experiences with the traditional Dakota religion and of his eventual conversion to Christianity. By telling the story of the Deloria family I can best illustrate what the establishment of Christianity among the Sioux meant to the Indian people themselves.

In the days of my grandfather the Yankton tribe must have been much larger numerically than it is now, perhaps five thousand people. Father told me the story of my grandfather Francis and how he finally went on a vision quest. And in telling me the story, he had to describe the way twice a year they had *oyate okiju,* "assembling of the people." Of course, nothing is perfect in this world, and so this does not mean that every single Yankton family came to such gatherings. But a good majority of them did come. Then they would camp in three circles of tipis, with a gap of about half a mile between each circle. My grandfather and family—that is, his parents and brothers and sisters—were camping in the middle circle.

On this occasion the Yanktons were camped in a flat bottom somewhere along the Missouri River. And one day the boys from the circle on the east end challenged the boys of the middle circle to a game of ground hockey. We call it shinny usually. There were about twenty players on each side. They started in the middle and played, we would say, probably about six or seven hours back and forth and back and forth. When they finally stopped, the sun was low on the horizon. My grandfather's team had lost, and good manners called for an invitation from the winners to a feast; so all these boys got together with their mothers helping them and had a nice, big feast. And afterwards—it was another gesture of goodwill and friendship—they had a big dance for them. So they danced. My grandfather was sixteen years old at the time.

Finally, past midnight sometime, Grandfather started for home. When he got there and bent over to open the oval door to the tipi, he heard a voice to his left. It was not that of a human or an animal or a bird—of that he was perfectly sure. He went to bed, but was unable to sleep for a long time. Next day and for·some time, maybe weeks, he worried and pondered about that strange voice and finally got over it—finally forgot all about it.

Then by and by another year came around. It wasn't a time when the people were all assembled, but there they were, camped somewhere—I don't know; Father didn't describe that. But my grandfather Francis, now seventeen, was fast asleep. He was a good sleeper, and suddenly he found himself awake. He sat right up, drew up his knees, and rested his arms on them. And I guess by that time he was really fully awake. And he said, "What did I wake up for? Why, I never have done this before." He was sitting there, thoughtless, when the voice came again. And so he jumped up and went outdoors. He saw the moon. So he checked it, and then he recalled the month of the year. It wasn't January, it wasn't February, it wasn't the month that you get sore eyes from the glare of March snow. So it must have been April. And he tried to remember that moon.

The next year he spent I would say a very attentive year trying to keep his experience in mind. So when it was once again getting near that time of year, he stayed up past midnight. I don't know how many nights, but finally the voice did come again. He was eighteen years old now. And with that third voice, Francis Deloria was convinced—or convinced himself—that it was the Great Spirit, or the Great Holy, or That Which Is Holy, calling him.

Father didn't mention the next part, but I guess Grandfather may have been planning when and where to go on a vision quest. About that time my great-grandmother wanted to visit the *Hunkpapaya,* whom we now call the Standing Rock people. They're the people to whom Sitting Bull and Gall belonged. (I'm afraid too many of us Indians today do not say this name right. *Hunkpapa* is incomplete—it should be *Hunkpapaya.*) So my great-grandmother wanted to go and visit these people. One of her daughters, with a three-year-old boy, and Brown Bear, a cousin of my grandfather who was about the same age as Francis, and maybe fifteen or twenty other families, set off on the trip. They traveled on the east side of the Missouri, planning to cross farther up. They camped near where Blunt, South Dakota, is today—about twenty miles northeast of Pierre. While they were camped there, Francis looked up at a big butte and said, "That is where I am going to go for my vision quest." And so his immediate family decided to stay there, and their other relatives and friends said, "Just a few of you should not stay here alone." So altogether about three or four families joined them and stayed.

Early in the morning he climbed up the butte and started his vision quest at sunrise. I have heard many times that when you go on a vision quest you stand or sit—there are two ways, to my knowledge—for four days, four complete days. And then if you don't see anything, if you don't have a vision, or if you don't hear a voice, you discontinue there and try it at some other time—try it again. So Grandfather stood there. They could see him from below, day after day. On the third day they saw him in the middle of the morning, but when they happened to look at noon, he was no longer standing there. Right away his mother told Brown Bear, "Get on a horse and go up there! He's been going like that for three days and he has probably fallen in a faint!" So Brown Bear rode up there. When he was reaching near the top, his horse would rear and want to come back down. There was a strong wind blowing. Finally, he noticed that the horse would snort and curve his neck, looking down. So Brown Bear looked down, and there were rattlesnakes crawling all over. But he wanted to see his cousin. So he kicked his horse and went a little farther up. Then he saw a whole pile of rattlesnakes, curling around all over on top of Grandfather, completely covering him.

Brown Bear reported back at camp. Immediately my great-grandmother, or father's grandmother, and her daughter went into mourning, cutting their hair and cutting their legs and arms with flint. But that evening at dusk, here my grandfather came through a few little trees growing there and arrived back in camp. He was really shocked to see his mother and sister in mourning. "What's the matter? What happened?" he said. So they told him the story, and he replied: "Why, no. There were no rattlesnakes up there that I noticed." Brown Bear had to go the rest of his life feeling that people were very skeptical about his report of the rattlesnakes. He even imagined that they concluded he had been afraid his cousin was dead, and therefore made this excuse. He went that way to his grave.

But here I want to insert how Brown Bear was later vindicated. Some years ago I told this story to a friend, who suggested that we visit the butte to see what it is like. So we did, and what we found was very, very interesting. There were stones, about the size of a man's fist, maybe some of them slightly bigger, placed in a circle with a diameter of about five feet. In the center you could see there was a depression in the ground, a place where somebody had gone on a vision quest and had dug a pit to sit in. And in a northwest direction there was a path, also outlined in stones, about three feet wide, zigzagging along for about fifty or sixty feet. So we followed it, and there at the end was the outline of a rattlesnake head, with his tongue sticking out. Right away I said, "Brown Bear was telling the truth! Somebody else came up here and had an experience with rattlesnakes."

So we go back to Francis Deloria. He did receive his vision. I don't know the full story, but I do know something about it. The first is the beginning of the vision, which must no doubt have been during that time he fell in a faint. In his vision he followed a path over the hills and through valleys until he finally came upon nice level ground. There, some distance away, he saw a black tipi. So he continued to follow the path, which led to the door of that black tipi. Inside it forked like a wishbone. At the end of the curved path on his right stood an unusually large black hawk. At the end of the curved path on his left was an unusually large white owl. The path to the right was red, and the one toward the left was white. Along the right path were four small purification lodges, sweat lodges. And along the left path were four skeletons sitting next to one another as if they were alive, their legs crossed, their fingers interlaced, keeping their legs supported; and their heads—or their skulls—were down.

Then he noticed that there was grass tied around the top of the skulls of each of the four skeletons, and grass was also tied around their wrists, hands, shoulders, backbone, and legs. And he didn't like that. But this beautiful red path was attractive. The minute he made up his mind to go on that, the hawk spoke to him in human language: "Come on. We knew that you were going to take that." And then the hawk said to the owl, "Come back over here now." So there he stood, the black hawk on his right, the white owl to his left, both facing him. The black hawk did all the speaking. He said: "You have just passed four purification lodges. That means you are going to kill four men of your own tribe, all Sioux."

That is all I know of the first part of Grandfather's vision. The other part I know is the end of the vision, where he found

himself a warrior of the skies. He found himself one of countless warriors on horseback to his right and countless warriors
on horseback to his left, and he also was on horseback. They
were on a cloud, the edge of a cloud, and they could see the
ground down below. Their horses were restless and reared in
the air, so that the riders had to pull them back and whip
them, then bring them back and try to calm them down, to
hold them in line. Grandfather asked, "Why are we up here?"
One of the warriors replied, "We're going to travel the length
of this land to the endless water" (*Mni wanca,* "endless water,"
the Atlantic Ocean). And Grandfather asked, "When do we
go?" One of the riders told him: "When there is lightning, followed by a little rumble of thunder. Then we'll go."

Grandfather looked down and saw an encampment, and he
noted there was a woman in a red dress who was very restless.
She would run around her tipi, run around her neighbors'
tipis, come back to her own, go inside, come out again—always looking up at the sky. Grandfather asked, "What's the
matter with that woman?" Again, one of the warriors replied:
"She promised to give us Thunder Gods a feast and she hasn't
done it. So when we move we are going to kill her." Pretty
soon there was that little flash of lightning, and that little
rumble of thunder. They took off, running their horses, but
never could get beyond the edge of the bank of clouds. Then,
when they went over the encampment, there was another
little flash of lightning—boom! They looked back and there
that woman was lying in front of her tipi, dead. When the
riders got to the endless water, they broke formation, and in
the air turned into yellow finches and started back. Flying was
a great deal of pleasure, maneuvering in the air. Grandpa had
never flown before, so he tried every trick that he could think
of. The birds flew up and down and around each other, and
eventually each went in the direction from which he had
come. Grandpa headed for that butte, and pretty soon he
could see himself lying on his stomach with one arm under his
head, and so he decided to land right between his shoulder

blades and down he came; and just as he touched himself, he woke up.

Now that's all I know about my grandfather's vision quest. I never heard the complete story.

Grandfather became, among other things, a medicine man (*wapiya wicaša*). All along he practiced medicine, using rituals, ceremonies, prayers, singing, and of course, regalia of a special nature that he had to wear. He had a pair of porcupine-quilled moccasins, both red, but on top of the foot in the center one had the outline of a black hawk, and the other a white owl. And Father said that in healing people, when he moved his right foot deliberately, the hawk foot, there was a hawk screeching in the room. When he moved his left foot, an owl hooted.

Of all his sons, Grandfather was especially fond of my father, Philip. He named him *Tipi Sapa*, "Black Lodge," after the black tipi in his vision. Whenever Grandfather went to heal the sick, he took Father along to carry a little drum. One time they went to minister to this very sick man who was lying in a log house. As he started to minister to him, Grandpa took the drum and sang this song:

He wakidowan can	Whenever I sing to him
Tiyata u we.	He comes to my dwelling place.
He naǧi ksapa wan	I call upon a wise servant,
Wa he wakidowan ye.	I sing to him.
He wakidowan can	Whenever I sing to him
Tiyata u we do.	He comes to my dwelling place.

When he finished, he handed the drum back to Father. Then there was a sound, in the southeast corner of the house. It was a gourd rattling, and when they looked, there were green sparks flashing from the rattle. Not too slowly, not too fast, the gourd rattle moved toward them until it got near my grandfather. My father said he forgot about the rattling sound and was sure that he heard whispering—they were talking to Grandfather in whispers. And when they were finished, my grandfather said, "*Ohan*," meaning "All right." As those spir-

its, or green sparks, began to move away, the rattling sound of
the gourd came back; and the gourd went out the northeast
corner of the house. And Grandfather said, "I'm awfully sorry,
but the spirits told me not to minister to this man." We don't
know why. At midnight my father said there was crying at that
log house. The man died.

My grandfather had a small stone, which must have been
given to him in his vision. It was wrapped in buckskin and was
tied to the base of the mane of one of his horses. A special
man had to lead that horse and not let the stone get wet—
unless with rainwater. One time the Yanktons were traveling—probably the White Swan band, or a part of them,
maybe twenty-five families. As they crossed a river, the horse
stumbled in the water and the stone got soaked. When they
got across, the man reported the accident to Francis Deloria.
Immediately, Grandfather said, "Where are the criers?" The
eyapaha, or criers, were usually old men. And he said: "Ho!
Give the cry! Put your tipis up and tie a rope to all the poles
inside at the top. Get a good stake with a little hook at the top.
Tie your rope there as tight as you can and hammer it down
into the ground. And drive the outside stakes around the tipi
cover deep into the ground because there will be a big storm—
wind, thunder, lightning, hail." It rained, thundered, and
lightninged—lightning flashed all around the tipis, but it
didn't hit anybody.

Grandfather used to be able to find things that were lost—
anything. I remember one story about a white man in Armor,
South Dakota, who had a crackerjack three-year-old race-
horse. He could beat everyone in the area. One day the horse
disappeared, and the man called on his neighbors for help.
Out they spread, but they couldn't find it. It was nearly a week
since the horse had disappeared, and Denny Moran, who was
married to a Yankton girl of the White Swan band, went to
the man in Armor. He asked, "Why don't you go down to the
Missouri River to that old man Deloria and ask him to find
your horse?"

"How can he find it?" he said.

"Well," Denny replied, "he sorta has mystical powers."

"Oh, I have no use for that hocus-pocus superstitious stuff. That's just practicing magic."

So Denny said, "Well, do you mind if I ask him?"

"No," said the man, "I don't care. Go ahead. It's not gonna hurt my horse one way or the other. It's probably dead by now anyway."

So Denny asked my grandfather. Father was still pretty young, but he was there. He said that his older brothers took everything out of their father's house. Then they brought in a pile of tanned buffalo hides and a lot of rope. And they tied my grandfather up in a bundle and laid him down. My grandfather, you know, was fat and round, so I guess he must have made a pretty high bundle. Then they shut the door. And my father said, "If we had had watches in those days, and I had known how to read one, I would say he walked out of there three minutes after they shut the door. And all those buffalo hides were just as they were when they were first brought in. I saw my brothers take one after another of those hides and tie my father up with rope. He couldn't have put those back in order in three minutes."

When Grandfather came out, he spoke to Denny. Although Denny was white, he could talk Indian. "Denny, hurry up," he said. "The horse is tied to a tree down toward the Missouri River, in one of the gullies going into the Missouri, in a fairly flat area. He's been going round and round the tree, so his track is finely powdered dust. He's been eating the tree bark and his stomach is pretty small. Take a bucket of water, soak a rag in it, and let the horse suck on the rag. Don't give him whole mouthfuls of water. Then he probably will go and lie down. Let him lie down."

They found him and did as they were told. The horse gradually recovered and got well. But he could no longer run.

Grandfather was married to three women. When his first wife was about twenty-three years old, she inherited a couple of new wives for her husband. They were just orphan girls, fifteen years old. But he waited until they were eighteen before he took them also as his wives. So from my three grand-mothers there were ten boys and twelve girls. My father once took me to see the place where my grandfather lived. It was only about forty yards from the bank of the Missouri. Father said: "Here is where my mother, the third wife, a Rosebud woman, lived. Your grandfather had log houses for each of his wives to live in and raise their children. About a good hundred yards away was where your direct grandmother lived, the Standing Rock woman, the sister of Two Pack. And over here, about a hundred yards up on this higher knoll, was grandma number two, the Crow Creek girl. And here, two hundred yards away, was a big square log house, and that's where your grandfather lived. His three wives took turns feeding him, and the daughters took turns cleaning house, washing for him, and so on." My father said that the children played all over that area. "I never felt that I had just one mother," Father told me, "I had three. Wherever I fell asleep, that's where I stayed."

Now let me tell about how Francis Deloria killed four Sioux men, according to his vision. One of his sisters was married to a man who beat her time and again. So Grandfather spoke to his brother-in-law and urged him to get along with his wife. But it did no good. Grandfather became angry and impatient with the man, and he said to him, "The next time you do this, I'm going to kill you." Sure enough, Grandfather heard his sister crying again. Grandfather rushed out and saw that his sister's husband had run into her and knocked her down, even though she was about near the time to give birth. So Francis Deloria rushed back in, took a double-barrel or something like that, and practically cut the man in two.

The second Sioux man he killed was one of his own sons-in-law, also a wife beater. After pleading with him for years, one day the girl cried again and called for her father. This time Francis just took his gun and went out. Then he saw that his son-in-law was forcing his daughter to walk barefoot over cactus. So he killed him, too.

The third killing took place after the Sioux uprising in Min-

nesota in 1862. Some of the Santees took refuge among the
Yanktons. General Alfred Sully came from Fort Randall to tell
the people that the government was very disappointed in
them. He reminded them that when Lewis and Clark had visited them in 1804, the explorers had wrapped a Yankton baby
born the day of their arrival in an American flag, and then
shaken hands with the leaders over the baby's body. By that
act the Yanktons had become allies of the United States government and people. The boy had grown up to be Struck by
the Ree, the top headman among the Yanktons. (The white
men like to call our leaders "chiefs," but we prefer to call
them "headmen," *wicaša itancan*. A headman might be defined as a person who serves his people in a special admirable
way in some area of need in human life.)

General Sully said to the Yanktons: "We have heard you are
sheltering some enemies of the people of the United States. I
am going to leave and be gone for two or three months. When
I come back I want to hear that you have shot a Santee. That
will prove you are our allies. I am supposed to drive all the
Santees out and open fire on them, but I'm not going to do it.
I want to be cooperative. But I must hear that you have shot
one." Then he left.

That evening Struck by the Ree, White Swan, Striker, and
all the other headmen of the Yanktons had a meeting. Struck
by the Ree reported the general's words. Then he asked one
headman after another if he would shoot one of the Santees
the next day. One by one they refused. Finally, he came to the
last one, Francis Deloria, and he said: "Yes, that seems to be
my destiny foretold. I'll kill one tomorrow."

The next day the Yanktons were on the move. Father didn't
tell me where they were going, but there they were, drag
poles behind their horses, some people walking on foot. My
father was about eight years old, and his cousin Baptiste Lambert was a year older. They were playing *painyankapi unpi*,
the hoop-and-pole game, as they went along. They rolled a
wooden hoop webbed in the center, and shot at it with short
spears, scoring points according to the location on the web-

bing through which their spears passed. Then two of Father's older brothers rode up. One said, "You two boys are supposed to go into those woods, and we are supposed to stand over there with you."

"Why?" they asked.

"That's our father's order."

"Why?"

Reaching for his riding whip, one of the older brothers started to get down from his horse, so the two younger boys ran.

"Can't you see up there on the hill?" one of the older brothers said. "See those men sitting up there on that hill, smoking? Can't you see our father, riding his gray horse, is going up there? He's going to shoot one of those men! One of those men must be a Santee."

That made it hard for the boys to keep their eyes away from the hilltop. The people as a whole all stopped what they were doing; the movement of the whole tribe stopped. When Francis Deloria got up there, the people could see a flash from the gun and the smoke from the barrel, and then hear the report. The men seated on the hill jumped up and ran off, all but one of them, who lay there kicking. All the people went up the hill, and the other brothers forgot to keep the younger boys back. So Father and Baptiste Lambert got up there, too. Father said the hill was covered with grass and the man lay there, bleeding out of the corner of his mouth. He kept rubbing his palm on the grass until his hand was full of ants. Father claimed he saw him swallow those ants. I guess the idea was that they would go down and mend his wound. But still he died.

So I heard that Grandfather handed over every weapon he had—gun, knife, bow and arrows—and got back on that gray horse. Then he rode over to the Santees and announced: "I'm going to sit here all night. Folks, I know that you are his relatives. I did a bad thing. You know why I did it. If you come up here and want to kill me, that will be fine. You will have no trouble." But nobody bothered him. That was the third Sioux he killed.

The fourth killing occurred after they were living on the reservation. Army officers were serving as Indian agents at that time. One day they called Francis Deloria to the agency. The army officer said to him: "Mr. Deloria, our government has been slow to deliver the wagons, harnesses, clothing, blankets, and food for the Indians." The goods were to be delivered at Wheeler landing, then transported to Rosebud, Pine Ridge, and various agencies. "A band of maybe two or three hundred people got tired of waiting, and now they are heading for Grandmother." That meant Canada, the country of Queen Victoria. "We don't know why the goods haven't been delivered, but we are going to give the Indians supplies from our own forts—food and blankets. The Indians will still get all of the other supplies when they arrive. We want you to catch up with those who have left, explain this to them, and bring them back. Captain Cunningham and sixty troopers will go with you."

Grandfather said: "No, I'd rather go alone. Those people will spot us and think that I am a traitor. They will expect the army to treat them in a rough way, as you usually do, instead of coming to talk to them civilly. So I would rather go alone." The captain insisted that the troopers must accompany him, but agreed that once they began to catch up with the fugitives, the soldiers would stay five miles behind and let Grandfather confer with the people alone.

So they went, and by and by Grandpa saw broken grasses and fires that had been put out. He told the captain that he would go on alone, the soldiers following him, but maintaining five miles' distance. Five days later, as Grandpa rode up on a hill, he saw the people moving camp. They spotted him and ran away, all but two men, one on a big, black horse, the other on a bay horse. They waited for Grandfather to come up to them. When he got to within hearing distance, one of the men said, "*Hun hun he*," in other words, "What do you know? What do you know? He is a Sioux." Then he spoke to Grandfather: "We scouts have been watching you for five days. There is one Indian riding ahead, but he has about a hundred troopers. When do you plan to attack us?" Pretty soon the man on the black horse lost patience. He wheeled that big horse around and came after my grandfather with a revolver. He shot twice, then as he pulled up alongside of him, he took another shot. All missed. He should have stayed behind and shot him from a distance. Grandpa lunged at the man, grabbed him by the wrist, and they both fell to the ground. Then he took the revolver away from him and shot him. Grandpa's gray was gone, so he grabbed the black horse by the mane, hopped on his back, and got away. The man on the bay horse didn't even chase him. So that was the fourth man he killed.

Grandfather was right. He should have gone after those people alone. The Indians so distrusted the soldiers that they would not even listen to what they had to say.

Francis Deloria and all the Yankton people settled on their reservation along the Missouri River. There were three communities there, from the three bands of the Yankton tribe. They were the White Swan band, on the north end; the Agency band, in the middle, near Greenwood; and the band on Shorter Creek, to the south. The Indians call this band by their name for the creek, *Nawizikicizapi wakpala*, "creek where two people fought out of jealousy." I suppose the whites called it Shorter Creek after some man named Shorter who lived there first. Grandfather belonged to the White Swan community, but he moved nearer to the Greenwood Agency.

After he killed the fourth man, Grandfather could never drink a cup of water or a cup of coffee in peace. The minute he looked into that cup, he would see the face of one of the men he had killed, with a sort of a snarling smile. So he used to shut his eyes to drink. And my father told me that the gray horse Grandfather had ridden when he killed two of the men would always come back from the herd. By healing people, being an Indian doctor, Grandpa had lots of horses. They gave him horses for his services, although he never asked for anything. Some people just gave him a pair of moccasins, and he was grateful. Others could give him nothing. If they were poor, he might give them something, besides healing the sick person. My father told me that many times he saw that gray horse with his own eyes, after Grandfather had turned him loose, come back at dusk and stand in front of my grandfather's log house. Every night he stood there until dawn, and then he would go back to the herd. Summer and winter. People asked Grandfather about this—it was known all over the White Swan community. He said: "The area of my power is like a circle, and he wants to come within that because otherwise the men I killed bother him." At least that's what he claimed.

When missionaries first came to the Yankton Reservation, Francis Deloria welcomed them with enthusiasm. He made some of his children attend the day school, and his son Philip— my father—particularly impressed the missionaries. Later they sent him to off-reservation schools to be educated. Grandfather had all of his children and grandchildren baptized, but he himself held back. Although he attended church regularly, he could not be baptized because he had more than one wife. One of his wives had died, and finally Grandpa arranged to send the other back to her people. Then on Christmas Day, 1871, he was baptized at last. In those days baptisms were public occasions. After the ceremony of baptism, the Indians heard speeches and enjoyed a feast. Grandfather told the missionary, Rev. Joseph W. Cook, of the Episcopal Church, that he had led a very wicked life, though he had acted out of ignorance of God's law. He said: "My friend, when you baptize people, you are accustomed to pour a little water upon them. I have been such an awful sinner that it seems to me you would need to take five or six barrels of water to wash away my sins." The missionary replied: "Never mind what you have been. Ask God to forgive you and he will take all your sins away." At the feast following the baptism, Grandfather picked up his cup of coffee. He thought, "I wonder which one will be looking up at me, smiling, snarling." But there was no face, no face at all. For Francis Deloria, his sins were gone.

After that, when my grandfather would go to church, Joseph Cook would ask him to stand up and tell people what Christ did for him. Father said he saw him do it several times. Grandfather would say, "*Hau.*" And from the pew he would get up and tell the story about having seen those faces. "I was living a very evil, bad life," he would say. "I didn't realize it. I didn't feel particularly sorry for taking the lives of those men. But now I feel really sorry. Those of you sitting here who have not been baptized, please get baptized. I know, I just told you from my own experience, that there is more to this baptism business than meets the eye!"

Grandfather remained a devout Christian the rest of his days. When he died in 1876 he was buried at Greenwood, in the big Episcopal cemetery on the hill. Before he died, he had the satisfaction of seeing my father made a deacon in the church in 1874. Later, in 1892, father was ordained a priest in the Episcopal Church.

Many of the Sioux entered church work in those early years. One man whom I remember well was Amos Ross, who was my uncle. I knew him in his old age when I was a missionary on the Pine Ridge Reservation, and he told me the story of his life. At the time of the Sioux uprising in Minnesota, he and his family, who belonged to one of the Santee bands, were living near the Canadian line. They were unaware of the fighting raging in the southern part of Minnesota. Nevertheless, they woke one morning to find themselves completely surrounded by soldiers. The commander ordered them to line up, wearing only the clothes they had on. They had to leave everything, including their tipis and horses, and they were marched south. It took two weeks for the trip. The military fed them once a day, in the evening.

Uncle Ross recalled a terrible incident from that journey. A woman had a small baby, nearly a year old. The baby was very sick. As they passed a fast-running stream, she called over to an interpreter so she could speak to the soldier who was marching along near her. She asked the soldier if she could run down to the stream and fill her cup with water to give to her baby. The soldier only smiled, jeeringly, and said "Here's the way to cure that baby." He jerked the baby away from its mother, grabbed it by its ankles, swung it overhead, and threw it into the bushes nearby. You could hear the baby hit the earth. That was the end. By the time they arrived at the end of their journey many of the people had worn out their moccasins and were walking on bloody feet.

They were placed in a military prison, an outdoor stockade, at Fort Snelling, Minnesota. Missionaries came to them, taught them about the Bible, and taught them to read and write. They also taught them about baptism. One missionary lined the Indians up and baptized them one by one, using a Bible to keep himself supplied with names. He must have been at the book of Amos when Uncle Ross knelt down. The missionary said to the interpreter, "Tell him that his name is going to be Amos. Tell him to say it." And so he said it, and then he was baptized.

Finally, they were taken to a reservation on the Missouri River. The missionary who had looked after them in prison came to visit them; his name was Bishop Henry B. Whipple, of the Episcopal Church. He was replaced by Bishop Clarkson of Omaha, and later, in 1873, by Bishop William H. Hare. Amos Ross worked at the agency. He was a wonderful carpenter. Bishop Clarkson interested him in becoming a helper, then a catechist, and then a senior catechist. Bishop Hare trained him as a deacon, and finally ordained him as a priest in 1892. Then he was sent out to missionize among the Rosebud Sioux and at Yankton. After he became a priest, he hardly ever worked among his own people, the Santees.

Uncle Ross did a wonderful job. Finally they assigned him the eastern half of the Pine Ridge Reservation, known as the Corn Creek mission. He worked there for many years and retired just at the time that I arrived in Martin, South Dakota, where I myself stayed for seventeen years. That's when he told me this story. At the time he retired he had eleven churches, eleven ministers, and a total membership of 1,776 people. He certainly did an admirable job as a priest for his Master.

My father told me how, when he was about ten years old (1864), an elderly missionary, a Catholic priest, came to the White Swan band. For about a week he preached to them throughout each morning about the gospel. Then he told them that in the afternoon after the last day's instruction they would be baptized. So the people stood before him in a mass, and taking a container of water, he sprinkled it to the right of them, to the left, over their heads, and at their feet. And he said, "That will have to pass for baptism. My intentions are good." I believe those people were validly baptized. I asked my father, "Was that man Father De Smet?" But he replied, "I'm sorry, I don't know."

There were four churches that were sent out to build missions among the Sioux: Catholic, Presbyterian, Congregational, and Episcopal. I must mention two of the early missionaries. One was a Congregationalist, Stephen Return Riggs. (I love that name, Return! That might have been an Indian name—*Kigla keš ake gli*, "Leaves but Returns.") The second was John P. Williamson, a Presbyterian. One of their great achievements for bringing God's message to the Sioux was their work in translating the Old Testament and the New Testament, not from the King James English version but from the French. An Indian mixed-blood, named Joseph Renville, assisted them. They sat for years by candlelight, translating the scriptures into beautiful Santee language. It gives me a thrill! The French could tell the word of God, the English could, and now the Indians could tell it, too.

Besides building churches and congregations and preaching the gospel, these four churches also went in for education. The Catholics had the largest number of schools. Next came the Episcopalians with four. The Congregationalists and Presbyterians together had that marvelous institution on the Santee reservation, called the Riggs Institute (the Santee Normal Training School). They also had the Riggs Oahe mission, and day schools as well. These mission workers are the men and women who established Christianity among the Sioux.

Let me tell about the Episcopalian Church's work, only because I know more about it than the others. Bishop Hare arrived in 1873. When he retired thirty-two years later, in 1905, he had ten thousand souls settled in one hundred chapels on the ten Sioux reservations, ministered to by six Indian priests, six white priests, and sixty lay ministers. Bishop Hare trained those Indian priests and Indian lay ministers by teaching them the Bible. He taught them the prayer book, and he gave them a booklet on the art of running a parish. That's all! But it thrills me how well he trained them, especially in the Old Testament. By teaching them the Old Testament he was really giving them a liberal arts education equivalent to a bachelor of arts, because the Bible contains all the subjects I had to study to get my B.A.: history, biography, poetry, social problems, economic problems, morality. The Old Testament is like a collection of all the experiences of three thousand years—like the brain of a man who has lived three thousand years and had all these experiences. This was the way their master, Jesus, learned. Like Him, the teachings of these early Indian ministers were simple, sound, sincere, solid, stimulating, and stabilizing! So that's how these early Indian ministers, who never went to school formally, received their training.

When Europeans first came to the New World, they admired the Indian people. Columbus wrote of their gentleness, faithfulness, and hospitality. But in time the white man's attitude changed. They came to see the Indian way of life as wrong and primitive. They believed the whole Indian way of life was the work of the devil and the powers of evil, wickedness, and ignorance. That's what the missionaries told us, and we believed them and gave it up—gave the whole thing up. And then what did Christianity do? Turn around and replace our superstitions with a set of their own. When an Indian prays over a stone and says he's made it holy, that's superstition and practicing magic. Why isn't it superstition when we pray over the water for baptism and the water suddenly becomes possessed of special qualities? The two things are exactly alike. The church calls its practices sacraments, while the Indian ones are only symbols.

During my career as a missionary I never questioned the Christian religion as reflected by the Episcopal Church. I was an orthodox Episcopal priest working among my own people.

I emphasized: "Christ saved you!" "He died for you!" "You are a sinner!" All my life I was basically what the church taught me to be, and I practiced all the rituals and ceremonies. But I never went in for the garb, the chasuble and so forth. I didn't have time for that!

Since my retirement I have come to look differently on the church. It seems to me now that the church leaders were wrong. There is too much of Saint Paul in their teaching—the Christ—and not enough at all of Jesus—the man. Christ the God and Jesus the man. So I set out to learn about the Jesus of history. There's my hero. Wonderful! It makes me feel enthusiastic to try to become like Him. I know I'll never get anywhere near Him, but it inspires me to strive. Although I am more than eighty years old now, I am still trying to grow, as Jesus did, on all four human sides: mental, physical, spiritual, and moral. The trouble with most of us is that we have developed only one or two sides, or if we have all four talents, each is weak. But I take comfort in the old Episcopal prayer book: "The world is made up of all sorts and conditions of men."

What I'm teaching now is not theology. It's just the art of living which we lost in the past. All we have to do is use some of the principles that are available to us through prayer, study, and thinking.

Maybe the recent movement on the part of us Sioux to revive our old religion, the religion of our ancestors, is a sign of the failures of the Christian situation. Today there is such a proliferation of churches that a lot of people get desperate. The church fathers ought to try to live the life of Jesus, but instead they are too busy revising the prayer book! The 1928 Episcopal prayer book is written in beautiful language, six hundred pages long. Now the new one is one thousand pages long! How on God's green earth can anybody worship God standing there thumbing pages? Page here and mumble words. This is not prayer. Now in desperation we blow balloons and let them go in church, and hug each other and kiss each other and add more and more ceremonies, as if that will give vitality to the church. But services like these are just programs and pageantry. I've been in faded Indian chapels where they sang simple hymns and said simple prayers and they read the Bible beautifully. Some of those catechists were real orators; they knew what they read, and boy, they moved you. And the singing just rattled the windows. When you would say, "The Lord Be With You!" the whole room rocked, "And With Thy Spirit!"

The Sioux are very spiritual people. They had spiritual strength before the white man brought them Christianity. We Christians need to shape up and think about where we're going if we want Indian people to remain in the church. For myself, I only know the gospel of Jesus. There in the words of Jesus lie the answers to the endless questions of mankind— what is the meaning of life, and how to live it. And that's as far as I can go.

6

The Catholic Mission and the Sioux
A Crisis in the Early Paradigm

BY HARVEY MARKOWITZ

SINCE their arrival on the Rosebud and Pine Ridge reservations in the late nineteenth century, the Roman Catholic religious of Saint Francis and Holy Rosary missions have ministered to what they have perceived as the spiritual, educational, and social needs of the Brule and Oglala Sioux. From the perspective of culture history, it is possible to deduce continuities and changes in the assumptions underlying these perceptions. By "culture history" I mean the examination of continuity and change in typical ways of thinking, believing, and acting, as well as the presuppositions that underlie these patterns. I will not present a chronological history of relations between the church and the Lakotas; rather, I will examine some of the assumptions that Catholic missionaries have held regarding Lakota culture, as well as certain practical orientations toward the Lakota people that have developed from these assumptions. This will be a partial culture history in that it focuses on only a few basic elements within the dynamic structure of symbol, belief, and action that constitutes the tradition of the Catholic mission at Rosebud and Pine Ridge.

The concept of Catholic mission is fundamental to an understanding of the history of relations between the Catholic Church and the Sioux. When conceived in the broadest sense, Catholic mission includes all those modes of thinking, believing, and acting associated with the evangelical outreach of the

Catholic Church. According to this understanding, it is the mission of the Church to spread the Good News of Christ's life, death, and resurrection through space and time. To the extent that the words and deeds of any Catholic reflect and make known Gospel values, he or she may be thought of as participating in Catholic mission.

Contrasted with this very broad understanding is a much more restricted usage in which the term Catholic mission refers to a particular stage in the development of indigenous churches among non-Western peoples. Fundamental to such a missionary stage are what are termed missions or "foreign missions"—socioreligious compounds inhabited primarily by nonlocal personnel and operated for the spiritual and temporal benefit of native populations. It is commonly held that if a local church is to mature, the pastoral-sacramental life of the people must progress from foreign control of the mission toward native direction. Elements essential to this maturation are the development of a viable Christian community (a parish) and an indigenous clergy. With the appearance of a self-sufficient local church, the stage of Catholic mission is properly at an end. All that remains is for the nonlocal staff to depart so that direction and leadership may be exercised by native laity and religious.

When speaking of Catholic mission among non-Western peoples, there is a tendency to identify it with the narrow sense of the term. The evangelization of such groups is generally assumed to entail the process of church development. However, examination of the history of Catholic missionary efforts among non-Western peoples reveals that evangelization has not always proceeded in accordance with the developmental model presented above. Rather, at certain times and in particular places environmental, historical, and sociocultural circumstances have demanded that missionization be theorized and practiced in ways other than the ideal.

Because so much of the theory and practice of missionary efforts among the Sioux can be linked to changes in mid-nineteenth-century federal Indian policy, a summary of the nature of these transformations serves as a starting point for the present study. Integral to this is a discussion of nineteenth-century theories of social development and assimilation on which both federal Indian policy and Christian missionization were based. Next, Catholic Indian mission—and more specifically, the missiology found at Saint Francis and Holy Rosary—will be placed in the context of these policy changes. Then the endeavor of Catholic religious at Rosebud and Pine Ridge to make sense of the discrepancies between their missiological ideals and the less-than-gratifying results of their labors is examined. A description of some of those conditions that the missionaries considered to be primary determinants of their failure constitutes an important part of this discussion. Finally, brief consideration is given to the recent call to rethink the nature and goals of Sioux missionization.

From its beginnings in the late 1700s until the middle of the nineteenth century, United States Indian policy revolved around the displacement of Indian peoples from their lands to allow for Euro-American settlement and the segregation of Indian and non-Indian populations in order to maintain peace. This era in federal Indian relations may be termed removal-isolationist. The Removal Act of 1830 and the assignment of various tribes to districts in the western territories represent the Indian policy of this era. (See Spicer 1969, Tyler 1963, Pommersheim 1976, Costo and Henry 1977, Deloria 1974.)

During the second half of the nineteenth century the federal government reoriented its policies toward Native Americans. Whereas the tradition of removal-isolation had cast Indian tribes in the role of autonomous "domestic dependent nations," Indians came to be considered "wards" of the government to be tutored in the ways of Euro-American civilization, then assimilated into the cultural mainstream. (See Prucha 1976, Priest 1942.)

This transformation of Indian policy may be attributed in part to a pragmatic encounter with the shifting demographics of Indian-white relations. Most of the treaties negotiated with

Indian tribes had assumed that, once removed and isolated, these peoples would hold title to their new homelands in perpetuity. However, the ever-accelerating tempo of white expansion, nourished by the credo of Manifest Destiny, soon demolished the illusion that tribes might retain permanent claim to any tract of land upon which Euro-Americans placed value. The removal-isolationist assumptions that had so long informed government policy could no more defuse the explosive situation between Native Americans and whites than could treaty promises of tribal sovereignty halt the encroachment of settlers on tribal lands.

It was under these critical circumstances that the federal Indian Bureau opted for assimilation—the policy of so-called civilization and Christianization of native peoples—as the most effective and far-sighted method for neutralizing hostilities between Indians and whites. This choice was not purely, or even primarily, a matter of expedience. For underlying the shift toward assimilation was a normative anthropology—a developmental social theory or philosophy of history—that simultaneously resolved the problems of "who the Indian is" and "what the Indian ought to become."

Fundamental to this normative vision was the basic presupposition that human society displays a pattern of growth as clearly defined and ordered as the ontogenetic structure associated with any particular species. Just as the normal development of an organism conforms to characteristic stages, social theorists believed that the lifeways of a typical human society pass through phases of maturation that run parallel to those of other nations. In other words, the normative vision presumed a unilinear development or evolution of human societies. At the furthest reaches of this developmental process were the habits and customs typifying Europeans and Euro-American societies. Lagging behind that standard in varying degrees were contemporary groups of what were called "barbarians" and "savages," non-European peoples whose social institutions were thought to resemble those of the Europeans' own primitive ancestors. (See Stocking 1968:110–32, Boller 1969: 47–69, Stanley, ed., 1972, Pearce 1971.)

In order to appreciate the importance of this philosophy of history to the theory and practice of midnineteenth century Indian policy, it is essential to understand some of its basic presuppositions. Among the most significant was the postulation of an unchanging yet dynamic human nature (Bidney 1953:192–98). On the one hand, human beings at every stage of cultural development were believed to be guided by the same basic principles of thought and action. That all societies of which there was record possessed some form of government, law, marriage, religion, and economics was taken to be both a consequence and evidence of the psychic uniformity characterizing humanity. The belief that human nature is unchanging made it possible to postulate structured change as typical of the growth of social institutions. Midnineteenth-century white Americans believed that human beings at a so-called savage stage of society experienced the world with a primitive mind and heart, while the functioning of reason and affectivity for civilized man was believed to be very different. But this difference was not considered to be one of essence. Just as we assume that an individual in his childhood and as an adult is in essence the same person, developmental theory considered human nature at both the savage and civilized stages of development to be one.

A complex expression of constancy in change characterized the relationship of human nature to the universal pattern of sociocultural development that was attributed to human history. Developmentalism emerged in late nineteenth-century social thought as a normative theory of cultural transformation; sociocultural development was identified with progress. The transition from savagery to civilization was not viewed merely as a neutral change from one cultural state to another, but as a movement through consecutive stages of advancement.

Such an evaluative reading of human history mirrors our view of the maturation of human beings from the innocence of infancy to the responsibility of adulthood. It is on that basis that nineteenth-century developmentalism became a normative as well as a descriptive and metacultural theory of human history. The prescriptive quality is best discerned in the dual meaning assigned to the term *civilization*, which was used to signify both the final stage of sociocultural growth and the entire process of development. In either case, the significance was predominantly normative—the belief that civilization represents a fundamental good through which nature develops the latent potential of human collective life.

A number of objections from the perspective of twentieth-century social science may be raised to these assumptions underlying nineteenth-century developmentalism. In the first place, we may question that any such pattern of human sociocultural history exists. In the nineteenth century an analogy with ontogenesis was repeatedly used to clarify this assumption; however, ontogenetic patterns are inductive summaries derived from numerous case studies of actual plant and animal growth, and the pattern suggested for sociocultural development was based on only one example, the history of Western civilization. Developmentalism as a prescriptive theory is no less immune to criticism, for the normative understanding of nature—the idea of progress—upon which it rests is, at the very least, debatable. There is no more reason to believe that nature is working for the best than to presume the opposite.

These objections underscore the weakness of developmentalism as a philosophy of history. Modern anthropology has shown that such a simplistic developmental typology is more an ethnocentric projection of Western history than an accurate account of social and cultural change. Moreover, the anti-metaphysical stance of contemporary philosophy has challenged the identity between development and progress so fundamental to developmentalism. The normative vision of nature needed to maintain such an identity is not in keeping with the twentieth-century temperament, which separates fact from value.

Despite modern objections, it is important to recognize

that most officials directly responsible for the theory and practice of midnineteenth-century Indian policy brought to their duties a firmly entrenched faith in developmentalism. From their perspective it is not difficult to understand why these officials chose assimilation as the logical solution to what they called "the Indian problem." Secure in their belief about the natural direction of social evolution, and confident that this direction was good, their primary task became that of finding the best means to train the Indian in the arts of Euro-American civilization and speed him along in cultural advancement. The more efficient the means the more quickly the Indian could achieve the civilization to which he was entitled. (See Berkhofer 1978, Prucha 1976.)

One of the most important elements in the government's plan to civilize the Indian was the reservation. As products of removal-isolationist policy, these tracts of land had been conceived as permanent abodes where the various tribes could continue their traditions without disrupting or being disrupted by Euro-American society. With the advent of assimilationist assumptions, however, the reservation was reconstituted to meet the new goals of federal policy. Instead of homelands to be held by tribes in perpetuity, these territories became way stations where the "civilizing" process might take place in a gradual and controlled manner. It was believed that once the Indian had achieved a degree of civilization comparable to that of his white contemporaries, he could be integrated safely into the cultural mainstream. At that point both the reservation and federal Indian policy as such would become obsolete.

A major springboard by which government officials hoped to catapult the Indian from savagery to civilization was the on-reservation boarding school (Tyler 1963:88–90). Officials believed that in such a self-contained environment children could be systematically trained in the habits of civilized society while being protected from the primitive conditions that characterized their homelife. The Indian Bureau therefore drew up plans to build, furnish, and operate a number of these institutions. Yet from 1869 until the last decade of the nineteenth century the bureau also encouraged Christian denominations to pursue the assimilation of native peoples. As an incentive, if a church would provide a school building, dormitories, staff, and supplies, the government agreed to contribute food (treaty-stipulated rations), clothing, and tuition for each student.

Among the denominations to receive this proposal was the Roman Catholic Church. Although suspicions ran high throughout the church hierarchy regarding the government's attitude toward the Catholic faith, the decision was finally made to accept the Indian Bureau's invitation (see Rahill 1953). A number of factors drew those in charge of Catholic Indian missions toward this favorable response. First of all, church officials realized that the monies which the government supplied for tuition could also be used to support other areas of missionization as well. Secondly, most of those religious and lay persons entrusted with the planning and execution of church Indian affairs had implicit faith in the social theory of developmentalism. In fact, their understanding of Church history reinforced developmental assumptions and suggested the pivotal role that Catholics might play in the "civilization" of the American Indian. After all, the church had long before succeeded in transforming the savages and barbarians of Europe into "civilized" nations; there was no reason to believe that this success could not be repeated in the New World.

Perhaps the deciding factor in the positive response of the Roman Catholic Church was the promise that on-reservation boarding schools, and the government's assimilationist policy in general, held for the propagation of the faith (Fritz 1963:87). For many years the church had been frustrated in its desires to establish mission stations among the native peoples of the plains. The earliest contacts between the Catholic Church and various Sioux bands had been made between the seventeenth and the early nineteenth centuries by itinerant explorer-priests such as Claude Allouez, Louis Hennepin, and Pierre Jean De Smet. None of these religious attempted to establish mission stations among the Lakotas similar to those founded by the Jesuits in New France and the Franciscans in the Southwest. Not only did the wilderness conditions in which they operated prohibit such an enterprise, but also the nomadic lifeways of the Lakota people were totally at odds with a stationary church structure. The evangelical activity of these explorer-priests was limited to brief sojourns among the various bands, during which they preached the Gospel, gave instruction, and performed baptisms. Reluctantly, the Catholic hierarchy had postponed plans to develop local churches until what they termed the "natural" conditions of Plains Indian society and its environmental setting were such that the faith could be planted. The sedentary patterns imposed by reservation life and the sociocultural changes forecast by Indian assimilation seemed to offer just those natural transformations awaited by the church. They were therefore prepared to cooperate fully with the government's policy of assimilation, viewing the latter as a natural tool for their own supernatural ends.

Numbered among those groups who were eventually to receive Catholic religious as missionaries and teachers were the Oglalas and Brules, two of the seven tribes of Teton Sioux, or Lakota, living in western South Dakota. In 1886 priests and brothers of the Jesuit Order and Sisters of Saint Francis arrived on the Rosebud Reservation, home of the Brules, to found Saint Francis Mission and Boarding School. A year later personnel from the same orders established Holy Rosary Mission and Boarding School among the Oglalas on Pine Ridge Reservation. From the day of their arrival these religious rigorously pressed forward the government's assimilationist policies. They hoped that by following a stringent regimen the Oglalas and Brules could be advanced from "savagery" to "civilization" in one or two generations.

The structure and operation of the Saint Francis and Holy Rosary schools typified the commitment of the Catholic religious to the assimilationist goals of federal policy (Goll 1919: 24–26). At the schools children were exposed to a curriculum designed simultaneously to divest them of Lakota customs while teaching them the habits of Euro-American civilization. This process of "cultural replacement" was an essential part of both the theoretical and the vocational training required of the students. During half of the day children attended classes in such subjects as reading, composition, and math; the rest of their time was devoted to learning the practical skills of "civilized" men and women. While boys were being taught the essentials of agriculture, animal husbandry, shoe repair, carpentry, and painting, girls received training in milking cows, sewing, cooking, washing, and other facets of home management. Instruction was given exclusively in English, and the children were strictly forbidden from and punished for speaking Lakota.

In keeping with the isolationist philosophy of the boarding school, home visits were prohibited. During the first year of operation it was policy at Saint Francis to allow the children to return to their parents' camps during holidays and on occasional weekends. But when holidays ended and Monday rolled around, many children would not return to school, and quite often they had to be fetched by the reservation police. What is more, once back at school their behavior convinced the missionaries that the children had been unable to resist the "savage" potency of life in the camps. Weekend and holiday visits were therefore terminated. The only breech in the assimilationist cocoons enveloping the students came during the summers, when they returned to the *tiyošpaye* (extended-family) camps. When school resumed each fall, teachers invariably despaired that their charges had tumbled backward in civilization. Yet they would begin anew, hoping that with an additional year's education the children would prove more resistant to the powerful influence of their parental homes.

The process of cultural replacement attempted in the school had its parallel in the missionary work carried out among the adults. While there were some Lakota customs that the missionaries believed they could adapt (for example, transforming the traditional men's and women's associations into the

Saint Joseph and Saint Mary's sodalities), they assumed that most native institutions would have to be abandoned. This assumption motivated the vigorous campaigns that missionaries waged against traditions they considered especially powerful in retarding civilization. For example, polygyny, a form of plural marriage valued among the Lakotas, was considered both illegal and immoral by the Euro-American mainstream. The *mastincala wacipi* (rabbit dance), since it took place at night, impeded the adoption of the "early to bed, early to rise" philosophy intrinsic to the Christian work ethic. And the *wihpeyapi* (giveaway) was antithetical to Euro-American concepts of rational economy; missionaries considered that this honoring ceremony divested individuals of the capital necessary to establish and operate self-sufficient households.

Missionary attitudes toward traditional Lakota customs are exemplified in the diaries of P. Florentine Digmann, an early superior at Saint Francis Mission. In an entry from 1896, Digmann wrote:

> Our Catholic Indians asked shall we contribute to the collection for the next year's Fourth of July celebration? "No" was my answer; the sooner you bury your old unprofitable customs of dancing and giving away, the better for you. One suggested that they should begin the celebration with a prayer and then have their old fun. "A new patch on an old coat will not hold." One remarked that the Agent was in favor of combining both, "wrapping up the old customs with religion" and so leading the Indians over but he would not succeed. [Digmann 1886–1922:73]

Of all the customs that the missionaries endeavored to supplant, however, they attacked none more consistently than the practices that they labeled interchangeably as "superstitions," "heathenism," "paganism," and "devil worship." Behind such rituals loomed a personality whom the missionaries believed to be one of the major obstacles in the Lakotas' path to Christian civilization—the *pejuta wicaša*, or medicine man. Catholic religious considered these traditional healers to be the devil's allies, whose control over the people had to be neutralized before the sacraments could make headway.

The missionaries at Saint Francis and Holy Rosary sought to replace Sioux social customs and spirituality with Euro-American civilization and Roman Catholicism. They believed that once the Sioux had adopted "civilized" forms of social life, suitable "natural ground" would exist for the planting and germination of the Catholic faith. It would be a mistake, however, to assume that missionaries understood their endeavors in religious development to run parallel to their work in social assimilation. Replacing Lakota religion with Catholicism was not, for the Catholic missionaries, a developmental process, since in a strict sense they believed that traditional Indians lacked religion altogether (Westropp ca. 1911). The missionaries assumed that God had revealed His true nature and the rituals and prayers necessary for human salvation only in the Judeo-Christian tradition. Although they acknowledged that "natural" systems of worship existed outside of the Judeo-Christian tradition, such as that practiced by the Sioux, they regarded these natural systems, the products of human reason and experience, as "heathenism." Although such systems of belief could contain a few grains of truth regarding the supernatural, their manifold "illusions" and "barbarities" were taken to demonstrate the susceptibility of man to the powers of Satan. The idea that "Devil-dominated heathenism" and Christianity might be phases of a single process of religious growth—parallel to sociocultural development—was totally unacceptable to Catholic missionaries. Instead, they viewed these two forms as antithetical. To replace Sioux heathenism with the sacraments represented a religious revolution, not evolution. Given such a perspective, missionaries rejected the notion that a Lakota could participate in traditional Indian ceremonies and simultaneously be a Catholic (*Indian Sentinel* 1919:4).

The early Jesuits at Holy Rosary and Saint Francis believed that they could rapidly make the Oglalas and Brules into civilized, Catholic peoples by means of a strategy of replacement. When, at the end of the nineteenth century, it had become obvious that the Sioux were not going to "civilize" in just one or two generations, the missionaries did not question the basic assumptions upon which their work among the Lakotas rested. As recently as the late 1930s, Father Eugene Buechel, who served as superior at both the Saint Francis and the Holy Rosary mission, wrote an impassioned plea expressing missionary belief that civilization was an exceedingly gradual process and asking that the Indian not be rushed. His statement encapsulates the developmental assumptions underlying Catholic missionization:

GIVE HIM TIME

Let me tell you how the Indian of today impresses me when placed beside the white man. The white man is the Indian's older brother, older by many years who long ago passed through kindergarten and grammar school, who in time went to high school and completed his fine education at the university and took his place in life doing very wonderful things.

And here is his wee little brother, just crawling from the cradle days of civilization. He was introduced to the classroom only yesterday. His thoughts run back to his playgrounds as he wrestles with the strange problems of the primary class. What a change for him! Still he tries and makes progress, too. There is no doubt but that in time he will be as well educated and as efficient as his elder brother, the white man—if he is given an equal chance.

But what a pity that the little fellow is being overcrowded, that it is expected that he be as efficient as his big brother. How could he be?

That is the Indian as I see him. His path to the white man's standard, which he must now attain, is beset with tremendous difficulties. We ought to appreciate them in order to judge him justly and charitably.

To begin with we should remember that the Indian was a nomad and up to two generations ago, knew no other way of making a living. As such he was forever following the tracks of the wandering buffalo, his daily food. With the necessities of life and a few "luxuries" he was happy and contented.

But were not our forefathers nomads, too? The story of the migrations of people in Europe and Asia is the story of our forebears. They turned to farming only gradually. And what crude farming they must have done in their early days. The Indian, however, is expected to grasp in a couple generations what the white man learned only after centuries.

Whenever I read of the man who was going to Jericho and fell among robbers who stripped him of all he had and left him half dead,

I cannot help thinking of the Indian. Men and circumstances have robbed him and left him half dead.

He is no longer the princely type of American he once was.

Poor Indian Brother, my heart goes out to you for being so misunderstood, misjudged and mistreated. Your "case" is plain, yet they will not see. May a good Samaritan come your way soon, not only to pour oil of understanding sympathy into your wounds but actually help you by giving you a chance to help yourself. [Buechel ca. 1930s]

Rather than questioning the validity of their approach, the Jesuits at Saint Francis and Holy Rosary blamed the failure of assimilationist missiology on external factors, thereby reaffirming faith in the traditional missionary understanding of Sioux life and the relationship of that life to Western civilization and Christianity. The traditional paradigm was judged incorrect only in its naïve optimism concerning how quickly changes in Lakota society and religion might be accomplished. Such a reflection on and reaffirmation of missiology was not peculiar to Saint Francis and Holy Rosary, nor was it limited to those actually involved in the missionary process (Digmann 1886–1922:107). Early twentieth-century documents from the Bureau of Catholic Indian Missions voiced a new realism with regard to the rate at which the Indian could be expected to "advance," but reaffirmed the basic assumptions of assimilationist missiology (Society for the Preservation of the Faith Among Indian Children ca. 1911). Again, the postulate that conditions external to the mission as such were responsible for the failure of Indian progress served to entrench the status quo.

Reconfirmation of that traditional paradigm likely served to heighten rather than alleviate the concern that missionaries felt regarding their lack of success among the Lakotas. For by blaming the failure on conditions outside the paradigm, the missionaries implicitly acknowledged a certain powerlessness. Such a hypothesis helps explain the loss of the ardor that had characterized earlier missionary writings. Replacing the zeal was a posture of reserve, at times chilled by tones of weariness and despair. This change of ethos is dramatically illustrated in a letter written in 1913 by Father Buechel, then superior of Holy Rosary, to Father William Ketcham, director of the Bureau of Catholic Indian Missions. Midway through his businesslike communication, Buechel paused to describe plans for the mission's upcoming silver jubilee: "We intend to celebrate the event before we dismiss the children at the end of June. It is true, we do not feel elated at the results of 25 years of missionary work—they are not such to make us feel proud—but we thought we would make a revival of it" (Buechel 1913).

From well before Father Buechel's letter, the writings of missionaries stationed at Saint Francis and Holy Rosary had revealed agreement concerning what they considered to be the major obstacles retarding Sioux "advancement." They fall into two main categories: intrasocial sources of Sioux cultural and religious tenacity, and the anti-Catholic bias of the Indian Bureau and its backsliding on assimilation policy.

Intrasocial sources of Sioux tenacity. To the religious of Saint Francis and Holy Rosary, the established norms of Lakota thinking, believing, and acting not only indicated the "savage" state of Sioux culture but also were a force that kept the majority from advancing and that continually threatened to demoralize those who had managed some degree of progress. Certain misguided whites—including anthropologists who idealized the primitive Indian, and showmen who exploited him in Wild West extravaganzas—were identified as standing behind this force, but the main agents of cultural inertia were seen as existing within Sioux society itself. Among them were the "blanket" or "non-progressive" Lakotas, so named because they refused to cooperate with the assimilation process. These individuals upheld traditional customs such as polygyny, dancing, and giveaways that the missionaries were anxious to supplant. The "non-progressive" Indians were considered most dangerous when they occupied a position of high standing or influence within an extended family. In such cases, other members of the group were less likely to participate in the programs designed to "civilize" the Oglalas and Brules. Moreover, students returning home during summer vacations to camps dominated by "non-progressive" elements were more than likely to backslide in "civilization" during the course of three months. Although the missionaries could point with pride to the example of a student who answered her father in English every time he addressed her in Lakota, the behavior of most children when they returned to school demonstrated that the rejection of things Lakota was the exception rather than the rule (Digmann 1889).

As disruptive as the "blanket Indian" was to their work among the Sioux, the missionaries believed the medicine man to be an even more formidable opponent. Whereas the former worked against the "nature" upon which the Catholic faith was founded, the latter demonstrated his partnership with the Devil by blinding the Lakota people to the first glimmers of true religion. Although the religious granted to these traditional healers a certain knowledge of herbs, roots, and other natural medicines, they believed that the medicine men's power rested on the frightening illusions and tricks that they performed at *lowanpi* (curing ceremonies) and other rituals. Henry Westropp, S.J., exemplified this point of view in his article "Catechist Among the Sioux," published in 1908. As one of the pioneer missionaries at Holy Rosary, Father Westropp had occasion to work with Nicholas Black Elk, the famous medicine man who eventually became the Catholic catechist referred to in the title of Westropp's article. In a brief biographical sketch, Westropp stated that Black Elk, "during many a year, fooled the people with his 'wakan' or remedies, supposed to possess magical efficacy. During the rising of 1890, at Pine Ridge he played a conspicuous part. The missionaries had not paid much attention to him, for the 'medicine men' are about the last class of Indians whom we impress" (Westropp 1908:113).

That missionaries did, in fact, pay attention to medicine men is vividly portrayed in a passage from Digmann's journal. In July 1887, Father Digmann was called on to baptize a dying baby at the home of a "pagan" Indian. After performing the baptism, he returned to the mission to fetch some milk and to seek the services of the mother superior, who was trained in nursing. On the journey back to the sick child Digmann reported:

Grace Kanyela met us saying, "The medicine men are conjuring the sick child, I do not want to be present." Arriving at the door, we heard their singing, beating the drum and without any compliments I opened. What a spectacle! In a corner of the room the father was sitting with the naked child in his arms. Along the walls four conjurors were crouching with their faces painted red and yellow. One of them had returned from an Eastern school, understood English fairly well, and spoke it tolerably. Him I addressed first. "George, you here?" He had asked me already to baptize him. Then I continued in Sioux the best I could do at the time, "Give up your Devil's work. The child is baptized and belongs to the Great Spirit." George said "Do you want that one of us shall die?" "You will not die, get out of here." They, however, continued their powwow singing and ringing pumpkin shells [gourd rattles]. On my repeated begging they finally kept quiet. Mo. Kostka examined the little patient and wanted to make hot poultices. . . . George flung the satchel of the sister out the open door. The scared mother took the baby outside [;] the Sr. followed. George, angry grasped my arm to put me out but I stood my ground. In the presence of them, I told the father of the child not to allow them to continue their conjuration, and not to let their leader to take the sick child to his house. . . . George became cool. He said that he himself did not believe in this powwow but there was money in it. My experience in this first encounter with them was a good *lesson,* teaching 1st, they themselves don't believe in their charlatanry, 2nd, that they are cowards (owing to their own bad conscience like all evil doers) and 3rd, that "money" is at the bottom of their superstitious practices. [Digmann 1886–1922:10–11]

Since the "blanket" Indian and the medicine man were the primary agents keeping Sioux traditions alive, the religious of Saint Francis and Holy Rosary saw them as two formidable opponents of their missionary efforts.

The anti-Catholic bias of the Indian Bureau. In the decades following its decision to participate in the government's program of reservation-based boarding schools, the Catholic Church could point to a number of actions on the part of the

Indian Bureau which it believed demonstrated anti-Catholic bias. Although prejudice against Catholics was undeniably an element in many of these actions, to what extent their actual planning and execution drew upon such sentiments is a matter of debate (Priest 1942, Fritz 1963, Prucha 1979). There is no debate, however, that certain policies of the Indian Bureau represented both a real and potential danger to Catholic missionary work among the Indian tribes.

The Catholic missions among the Brules and Oglalas were founded between two turbulent periods in which the Roman Catholic Church believed its presence among Native Americans to be seriously compromised by Indian Bureau policy. The earlier of the two confrontations had revolved, ironically enough, around the implementation of the very policy that sanctioned federal support of church-run schools on Indian lands. A significant feature of President Grant's Peace Policy of 1869 was that it passed the administration of reservations from the hands of government-appointed agents to those selected by Christian denominations involved in Indian mission work (Fritz 1959–60, Rahill 1953, Utley 1953). To this end the Indian Bureau divided up the reservations and their occupants among the churches. The equitability of the distribution was guaranteed by choices the churches already had made by themselves: the religious body that had expended most time and energy among a particular tribe received exclusive control over the governance of its land, including the right to choose Indian agents, select teachers for reservation schools, and prevent members of other churches from evangelizing among its people.

The Grant Peace Policy assumed that all denominations would push ahead with the important business of civilizing and Christianizing the American Indian. But criticisms of the theory and practice of church-administered reservations were not long in surfacing. Among the most vocal critics was the Catholic Church, whose officials complained that Protestant bigotry had precluded a fair distribution from the very start (Prucha 1979, Rahill 1953). Instead of receiving the thirty-eight reservations to which it believed itself entitled, the Roman Church was awarded only seven. The Catholic hierarchy argued that, the Peace Policy notwithstanding, the church was obliged to minister to Catholic Indians, regardless of where they lived, and that for the government to deprive any Indian of the sacraments was a grievous breach of religious liberty. Furthermore, Catholic officials believed that neither heathen nor Protestant Indians should be deprived of the opportunity to embrace Catholicism merely because the government failed to recognize the essential difference between the Roman Catholic Church and other denominations.

After more than a decade of turmoil the Grant Peace Policy was finally rescinded in 1882. In the meantime, perceptions of the anti-Catholic tenor of federal Indian policy had motivated the church to establish the Bureau of Catholic Indian Missions (Stephan 1895). Located in Washington, D.C., this organization was designed to lobby on behalf of Catholic missionaries and to serve as the official intermediary between individual missions and the federal government. Church officials believed that without such a bureau the rights of Catholic Indians and the church itself would be violated by the pressures of Protestant interest groups.

The repeal of the Grant Peace Policy signaled a period of relative tranquility in relations between the Catholic Church and the federal government. During these years the Bureau of Catholic Indian Missions was able to secure governnment support for additional on-reservation boarding schools. Since religious denominations no longer administered the affairs of Indian reservations, the building of such institutions among groups formerly assigned to Protestant Churches was possible. It is to this period of expansion that the Saint Francis and Holy Rosary mission schools trace their origins.

This era of prosperity was to prove merely a calm between two storms. Even while the growth of Catholic education among Indians was experiencing its peak, a new conflict between the Indian Bureau and the Roman Church was taking shape. In a sense, this second confrontation was centered on a danger even more serious to the status of Catholic boarding schools and missions than the perceived bigotry of the Grant Peace Policy. For whereas the Peace Policy had set what were thought to be unjust limits on how many such institutions might be established on the reservation, new decisions by the government threatened the very existence of the Catholic presence among American Indians.

The storm broke in 1889 with President Benjamin Harrison's appointment of Thomas J. Morgan as commissioner of Indian affairs. Without delay, Morgan proceeded to initiate a policy intended to replace reservation schools administered by churches with government-run boarding and day facilities. The two commissioners following Morgan, Daniel M. Browning (1893) and William Jones (1897), continued their predecessor's campaign against federally supported sectarian Indian education. The Browning Rule (1896), which stipulated that the schools of the federal government be filled before Indian students were allowed to enroll in church-operated institutions, exemplified the push to federalize completely the Indian school system. This push culminated in a series of congressional acts sanctioning the gradual withdrawal of government funding for sectarian education. Beginning in 1896, the yearly allowance for such education was cut twenty percent. By 1901 schools like Saint Francis and Holy Rosary found themselves completely without federal monies.

The Indian Office argued its case for an exclusively federal system of Indian education on the principle of the separation of church and state. It reasoned that to the extent that public funds were used to support sectarian schools, the government was in violation of this principle. In mounting a challenge to the withdrawal of federal support for its reservation schools, the Catholic Church upheld the sanctity of the very same separation. Indian education, it observed, was not financed through gratuities awarded by Congress for this purpose. Rather, it was supported by federally administered treaty monies or "trusts" belonging to the Indians themselves. The government thus had no right unilaterally to deny their use for sectarian schools. Far from safeguarding the principle of separation of church and state, Congress and the Indian Bureau were infringing on the religious liberty of the Indian parent who desired to give his child a parochial education.

In 1904 the Catholic hierarchy presented its position to President Theodore Roosevelt. Convinced of the validity of the church's argument, Roosevelt issued an executive order restoring Indian trust funds to sectarian schools. This order, however, was challenged in 1906 by the Indian Rights Association. The respective points of view of the Roman Church and the Indian Rights Association were pleaded before the Supreme Court in the case of *Quick Bear* v. *Leupp,* and in 1907 the decision of the court fell in favor of the church. The Catholic Church's right to federal treaty monies for the sectarian education of Indians was definitely reaffirmed, and distribution of the funds recommenced.

Except for a brief period between 1904 and 1906, Catholic Indian schools had existed without federal support from 1901 to 1907. With the return of such support, the church surmounted the second threat that government policy had posed to its presence on the reservations. Yet Roosevelt's order had occasioned some radical changes in how Indian trust funds were awarded to parochial schools. Because these were Indian monies, and under the assimilationist policy Native Americans were considered as individuals rather than as tribal entities, signatures had to be obtained from those parents who wished to send their children to sectarian schools. This procedure continued, essentially unchanged, until the Indian Reorganization Act of 1934.

Ripples from battles waged on high between the federal government and the officials of Catholic Indian missions can be detected in the writings of missionaries stationed at Saint Francis and Holy Rosary. In what may appear as an irony of monumental proportions, these texts often portray the policies of the Indian Office and its reservation arms as greater obstacles to Sioux "advancement" than the "blanket" Indian and the medicine man.

Although they were no longer officially Episcopal peoples as they had been under the Grant Peace Policy, the Brule and Oglala continued to be administered by agents of Protestant denominations. The intentions of these agents with regard to the missions and their schools were thus matters of deep concern and suspicions for the Catholic religious. The following statement by Aloysius Bosch, S.J., demonstrates that an agent's actions might justify a missionary's worst anxieties. Writing in 1898 as the superior of Holy Rosary to the Bureau of Catholic Indian Missions, Fr. Bosch related:

At the opening of this fiscal year, several parents wanted to place their children into our school, but were refused to do so by the Agent. Nay, several children were taken out of my school in order to fill the day school in my nearest neighborhood. Once I was with the Agent and asked him, how he would act with regard to such parents as wanted to send their children to our school. I have heard, I said, that the rule of Commissioner Browning was abolished. He said, that he is boss here. . . . the agent is a bitter enemy of our school, he is a bitter enemy of the freedom of the parents, to whom he denies conscience and judgment; if he prevails our school will be reduced more and more and our influence and our work among these Indians dwindles [*sic*] down to a minimum. If the freedom of the parents in selecting the school is not proclaimed, I have a school which depends solely on the good grace of the Agent and not on God's will and God's order. [Bosch 1898]

Government agents not only expressed overt hostility toward the missionaries' work. Equally dangerous to the Catholic cause of Indian advancement was the indifference attributed to some officials. Thus, Father Digmann wrote, referring to Saint Francis Mission, "Our success could have been greater if we had had an agent more interested in our school" (Digmann 1887).

Because they assumed that prejudice against Catholics permeated the entire structure of the Indian Office, it is at times difficult to know how much congruence there was between the missionaries' readings of antipathy and the actual sentiments of a particular agent. Yet it is important for understanding how the religious interpreted and reported the action of agents to know that they made such an assumption. At times they attributed bigotry to the personalities of the officials in question. On other occasions it was assigned to the more impersonal and institutionalized locus of "the government." Thus an entry in the diary kept by the Franciscan Sisters of Saint Francis reported:

The Government Boarding School remained half empty and some of the day schools had to be closed entirely. The Government tried to force the children to return to other schools, but their parents opposed very much and refused to send their children back but the Goverment sent their policemen and packed them into a wagon and forced the children to return to the Boarding School. [Sisters of St. Francis 1886–]

The Catholic religious considered the institutionalized anti-Romanism that they attributed to government Indian policy to be a major obstacle in their work among the Lakotas. It was not, however, the only problem posed by the federal government. The government was also lax in pressing forward the process of cultural replacement. The Catholic religious found the lack of backbone or misconceived plans of local agents vexing enough, but they considered backsliding on the policy of sociocultural assimilation particularly reprehensible and dangerous to Sioux progress when it was expressed in official issuances of the Indian Bureau. Thus Father Digmann wrote:

Whilst the government before with pharasaicle [sic] zeal tried to abolish the old heathen customs, it now revives them on the occasion of the Fourth [of July]. Commissioner Morgan had issued a circular to the Indian Agents to instill patriotism in the Indians and have them celebrate the legal holidays especially the Fourth of July. In olden times the Indian used to have their sundance with all its cruelties and superstitious practices at the time of the summer solstice. For the non-progressive Indian the order of the Commissioner proved only an invitation to fall back into their old habits. The Omaha war dance, sham battles, the give-away of property on a large scale revived and increased so, that a progressive mixed blood made the remark: "We need only the sundance and we have it all back." [Digmann 1886–1922:75]

Governmental inconsistency and backsliding were seen to lend encouragement to the "non-progressives," and the missionaries reported the discouragement and cynicism that they engendered in those trying to assimilate. Father Digmann wrote in his journal that one member of the Saint Joseph Society complained: "'Dress like an Indian and dance with them and you will have them [the agents] at your feet.' He was [using] sarcasm; he meant the Agent should use a stronger hand and abolish the old customs hampering their progress" (Digmann 1886–1922:106). Thus in their attempts to civilize and Christianize the Sioux, the missionaries of Saint Francis and Holy Rosary often found the Indian Bureau, including both official and unofficial representatives, to be more hindrance than help.

The early crisis in Catholic missionary efforts among the Oglalas and Brules revolved around the failure of a missiological paradigm that sought to replace Sioux cultural and religious traditions with the institutions of Euro-American society and Catholicism. Underlying this strategy of replacement were two basic assumptions concerning the nature of Lakota social structure and spirituality. First there was the supposition that Sioux lifeways belonged to a stage of human collective life inferior to that of European and Euro-American nations. To Americanize the Sioux meant to advance them in civilization. Americanization was also considered the prerequisite both for assimilation into the cultural mainstream and for acceptance of the Catholic faith. Secondly, Catholic missionaries understood and evaluated Lakota patterns of worship in terms of a theological split between natural religion, on the one hand, and the revealed Judeo-Christian tradition on the other. Replacing the beliefs and practices of Sioux spirituality with Catholic ritual and prayer signaled for the missionaries a revolutionary victory of Christ over devil-dominated heathenism.

On the basis of these assumptions a unilateral relationship evolved between the missionaries and the Sioux. Missionaries presented a set of social and religious ideals, and thought that there was nothing the Lakotas could offer in return except willing acceptance of those ideals. The persistent refusal of numerous Sioux to respect the conditions of this relationship represented to the early missionaries of Saint Francis and Holy Rosary the failure of their missionary efforts. They adduced a number of conditions and obstacles to explain their failure. Though apparently different, these conditions shared one thing in common: all of them were external to the basic mission paradigm. In such a manner, this paradigm was reaffirmed and continued unchallenged until the Second Vatican Council in the early 1960s.

Since Vatican II, efforts have been made at Saint Francis and Holy Rosary to rethink the nature and goals of Catholic mission among the Sioux. A starting point is the basic recognition that the failure of missionization can no longer be attributed to external conditions. Rather, the paradigm itself is in need of a fundamental shift. It is too early to tell what form and content this shift will have, if it occurs; however, the turning of a critical eye inward rather than out represents a significant break with the past.

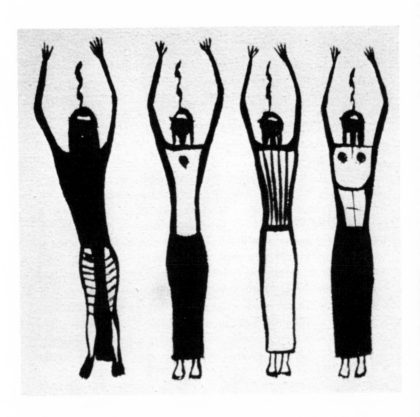

7

Contemporary Catholic Mission Work
Among the Sioux

BY ROBERT HILBERT, S.J.

THE TOPIC I am to address is contemporary Catholic mission work among the Sioux, but I would like to begin by restricting that considerably. I am not a scholar, nor have I made a general study of contemporary Catholic missions among the Sioux. I know something of Catholic mission work among the *Sicaṅgu* (Brules) of the Rosebud Reservation, since that is where I am working. I also have some knowledge of the work of Jesuit establishments on the Pine Ridge Reservation and in Rapid City, South Dakota. But I do not pretend to speak for missionaries in general. What I have to say represents my personal understanding, and others might give different views. And I certainly cannot speak for the Sioux people. I do not know directly how they view our work, nor what the faith experience of individual Sioux people might be.

A few years ago Bishop Harold Dimmerling asked priests in our area working among Indian people to respond to certain questions. One of these was how the Indian people view the church's ministry. The priests at Saint Francis met to discuss the issue and to offer their impressions of how the Lakota people look on us and our work. Please, understand that this is not based on a study made among the people, but represents impressions the priests have developed from their experiences in their ministry.

The most common feeling among Jesuits at Saint Francis

Mission is that the people are generally indifferent to us and to our apostolic efforts. The following were some of the opinions expressed along this line:

—The people are confused and feel that we are incompetent to bring meaning for their lives out of the confusion.
—We are inadequate to fulfill the perceived needs. We are mainly trying to acculturate them to white society. They do not understand the genuine meaning of our lives and work. We are viewed as somewhat harmless rather than positively helpful or harmful.
—We work from a legalistic theological standpoint, whereas they have need of a positive theological ministry based upon their culture.

A less common but solid feeling among the Jesuits is that the Sioux people view us as needed but not to the extent that we would hope. Some of the opinions expressed along this line were:

—We are needed to provide somewhat superficial religious identity for them, especially through baptism.
—We are needed to prepare them to enter the mystery of death and afterlife.
—We are needed as a kind of supplementary welfare agency.
—We are needed as a kind of traditional security blanket.

The feeling least commonly expressed by the Jesuits is that the Lakotas have a deep respect for the church and us as its ministers, a deep-felt need for our ministry, and a trust that we will help them through spiritual means to find genuine meaning for their lives even in these times of confusion.

Mission theory and practice have developed extensively in recent decades. I must limit my focus to only a few points. My choices may be given some perspective by presenting the circumstances of my own involvement in mission work.

When I joined the Jesuits, I was interested in engaging in the teaching work of the order and had no personal desire to do mission work. With the kind of organization we have, I came to know men on the Indian missions and something about their work, but I was more inclined to teach in Jesuit college prep schools.

During my years of education and teaching I had two very

important and formative lines of experience. In the middle 1950s, I spent two summers working at Saint Francis Mission. I did it as a way of avoiding the usual summer program for Jesuit theology students, rather than out of any specific interest in the mission. I worked not in church ministry but in doing plumbing work, installing heating, water, and sewer lines in the school buildings. What was very fortunate about those summers was that my associates in the work were two Indian men. One of them particularly, a man about my age, was a great help. He was a full-blood, raised in a traditional family; and he very much enjoyed talking about Indian ways and values and activities.

I found the experience fascinating, not particularly because I was learning about Indians but because it suddenly revealed to me the profundity of culture in determining the outlook and values and the ways of any of us. I could work beside this man all day, go riding with him, and have a good time in his company, and at the same time grow more and more conscious that we looked on the world in vastly different ways. This began an interest in cultural differences which has developed over many years.

The second line of experience that was strongly influential for me was that the schools in which I worked involved me in conflicts over racial prejudice. Through acquaintance with some of the black students I taught, I became aware of the prejudice that surrounded them. Through visiting families in Milwaukee's inner city, I saw firsthand some of the problems the city imposes on poor blacks.

For a time I was in charge of a Jesuit boarding school. In trying to modify it so that we could legitimately accept black students and accommodate some of their needs, I found that we were a racially biased institution and that there was strong pressure from within the institution, as well as from outside forces, to maintain the bias. In the course of the ensuing difficulties my understanding of American society and social institutions went through a major change, and I began to have some sense of how they might appear to those on the bottom.

After some years I began to be more and more affected by

the scriptural phrase "the Good News to the poor." I had been a priest for a good number of years; that phrase seemed to be at the core of what it is to be a priest; and yet I felt I really did not have any sense of what the phrase meant. So when I was due for a change of job, I told my superior I thought I would like to live among poor people for a while to see if they could teach me what God's Good News is about. The result was that the superior sent me to take a job as a math teacher at Saint Francis Mission.

There are two reasons for my having gone into this personal history. One is to offer some indication of what might be the attitude of a present-day priest in ministry among Indian people. The other is that not only in me but in other missionaries and in the teaching of popes, bishops, councils, and other church authorities, two of the areas of thought that have undergone the most change are the areas I have mentioned as affecting me—awareness of the profundity of cultural formation in people and concern about the institutionalized injustice of social systems.

In the nineteenth century, when Saint Francis Mission was founded, it was common in missionary circles to speak of "Christianizing and civilizing" non-European peoples. In contemporary terms, this meant to persuade them to accept the ways of Europe and European-Americans. I hope there is sufficient general awareness that such ministry aims are of a bygone era. The church today affirms the right of all peoples to live in accordance with their own culture. Allied with this is the teaching of respect for the religious traditions and beliefs of all people.

This is not to say that religious and cultural pluralism is an easy matter. Neither in the church nor in civil society have we found ways to live in a pluralistic world. But as an aim or ideal, we do affirm this direction.

In relation to mission work, there are two elements of pluralism. One pertains to the attitude of missionaries toward religious traditions. The missionaries in the first three-quarters of the history of Saint Francis Mission generally considered traditional Lakota religious acts and beliefs to be in opposition to Christianity.

The second element relates to the attitude toward forms of Christianity. As is evident from the churches built and ceremonies followed, ordinary western European forms of Roman Catholicism were considered to be the proper—probably the only—forms in which Indian Catholicism should be expressed.

What about the situation now? When I came to Saint Francis in 1973, the priests and the medicine men had started a series of meetings to discuss various aspects of Sioux traditional religion and the Catholic religion. From the perspective of the priests, it represented an effort to come to some understanding of Lakota traditional religion as currently practiced. This approach differed sharply from the judgmental attitude of earlier years.

One of the facts that has to be taken into account by the missionaries is that a number of medicine men are also practicing Catholics in good standing. They experience no opposition between the two religious systems. A number of the priests also engage in some portions of traditional Lakota ceremonies. Several quite regularly participate in sweats. One has made a series of three or four vision quests. One of the medicine men even requested that a priest be on hand for counseling during a Sun Dance. All this, clearly, is a considerable change from the days when people were expected to confess as sinful their participation in traditional ceremonies.

This does not mean that all questions are settled. Many areas of confusion and disagreement exist, and many Indian people would consider the two religions in opposition. But there is a major change in mission attitude.

Regarding the possibility of some non-European cultural expression of Christianity, there are various theological positions. A paper by one theologian distinguishes twenty-nine positions. I'll simplify by suggesting three, which I will call *accommodation, adaption,* and *inculturation.*

All three approaches involve acceptance of the notion that God is and has been at work among the Lakotas (or any other cultural group), revealing (communicating) Himself, leading them both individually and as a people to respond to Him in faith. This would mean that their culture and the traditional religion are not formed just by the "natural" light of reason, but are "graced"; that they have come, however imperfect and mixed with evil, through the saving action of God in them.

Those who follow all three approaches would likewise assume that God has most fully revealed (communicated) Himself to man in Christ, that Christ is, in some way, the fulfillment, or the final stage, of the process of revelation and the establishment of a covenant relationship with the Lakota people as with other peoples.

Accommodation implies that the Roman Catholic Church transcends culture and is to be accepted in its entirety as the universal church, univocal in form and doctrine and law and sacrament for all peoples of the earth. The process of growing into the fullness of the life of that church differs, depending on culture and tradition. Since we are pilgrims on the way to this fullness there will be in any historical period differences among us. These differences arise from the inadequacy and incompleteness of our assimilation into the one people of God, not from any differences in the goal or term of our pilgrimage.

Adaptation implies that there is a central transcultural core of the Roman Catholic religion around which are gathered certain cultural accretions—accidentals—which can be shifted as the Church comes into being in various peoples. Differences come not from inadequacy and incompleteness but from variations in values, attitudes, customs.

Inculturation takes as fundamental the idea that Christianity—and Christ Himself—can exist only in cultural form. This is not to say that cultures are disparate, without similarities, nor that they cannot intermingle, adapt, assimilate, change; people of different cultures can appreciate one another and learn from one another. But what they learn or assimilate from one another is modified and reexpressed according to the culture of each.

God is not within the limitations of human culture, but any

man is. A man, or a woman's, understanding of who God is, what his or her relationship to God is, and how this relationship is to be lived and expressed, are necessarily cultural, because human perception, concepts, and thought processes are culturally developed. This is not to say that Christianity is simply identified with culture; the Christian message will challenge any culture, for it will always conflict with the evil that inevitably is incarnated in human culture. Still, the Christian message can be encountered and expressed only within a cultural context. Christ was a Jew; He lived as a Jew, He thought as a Jew, He prayed as Jew—although it is also true that He was such a challenge to His own people that He got Himself killed.

To the Jews the Cross was a stumbling block; to the Greeks it was an absurdity. Those, I think, are different reactions because the cultural base was different. What to the Jews conflicted with their sense of history of God's covenant relationship with His chosen people, to the Greeks conflicted with the wisdom of the philosophers.

Christ died and rose, that is a fact; but the perception of the fact, the meaning of the fact, is cultural.

Inculturation of the faith and life of the church seems to me to apply to the whole of it, even the most basic elements. It can be accomplished only from within a culture. Someone from a different culture can present the witness of his own encounter with Christ and His message, but can reexpress it in another culture only to the degree that he is immersed in that culture.

There is no central core of Catholic Christianity which is completely transcultural and univocal for all peoples and all times. But just as cultures are not totally disparate, neither will various cultural expressions of Catholicity be. They will be analogous expressions.

The universality of the Church is verified not in the world-wide acceptance of one cultural form but precisely in the pluralism of its incarnation.

To shift from general theoretical considerations to practical application, consider the implementation of the revised penance liturgy among the Lakota people.

The approach of accommodation would not consider whether a different ritual might be more proper for the Lakotas. The only questions would be how to present this ritual to the people in a way that enables them to see its continuity with their values and customs, and possibly, what gradation of stages might be necessary to lead them to the practice of penance in the new form.

The approach of adaptation, on the other hand, would consider which elements of the rite are part of a transcultural, invariant core and which are cultural accretions. Preserving the core, one would consider how Lakota people might develop their own cultural mode of the accidentals. The prayers, for example, might be recast in a Lakota thought pattern.

An approach of inculturation would look upon the entire sacrament as a cultural incarnation, a cultural signification of the experience of reconciliation with God and the community. Obviously, it is a fundamental truth that in Christ men are reconciled to the Father and to one another, that in His church Christ continues to exercise and make effective that reconciliation. But the perception or understanding of that mystery and the expression of signification, or sacramentalizing, of the reconciliation are formed within the life of a culture. Just as the sacrament has varied enormously through the history of the Roman Church, so it might vary among different peoples today.

This is not to assert that the revised penance rite is unsuited to Lakota culture. It seems to me quite probable, in fact, that it is far more suited to present-day Lakota culture than such a ritual of reconciliation as the *hunka* ceremony in Black Elk's description (Brown 1953:101–115). But an approach of inculturation would not assert a priori that the revised penance rite or any part of it, even the parts considered most essential for validity, are transcultural and necessarily to be adopted by all peoples in precisely the same form.

I wish to touch briefly on one other point of change—the concern for social justice.

The Christian tradition, like any other, has always been in favor of justice, and against injustice in the abstract; concrete applications have suffered many painful and slow developments. Our basic understanding today comes from our sense of the meaning of social structures. They are formed through human choices; they reflect and incorporate human values, some of which are unjust and oppressive in their impact. Furthermore, social structures in many ways practically determine the choices of those who are involved in them. A teacher's freedom of choice regarding who will be taught, what will be taught, and how it will be taught is very limited by the school system. A priest's freedom of choice regarding inculturation is very limited by church structure. When a structure is unjust—racially biased, for example—individual officials have very little chance to act justly.

A second key idea is that the justice spoken of in the church today takes its inspiration from the biblical tradition of special concern for the poor, the little ones, the *anawim*. It is based more on need than on philosophical or legal rights.

A third point, strongly emphasized in the document on justice of the 1971 bishops' synod, is that faith and justice are integral to one another. "Action on behalf of justice and participation in the transformation of the world fully appears to us to be a constitutive dimension of the preaching of the Gospel."

It is in this spirit that Saint Francis Mission established an Office of Social Concerns. It is not intended to be only one effort among others, but is intended to establish concern for justice as the integrating factor of all our ministry and of our own lives as individuals and as a church community.

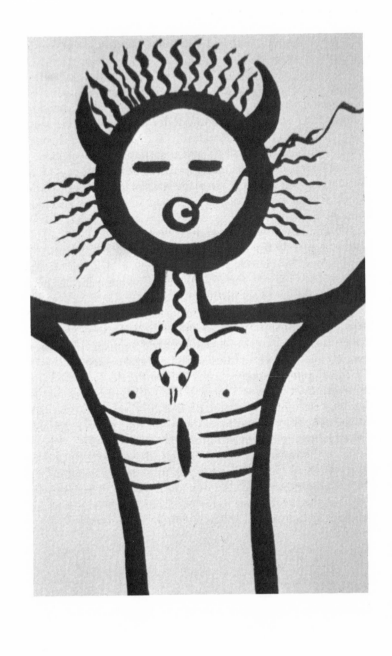

8

Christian Life Fellowship Church

BY MERCY POOR MAN

I LIVE on the Rosebud Sioux Reservation at Antelope Community in Mission, South Dakota. There I belong to a relatively new church which we call the Christian Life Fellowship. It is composed of Assembly of God believers. The church sponsors a home for troubled boys, and soon will be taking in girls, too, to give the children a good home and a good Christian education. We believe in Jesus as our personal Savior.

I wasn't raised as a traditional—I was brought up in the white man's church. Some of my grandparents converted to the Episcopal Church. My grandfather and mother were Catholics. So I was ecumenical from the beginning! I believe there is one God; we all serve Him. When Sunday came around, the minister took us to church. My father would say, "Today is Holy Day (*anpetu wakan*), go to church today, God's day!" and he always went with me. I remember making the sign of the cross, "in the name of the Father, the Son, and the Holy Ghost." We always talked about God the Father and Christ the Son, but we never heard about the Holy Spirit. When I was a little girl I went to Catholic school. I remember the teachers always told us that if we weren't good, we would go down to Hell. So I tried on my own to be good, and finally I came to know the Lord.

The way in which I have grown up and lived has all come about because of my family. I was very lucky: I saw two of my great-grandmothers and one of my great-grandfathers. I was just a little girl then, but I was lucky to know them. And of course, I had my grandparents as well as my parents. It is important that parents live in such a way as to be examples to their children and grandchildren. I wanted to live just like my grandparents did—to be kind, good, and to love all the members of the family. My grandparents always told me to be kind to everybody, and that way, they said, I wouldn't have any enemies. So I live by that.

In Lakota culture all of your relatives teach you what to do. I was scolded once in a while, but I was trained. My grandmother used to sit me down and cut out blocks of cloth for me, giving me a needle and thread to stitch them together. This was a way of teaching me to complete things, and to sit still.

There are many ways to teach children. The Sioux tell stories for this purpose—some are even dirty stories! Christians are not allowed to read books that are bad. But when Indian children hear those bad stories they are embarrassed and think, "We'll never do that when we grow up!" This is a way of teaching children what is bad.

My father, my grandfather, and one of my grandmothers were storytellers, and many of their stories had morals. There is a story about a meadowlark that teaches about obedience. Once there was a little bird whose nest was on the ground. Snakes always came around it. The mother bird had two children, Yellow Belly and Black Necktie. One way when the father was away, the snakes came around and lay waiting. So the mother bird said, "Yellow Belly, why don't you go look for your daddy? He has a lot of meat." So the little bird flew away. Then she spoke to the other child: "Black Necktie, why don't you go look for your daddy, too?" So away he flew. And right away the mother bird flew off as well. The children were obedient. A lot of little children would stop and sit there and say, "Why, Mommy? Why?" And in the meantime the snakes would have come and eaten them up. A lot of stories taught behavior in this manner.

When I was a small girl of four and five years old I remember that my grandparents were always praying. For every meal they put down an old canvas, and we all sat around it, and then my mother and grandmother passed the dishes and we filled up our plates. My grandfather at that time was head of the *tiyošpaye* (family). He prayed for every meal, three times a day. He thanked God for what we had to eat. My grandfather really affected my life. He wasn't a chief or a spokesman, he was never seen in public, but God saw him every day.

One of my grandmothers was a Cheyenne, not a Sioux, but she loved my grandfather and married him. I don't know how she managed, but she learned to speak the Lakota language. When I was in my teens I used to stay with her. She was blind, and the two of us would go to visit our family on foot— the whole family lived within a couple of miles of one another. One day we went over the hill to visit my aunt. On the way home my grandmother became tired and said, "Grandchild, let's sit down." Because she couldn't see, she probably thought we were only halfway back, but in fact we were only a little ways from our house. So we sat down, and what she told me during the next five or ten minutes has had a great influence on my life.

She said to me, "Granddaughter, because you are a young woman now, pretty soon you're going to be getting married. I heard something I want you to remember when you get married. Your children are the most important possession in your life. Raise them up right and have love for them and they'll grow up right." And she said, "Never forget that." This has stayed with me and has had a lot to do with the raising of my children and my grandchildren.

I saw my grandmother pray, I saw my mother pray; they must have had experiences. I'm a very lucky woman.

My husband, John, is a good Christian. He is ten years older that I; when we were first married he was more like a father to me. He was a good father for our children. My children never came home to be slapped or kicked around because their father was drunk—that never happened. He was a warden in the Episcopal Church. Now he is seventy-two years old.

When my husband and I were married and started to have a family, we were so poor that we didn't have a home of our own. It was then, at the point when I was pooorest in my life, that I had an experience and came to know the Lord. One day I knelt and prayed with my little children on each side of me—the oldest was eight years old. I told them, in Indian, "You children kneel with me and I'll give my heart and my life to the Lord." I knelt and prayed and something happened to me—I had an experience. I got off my knees and knew I was free, free from bad things. I sang a hymn, "The Lord Set Me Free." I'm so thankful the Lord Jesus made me a mother. I used to think I owed myself a good time, but as soon as I had this experience I gave up all my bad habits. Before I had that experience I struggled. I wanted to be a Christian, but it was hard. I really believe that when you experience the Holy Spirit you don't have to struggle any more.

I had eight children, and after they had all grown up, I went back to school. I was in my forties when I decided to go to classes and I got my degree in education. I am a teacher now.

About four years ago I lost one of my family members; that was the hardest thing I've had to go through in my life. But the Lord helped me through. I know Him because I pray. Life without the Lord is miserable. Although you may make ends meet and enjoy life, only when you know Jesus Christ can you have a full life. The years that I have been a Christian are very precious. I try to live as an example for my children.

When you know the Lord you love people. I enjoy meeting and talking to people. I am frequently asked to talk at meetings and workshops because I know a lot about Indian culture.

Church is very important in my life. I used to belong to the Lakota Chapel in White River, South Dakota, until I moved to Mission. Then I went to church at the Assembly of God. We didn't have a pastor, so I led the congregation for a while. I always leaned toward the Assembly of God because of their morals and their belief in Holy Spirit baptism. Our new church, the Christian Life Fellowship, is no different from the Assembly of God except that we support a home for troubled children.

We have only about thirty members now. We have our own charter. We are of all ages, and we want to have a mixed Indian and white church. There are now about three white members.

We start our services with Sunday School classes at ten o'clock; we have an adult class and a children's class. I am one of the Sunday School teachers. Our worship begins at 11:00 and lasts until 12:00 or 12:30. Our services are open, and we usually have guests from other churches. Anyone who wishes to may stand up and share something with the congregation.

Our church services are very, very simple. We start with singing—we do a lot of singing. Sometimes we feel the Lord's presence because we're singing. The Bible tells us that when we're depressed we should sing hymns and songs of praise. It brings up our self-esteem, it refreshes us to go on.

Then we have prayers. The pastor asks for prayer requests, and we name the individuals for whom we wish to pray. Usually we pray for young people, and for those who don't know God. Sometimes when I'm leading the service I pray in Lakota. If I see some Lakota speakers there I pray in Indian.

After we have these prayers and finish singing, the minister preaches to us about the day's message. I am an assistant minister—minister of Christian education. So after the singing I'm the one who always reads the scripture and expounds on it a little bit.

Next the minister comes and sings again, and then he preaches about the day's message.

After that we go up and pray for people who are sick, whatever healing they might need. We lay our hands on them and ask God to heal them. We only sit still during the minister's preaching. After this we can go up to the altar and touch people as we pray for them. We have to believe and accept that God will heal them.

We always end up our service with a meal—we're still Sioux!

On Sunday night at 7:30 we go to church again. People in the audience speak a lot during this service, praying and giving testimonials. And we sing a lot. Sometimes, when we're really blessed, we raise our hands to sing. It's a very happy time. Individuals get up when the time has arrived for them to give testimony about what the Lord has done for them. When the Lord blesses you, you can't just sit still and keep quiet. We recognize the things that the Lord does for us in our lives, even the littlest things. We thank Him because He is our God.

After the testimony is over, we give offerings. We have to support our pastor and we have to pay our rent and other bills. We believe in tithing, giving to God one-tenth of whatever we earn. Those of us who have gardens take the first things we pick to the church as offerings.

We are a church, but we don't try to convert people—we don't ask people to join our church. We want to reach the ones who are having problems. When people come to our church we greet them and thank them for coming. But we don't try to get anybody to leave their own church to come to ours. We just try to reach the people who are wandering around.

Many people are very depressed, and so they drink. You can overcome depression if you think about the good things, not the bad. You can develop self-esteem if you pray. Don't try to change yourself, just depend on the Lord. It takes God to change you. We try to tell people who drink heavily about Jesus. Many people know that I am a Christian and they come to me. I tell them that they must believe that God can change you—you cannot change yourself.

We believe in the Holy Spirit. If we're trying to become a Christian without the Holy Spirit we struggle. The Devil is strong and we are tempted. When the Holy Spirit baptism comes upon us we are stronger, we have the power to resist the Devil. I urge people to recognize the Holy Spirit, which is most important in a person's life. We say *wanaǧi*, the spirit; the Holy Spirit is like that, only it's holy, sacred, *wakan*. The Holy Spirit is the power in the Christian life.

The Bible tells us not to provoke our children to wrath. Many people take out their anger on their children. We have to nourish them and nurture them. We have to train a child in the way he should go. Even if he departs from the way for a time, he will always come back. To raise our children we have to depend on the Lord.

I tell young people about Jesus. I say, "God loves you and He forgives you. It's through Him that we go to heaven." I tell them marriage is for life. One young girl here got in trouble and had a baby when she was only fourteen years old. Her relatives, who are educated and are outstanding people on our reservation, all wanted to send her away to school, take her baby, and adopt it out. But I said no, I wanted that baby to be here with the mother and the father. I talked to both of the parents, and they wanted to get married. Finally they did. I wanted them to start right, so I took them to church. I told them never to be jealous of one another, to share everything, to trust each other, and to be Christians. Marriage is difficult today because everything costs so much, but when Jesus touches our lives we are happy and we care for our families.

We do have weddings in our church, and I can marry people. I am a licensed minister, but I don't have a special title. Once they printed in the paper that I am a reverend but I said no, I'm a sister—Sister Poor Man. It's great to be a Christian, and I am happy serving the Lord.

You have to read the Bible to know where you stand, what you should do in life. Everything is recorded in the Bible about how to live. When you read the Bible, that is God talking to you. When we pray, we're talking to God. I believe in formal, written prayers like the "Our Father," but it is also necessary to say your own prayers. I believe strongly in prayer. Sometimes I wake in the middle of the night with a kind of a burden. I don't know what I'm supposed to do. Then I pray. Although I'm an old lady now, I don't feel like one; my feelings, my mind, my physical actions are not like that. I love the Lord so much. He's my strength and He's my life.

PART THREE

TRADITIONAL RELIGION IN THE
CONTEMPORARY CONTEXT

9

Indian Women and the Renaissance
of Traditional Religion

BY BEATRICE MEDICINE

IN DISCUSSING the roles that American Indian women have taken and should take in the current revitalization of traditional religion, I will speak from a dual perspective, both as an anthropologist and as a Lakota woman. Those of us who have gone into academic disciplines to become teachers, not only of our own people but of other people as well, have had to learn to meet professional criteria. We use the theories and methods of the humanities and social sciences, even though these fields have so far neglected to foster native perspectives for understanding the social systems of which we are a part. In a sense, I believe that the scientific method has dulled my perceptions in terms of the way I was socialized. My intuitions and perceptions of the unknown—the *wakan,* if you will—have been sublimated in an acknowledgement of objectivity.

Living in a bicultural world, it has been difficult for me to maintain a native perspective and simultaneously maintain the standards of excellence required in academia. Yet I think it is entirely possible to do this, to be a Lakota person and yet be a professor. Those of us brought up within strong families (*tiyošpaye*), with strong Lakota beliefs, are able to function in two worlds. There is something intrinsically valuable about the Lakota life-style. That view persists, no matter what kinds of culturally repressive measures—intellectual, social, or religious—we have had to endure. This is what is so important to

us when we hear Lakota songs, such as Sun Dance songs—
Lakota hymns, really, because they are about cultural values
and attitudes. The words of the ceremonial songs and the
dances convey these values and attitudes. Surely this is what
Lakota rituals and belief are all about. They are tied in with
the way we perceive a world that is ours, a world that many
outsiders try to penetrate by way of history, anthropology,
education, or psychology. I have always wondered what it is
about the Lakota way of life that is so attractive to all the
countless numbers of people who research us constantly. We
must have something important.

It is counterproductive, however, to dwell on the inequities
of academia. Some very powerful and credible academics have
helped us in our research for treaty rights cases. Those of
us who are very strongly based in Lakota culture have the
strength to make the adjustment to a life-style in academia—
or any other life-style we might choose—because we have a
good sense of who we are. A recent study by Trimble and
Richardson (1983) validates the strength of Indian peoples' concepts of self. Yet educationists have always claimed that Indian
peoples' self-image is extremely weakly developed. We must
transmit a strong identity as *Lakota* to our children. Whether
we are biological or sociological parents, we are embedded in
the *tiyošpaye* (the basis of the extended family), and this relationship factor is extremely important to us; through it we are
all related. Thus we pray, *mitakuye oyas'in*, "relatives all."

In my work as an academic I have advocated treaty rights
for our people as well as the rights of women and children.
I am an extreme advocate of feminine perspectives in anthropology. I believe that women's activities and women's orientations to Lakota life-styles have been slighted, both in the
ethnographic literature and in contemporary studies. This is
true of the totality of women's activities and women's orientations to Lakota life-styles. I am aware that there is currently a
trend to undertake research on Indian women—a concern
that is tied directly to funding sources. It seems to me that
much of the research that we should be doing independently

is hampered by funding requirements, which do not always allow us to take those broader perspectives on research that might seem to us most productive. History is fashioned by events and relationships in the lives of both women and men within a cultural milieu; this holistic picture should be the concern of our research. For one attempt to demonstrate this, see Albers and Medicine, editors (1984).

I once commented that I was interested in the dyadic relationship between men and women (in the published version, edited by an Indian man, this came out as *"didactic"* relationship! [Medicine 1979:4]). We must see this relationship between the sexes in equilibrium to understand truly the changes in Lakota society. We must also elucidate women's lives—the events and their meanings that yield new perspectives on women in the ritual realms of Lakota life. This means simply that we should look at the complementarity of the sex roles in Lakota life. Then we can appreciate the sense of harmony reflected in the way Lakota society functioned in the past and how it still functions today. But before we undertake this study, we must be acutely cognizant of who we are as individual Lakota people.

To concretize this notion, I suggest that the *hanbleceya* (vision-seeking) ceremony for adolescent boys as a transition to manhood was counterbalanced by the ball-throwing ceremony for Lakota girls at puberty. These ceremonial events imprinted upon the minds of each sex the duties and responsibilities both to self and to *tiyošpaye*. Each was an intensive rite of passage out of childhood. More contemporary examples might be the ritual *inipi* (sweat lodge), performed separately for each sex, and the possession of a pipe as a means to participate in the sacred realm.

All of us brought up in the Lakota way were instructed never to be stingy, always to share. Girls were repeatedly told that they should take care of others, especially their brothers. Industriousness and patience were lauded in the behavior of young females. As one grew older, critical remarks such as *"That* woman was screaming when her baby was born!" often had a forceful impact. Offhand remarks such as, "She respects old people," or, "She listens to her grandparents," were effective in reifying virtuous behavior. By introspective assessment of our own socialization, it is possible to delimit the patterns by which values were transmitted to shape behavior. I recall my grandmother telling my younger sister and me that our father worked hard and therefore we should remove his boots for him when he returned home in the evening. My sister and I vied for this chore, and we were not surprised when we saw our mother rubbing our father's feet to relax him.

I feel strongly that we must be aware of how we were socialized in our cultural milieu. Whether we grew up in a full-blood or a mixed-blood family, we should try to understand what motivates us to involve ourselves in Lakota religion. We need to think about the ways in which we were taught the Lakota values that are so much a part of the religion. Sharing and generosity are the first things that come to mind, the first of four great Lakota virtues; the others are fortitude, wisdom, and bravery. These virtues must be realized in our lives as individual men and women; we have to make them *real*. I was brought up with the understanding that no matter who came to your house, if you have nothing else to give them you must at least offer. them a cup of water. My father said this over and over, imprinting the value of sharing in my mind. When Lakota people become adults, they try to live up to this value throughout their lives, even though it can be difficult.

It is important to understand contemporary religious revitalization within the historical context of the cultural repression that Lakota people have endured. In a recent paper I presented material on the revitalization of the Sun Dance, which I will not reiterate here (Medicine 1981). But I do want to comment on some significant aspects of Lakota women's roles in ritual. In the Sun Dance virgin girls still ritually chop the sacred tree, and their role is highly valued. Although the status that this formerly gave to the *tiyošpaye* is somewhat eroded, many families are nonetheless honored when a daughter is chosen for this role, although many families today are hesitant to participate if they are financially unable to provide an impressive giveaway. The role of the Sacred Pipe Woman is very prestigious, and many Lakota women, both young and old, vie for the honor. Of course, the work of Lakota women in organizing ritual and in making ritual and giveaway items is overshadowed by the prominent roles of the male participants. However, there is a decided increase in the number of females who parallel the men's sacrifices in the Sun Dance by making flesh offerings from their arms. The question of disparate sex roles in ritual has been at issue at least since the 1950s when the Sun Dance began to reemerge, but has become increasingly important since about 1963, when the Sun Dance began to function as a revitalization movement among the Sioux. Today the Sun Dance has assumed an almost intertribal character as a nativistic movement. We see more and more native participants returning from urban areas, or coming from non-Lakota reservations, to take part in the ritual. They come and are in a sense instructed in the ritual while they participate in it. The result is that norms and values are not always well integrated in the participants' lives so that they are able to sustain them throughout the year.

There are many reasons for the emergence of the Sun Dance as a nativistic movement. On the one hand, it met the requirements of the American Indian Movement. The reemergence has had an effect on one segment of Lakota society, and from there it has reached out to other areas and other tribes. Indeed, when I was teaching at the University of New Brunswick in 1976, many of the Micmac Indians felt that they were not Indian unless they traveled to South Dakota to participate in a Lakota Sun Dance. You can appreciate the attraction of the Sun Dance for Indian people whose cultures today lack any such rich and well-detailed religious rites. On the other hand, some of the Anishinabe—the Chippewa in Michigan—told me that they had no intention of participating in a Sioux ceremony, because they knew it was not part of their own tribal religious tradition. We therefore find tremendous variation on an intertribal level in native views of the Sun Dance. This variation is also found among the Lakota people themselves. There are many Lakotas who say, *"Inše škatapi,"* "They're only playing (at the ritual)." I understand their perspective and realize that in any Indian group there is no monolithic agreement about the direction ritual should take. Certainly, among the Lakota people there has always been variation in the practice of the Sun Dance, and this is still very apparent today.

We also should consider the effects of other social movements on the Sun Dance. I mentioned the American Indian Movement. For a time there were many members of AIM who did not feel that they were Indian until they took part in the Sun Dance and were pierced, no matter what their tribal affiliation. I think this is a matter for concern. To be considered also is the emergence of what we in our *tiyošpaye* have called "self-styled" medicine men and women. Partly because of concern over them, a group of us put away the Sacred Pipe for seven years. There are certain problems inherent in believing and belonging to a native religion, just as there are in any religion. I think that the American Indian Religious Freedom Act (1979) is going to have a great effect on the direction in which native religion is headed over the next ten years. This legislative support of native beliefs is going to be extremely important. I think that throughout Native North America we will see people reading ethnographic accounts of the traditional religious rites of their tribes and performing them. No matter how tolerant or how inclusive Christian sects may be—for example, using the Sacred Pipe in their rituals, and Indian designs in their churches and priestly garb—there is always something lacking for American Indian people, who are searching not so much for identity as for a viable, believable system—an orientation to something that will guide them through their lives. The sacred sphere of native life must be restored.

Those of us who know the native language can never forget how intrinsically it is tied in with the values and beliefs that should be enacted in behavior. We see here the anthropological truism of the interweaving of all the elements of a cultural system. I believe that we are now observing the development of an apprenticeship system among the Lakotas, whereby an elder person willingly takes an apprentice and teaches him or her those things that need to be done. This is an effective way of recapturing the traditional learning process. Learning the native language will enhance this process tremendously, much to the benefit of the continuing ritual system. In my view, there is at this time, the 1980s, almost a transformation of *wakan* from an abstract concept to an active construct. Through increased participation in such rituals as *yuwipi*, naming ceremonies, and the Sun Dance, the *wakan ki* is actualized and assumes a more functional role in the ritual lives of the people. There is a heightened awareness of the efficacious attributes of *wakan*. This comes through very clearly when Indian people talk about their experiences and the philosophical bases of the whole ritual structure. But this transformation of *wakan* has to go beyond mere ritual. It should, in a sense, be enacted in the way we socialize our children and the way we present ourselves not only to other Lakota people but to the dominant society. Surely we must look at the contours of spirituality in our Indian communities.

In our *tiyŏspaye* we had a discussion about the erosion of *wakan*, and especially of the introduced patterns of imbibing alcohol and how this has affected our culture. One person said, "Well, you know, drinking was not a part of native village life." We thought this was an important point to consider when discussing *wakan*. What is occurring now among many Lakotas is a reorientation of native belief and a redirection of contemporary life. Means for making this more functional could herald a true revitalization in everyday life.

A paper entitled "Wakan: Plains Siouan Concepts of Power," by DeMallie and Lavenda (1977), utilized published and unpublished sources to describe how the concept of *wakan* permeated Lakota life before white contact. Although their paper presents a very cogent summation of the previous descriptions of this power concept, it made no attempt to consider

this cultural construct among contemporary Lakotas and related Siouan groups. How *wakan* is manifested in present-day
rituals is important for us to understand, especially for those
who are believers and who participate in such rituals as *yuwipi*,
the Native American Church, or the Sun Dance. We must
understand exactly what this concept of *wakan* means to us as
individuals and what it means to other people enacting their
roles in Lakota culture. We should examine what have been
called in anthropology the emic or native categories. We must
see precisely how we can actualize *wakan* in our daily lives.
The Sun Dance itself, for example, is held by a community
only once a year. What other kinds of ceremonies will help us
keep to the four cardinal virtues throughout the year? How
can we talk about generosity as a Lakota norm if we do not
practice reciprocity within our own *tiyošpaye?*

These are the issues we must work through if we are to consider ourselves as traditional Sioux people and as believers in
the native religion. In my work with mental-health personnel
on various Lakota reservations, I found that many people were
somewhat bewildered because they were unable to translate
mental-health concepts into the Lakota language. These individuals are generally psychologists, psychiatrists, or mental-
health educators, some of whom are native people themselves. What is the state of well-being, the major concern in
an individual's mental health? For the Sioux this is best described as living in harmony with the *Wakan Tanka*, the Great
Mystery. Thus the concept of well-being must be understood
within a cultural milieu and within a culturally specified perception of personhood, both male and female.

The ritual context is an important one in which to understand individual motivation. We must ask why an individual
participates in a naming ceremony or a *hunka* ceremony or a
hanbleceya (vision quest). Is he doing this for the good of the
tiyošpaye, or does he feel he needs to do this in order to be
recognized as a person? Is participation in these ceremonies a
sincere attempt to change a person's life-style, or is it merely a
sign or ethnic marker? I once studied the motives expressed

by participants in a Sun Dance, and I was amazed to learn that many of them had joined in the ceremony either as a means of gaining recognition or in order to rid themselves of addiction to alcohol.

It is important to understand individuals' reasons for participating in ceremonies if we wish to chart the direction in which our society will be going. For example, naming ceremonies were traditionally held to honor a child and his family and to make the child realize that he or she was a part of a larger ongoing cultural group. Some ceremonies I have attended, however, have simply been a means of showing people that the family was financially able to sponsor a giveaway. None of the religious aspects were involved. There was no recounting of family history or discussion of the responsibilities of being Lakota. When we talk about memorial feasts and ghost-keeping ceremonies, we must ask how successfully they function to reintegrate the people who are mourners and exactly what benefits the ceremonies produce for the larger group. Is it a mere display of giving away? The same questions can be asked about the sweat lodge, the *inipi*. Some people feel the only function of this ceremony is to go and have "a sweat," as they call it. Many brag about how many hot stones are used, and how much heat they can tolerate. Even the term "sweat" has so little significance compared to the Lakota name, *inipi*, which is laden with values in our native culture. It means "to live again." Usually in a sweat lodge a person thinks about his life and the direction in which he or she wants to go. But many participants do not think these things through. The same lack of proper ritual attitude appears among participants in *yuwipi* and in the Sun Dance.

In connection with the Sun Dance, I would like to mention a few important symbols. The Sacred Pipe Woman who participates in the ceremony symbolizes White Buffalo Woman, whom we recognize as the culture bearer. She gave us this most important ceremony. This is exactly contrary to an analysis I heard recently at a professional meeting in which a psychologist commented that the Lakota people, even though they were a warrior society, had a female god. He completely misconstrued the role of the White Buffalo Woman in our mythology and belief system. This warns us that we must develop our own interpreters of culture, something I now see happening. We want to understand the ways in which our society functioned in the past, as well as the ways in which it functions today, and to make a record for the benefit of the generations that are yet to come.

It is beautiful honor to be selected as a participant in any part of the Sun Dance. The Sacred Pipe Woman, the four virgins who cut the sacred tree, the people who do the work—all consider it an honor. They are seen as valuable members of society and are appreciated as the repositories of ritual knowledge. This reflects the intensity of the experience of participating in the Sun Dance ritual, and it expresses a continuing commitment to Lakota ways. No matter how far you are away from home, this commitment is something you can never forget. This is the real function of ritual and belief. For these women and men there is always the *tiyošpaye* functioning as a social support group. It helps the individual when he has a giveaway, when he gives to the elderly, to the unfortunate, and to the *wašigla*, the mourners. At the Sun Dance those who have lost a relative during the previous year are fed a ritual meal and thereby reincorporated into the ordinary activities of Lakota society.

Despite the present interest in revitalizing traditional religion, one ceremony that has so far been overlooked is the girls' puberty ceremony, *išnati* ("living alone"). Such ceremonies are still ongoing among the Apaches, Navajos, and many other tribal groups, but they are curiously absent in Northern Plains revitalization movements. Yet in any ceremony that one attends, there is always the request that women who are in "that phase of the moon" remove themselves. When something goes wrong with the ceremony, there is always the subtle underlying accusation that its failure can be attributed to the presence of an impure woman—even though there is never any way of determining if this was so. The *išnati* ceremony has to be appreciated for its present-day connotations as well as traditional ones. In the past a Lakota woman removed herself from the *tiyošpaye* at such times because her *wakan*, her creative force, was so powerful that it interfered with other sacred activities.

Lack of the girls' puberty ceremony creates dissonance in the present ritual revitalization because it was during this ceremony that women were instructed in their social roles, procreation, and the care of children. I think that much of the erosion of family responsibility that we see on the reservations really could be averted if we talked to young people about their responsibilities as functioning members of society. In the days before contact with Europeans, there was ritual avoidance between husband and wife after a child was born, so this served as a natural way of spacing children. In the old days we did not have large families because the child's life depended upon the avoidance between his father and mother for two or three years during the lactation period. This religious sanction allowed for a smoothly developed relationship and protected women from a very tedious pregnancy every year. They had to move, to live in a nomadic way, and this sexual avoidance allowed time for the child to grow. Psychologists realize that the period up to age four or five is the time when a child's mind and body have the greatest capacity for development. It seems to me that the roles of men and women in Lakota culture were beautifully set up for the care and nurturance of children. The very name for children, *wakanyeja*, emphasizes their *wakan* aspect. They were a powerful part of this Sioux world. We should consider this in our child-raising methods. It is upsetting to witness child abuse on reservations today. Traditional Sioux people brought up their children to cherish, not mistreat them. We must understand and recapture this as a tremendously important means of revitalizing the best of our values.

Other traditional Sioux ceremonies that were important for women so far have failed to be revitalized, such as the bite-the-knife ceremony in which only older women who had lived faithfully with one man were allowed to participate. When the woman bit the knife, her truthfulness could never be questioned. She would then have a feast for her age mates, and she became one of the most honored women in the tribe, regarded with the greatest respect. Such a woman chose never to remarry after her husband's death. In sacred rites these women filled the special role of preparing and serving the ritual food. As symbols of purity they were related to the virgins of the Sun Dance.

The fact that women are the primary socializers of children underlies their duties as teachers of values, language, culture, world view, rituals, and practices, and underlies the beliefs and behaviors of the Lakotas. As Lakota women and men, we must constantly keep in mind the meaning of our word for children, the "sacred ones." By valuing the Lakota way and teaching it to our children, we will ensure that this lifestyle that we cherish will continue.

If the picture I have presented seems idealistic, we must realize the everchanging roles of Lakota women. Women's roles as household provisioners have retained a certain stability. Women continue to maintain the house—to cook, clean, and care for children. Because of the socioeconomic situation in most native communities, women are assuming a greater share of work as economic providers. This may be due to several factors: the transitory nature of marriages, the lack of jobs for males, the adaptive aspects of motherhood for purposes of financial support (welfare checks from Aid to Families with Dependent Children), and a racism that appears to be more focused on Indian men than Indian women. Women also tend to be better educated, which also accounts for their greater ability to obtain and hold jobs.

Alcohol abuse has also had a detrimental effect on native families. In many cases belief in male superiority continues. The disorganization of male-female relationships is reflected in spouse and child abuse. The weakening of the *tiyošpaye* is also a factor. Lakota women are imbedded in that social nexus. A biculturalism with resultant segmentation of self is a common characteristic of the contemporary Lakota woman. Selective attention to sex-role enactment may be what distinguishes the Lakota woman from her Anglo counterparts. She must develop adaptive strategies to allow this flexibility.

A common phrase heard at Indian women's gatherings is this: "We are the carriers of culture." This belief may provide Indian women a mandate to transmit cultural viability, engendering a sense of identity with a unique and satisfying cultural group. It is this that gives Lakota women the strength to operate in both the native and the non-native life spheres.

10

The Contemporary *Yuwipi*

BY THOMAS H. LEWIS, M.D.

FEW peoples throughout history have been without healers. Once the need for a special skill or function is recognized, someone arises to provide it. Social roles are thus defined and filled. When problems of pain and injury and illness arise, those individuals emerge who learn to cope with such problems, who profess or eventually assert a competence in their solution. The assumption of competence, and whether such competence is to endure and be recognized as worthy, depends always upon results. Today science endeavors to evaluate medical results objectively. Earlier healing arts frequently were not as objective, and sometimes, then and now, healing was more concerned with the process than with the careful measure of effect.

Oglala healers, with few exceptions, were and are senior men and women who come to their generalist or specialist practices late in life, when their accumulated knowledge and long experience would place them, in any culture, in advisory positions. Oglala healers tend to have a family tradition of specialized ritual-medical knowledge and of special spiritual powers. But whether the father or an older relative was a medicine man or not, the calling depends upon the individual's dreams or visions, considered to be beyond individual control or ambition, which directed, obligated, advised, or commanded the dreamer to begin healing work. Preparation—a

better word than training for Oglala healers—encompassed
the healer's entire experience with religion and life. To have
seen and felt injury and illness, to have watched death, to
have achieved some equanimity in the presence of pain,
to have attended ceremonials and night sings, and to have
finished with the vigors and labors of youth—all that went before is preparation for the life of the sage, the seer, the advisor. A healer may undergo an extended period of learning
the songs and techniques of ritual with a recognized mentor.
Sometimes medicine bundles or rituals are purchased or bequeathed. An aspirant may attend sings (healing or divining
ceremonies) for years as an assistant or a singer or one of the
drummers to an older shaman. He may be a Sun Dancer year
after year, accumulating power and reputation. But the keys
to the process are the achievement of a sense of personal ritual
power—the feeling that one possesses important spiritual
helpers and can safely represent the spirit world to humankind—and the assertiveness to present oneself as effective.
Results count, and successes are recounted in the age-old way
of recounting prowess in war and in ritual. And reputations
grow—or wither.

A Lakota healing session is arranged through a meticulously
formalized approach procedure. The patient-client begins by
discussing his problem with family or friends, with an advisor
or intermediary, or with the healer himself. Haste is unwise,
likely to give offense, likely to rupture the fragile fabric of eti-
quette and correct procedure. Indeed, an unhurried contemplation of all the implications of the problem by the community is often part of the procedure. It is important to see
the right specialist. It is important that the healer, the dis-
order, and the treatment procedure are harmonious. Once
those elements of the healing session are settled, the applicant sends his emissary, or goes himself, to make a dignified
formal visit, carrying the pipe to the medicine man. Several
visits may be needed. The pipe carrier enters the house in a
slow respectful manner, observing the elaborate visitor's eti-

quette of moving always to the left. The filled pipe is carried horizontally in extended hands. The pipe is presented in that position and may be ritually refused three times. A fourth refusal is final and irrevocable. If it is accepted—and that is rarely on the first visit—the pipe carrier is seated, and his problem is recounted in proper terminology. Contemplation follows, and finally the healer offers advice on recommended preliminary actions, which may include fasting, vision seeking, abstinences, prayers, preparation of offerings or feasts, or enigmatic delays covering weeks or months. If the problem is considered unsuitable, frivolous, or in any way inappropriate, the healer's refusal to act is firm.

Once accepted, the pipe obligates the healer to a full commitment to the task at hand, to the appropriate ritual, time, and practical procedures. The patient-client may have traveled miles or days for these preliminary meetings. He is spared the agonies of the waiting room, at least, and if all goes well, he has the assurance of a firm treatment contract, a therapeutic alliance he can depend on. The personal-history taking embedded in the first encounters may be prolonged, and may include discussions with not only the patient-client but also his family and friends, tribal officials, incidental informants, or even persons inimical to him. As in small towns anywhere, everyone knows everyone else's business. The patient's troubles and his likely arrival at the medicine man's home may have been announced by the moccasin telegraph long before he appears in person.

The applicant for healing services shares a wealth of understandings with the healer. He expects that the healer will define the problem and clarify it in terms of a shared vocabulary, a shared religion, a shared theory of causality and importance. He expects the healer to be more experienced and more powerful vis-à-vis the forces which he believes affect his life. He assumes the benevolence, sagacity, and commitment of the healer because name and title, like all aspects of language, condition his thinking and preformulate his perception. He understands that all the participants in the ritual, not only the healer and himself, have his best interests at heart.

The applicant values a sense of wholeness and harmony above science and logic, and this enables him to let his possible scepticism float freely. He expects to gain a richer comprehension of himself and his relationship to the world, his tribal group, and the other world beyond the ordinary boundaries of reality. He expects to achieve a greater harmony within himself and an integration of inner and outer experience, a lessening of nameless fears, an increase in self-value, identity, and community acceptance. He assents to the healer's greater authority and wisdom. In matters he might well handle rationally in ordinary life, his expectations of good override disbelief. Although he may be disdainful of the conjuring tricks of a clumsy shaman, or amused by the accidental betrayal of the mysteries, his confidence in what he sees as helpful in the procedure as a whole will not be weakened in the least.

The healer, on his part, has well in mind the principles known to physicians since the world began—that time is a great healer, that fears and passions fade, that problems pass, that benign neglect sometimes suffices, that all therapeutics help at first or to some degree, that patients get well irrespective of theory and in spite of practice, and placebos are not inert. The presence of the healer, in itself, arouses hope and quiets fear. When he comments with the sagacity of his years, he affirms the patient's identity and sense of belonging in his world. If to this he can add specific remedies, all the better.

Assessment of the effect of treatment has to keep in mind a Lakota viewpoint, not a laboratory viewpoint. Many times the results are what the patient and the therapist say they are, and measurement is impossible by any other criteria. A surgical procedure or a unit of some drug may yield an observable effect, and the effect is a measure of efficacy in at least a narrow sense. The Oglala healer and his patient are more inclined to feel that the process of examination, identification, and ritual are ends in themselves.

Understanding *yuwipi* is central to understanding the many semisecret healing rituals of the Lakotas. Although *yuwipi* has ancient origins, it also contains more recent accretions, as it embodies syncretistic and revivalist elements of Sioux religion and pan-Indian movements. Politicians seeking popular support subscribe to it. Christian groups and health projects approve it, oppose it, or try to integrate with it. The principal and powerful and prominent medicine men, by and large, use *yuwipi* procedures.

Yuwipi refers to the supernatural escape from inescapable bondage of the human shaman, his prayer powers, his flight through the air with his spiritual helpers, and his eventual return with wisdom and instruction. In the special terminology of the Oglalas, *hanhepi woecun*, "night doings," refers to all nighttime ceremonies, while *yuwipi* refers to the wrapped and tied healer who is to be dramatically released by the spirits, as well as to the belief system as a whole. Using—but transcending—conjuring, magic, and variations in ritual, *yuwipi* healers give authoritative medical advice and general guidance in life's problems, and the *yuwipi* ritual powerfully reinforces Indian identity.

Healing meetings are held as often as nightly at the request of petitioners, who carry a pipe to the *yuwipi* man, the *wapiye*, or healer. The healer professes a power achieved by dreams, vision seeking, purification rites, and prayer. Like many other healers, the *yuwipi* medicine man emphasizes his personal weakness, insignificance, and humility in comparison to the gods and powers (the *Wakan*), while simultaneously practicing an attitude of omnipotence and omniscience.

During the years that I lived and worked on the Pine Ridge Reservation, Frank Andrew Fools Crow was one of the most powerful of the *yuwipi* healers, a politically powerful medicine man and sage. He is the *wicaša wakan*, the *wapiya wicaša*, the *yuwipi wapiye*, the one who conducts the ritual aspects of the Sun Dance, the priest, the medicine man. He is also the *pejuta wicaša*, the medical practitioner of his district.

In 1968 he was seventy-six years old, a pleasant, thoughtful, friendly, toothless man, heavy of body, sedate, shrewd, good-natured. It was to him that I went in order to learn about the Lakotas' healing techniques in the *yuwipi* ceremony. When we talked, his speech moved from subject to subject, sometimes with disjunctures which eventually got closed as long as you listened patiently. Of his powers he once said to me:

I can find things that are lost or hidden. One man lost a new harness. He looked and looked. He came to me. I took him (after a *yuwipi* ceremony) on horseback where the vision told me. There were two holes in a bank. They had put one in one of the holes and covered it very good with grass. He wanted me to tell who did it but I said, "You have the harness back. Be happy. That's what you wanted. That's what you came to me for. No use to get anybody in trouble. You got the harness back."

Fools Crow showed me a small metal trunk containing his ritual equipment. There were rawhide thongs for binding his fingers; a rawhide rope and a quilt for binding his body; rattles which the spirits animated during *yuwipi* ceremonies; several small hoops with crossbars, *cangleška,* symbols of the universe, which were decorated with porcupine quillwork and plumes; and a large sacred pipe. He described *yuwipi* for me in great detail, and he said:

It is more important to know that spirits are all around. One gives tobacco and food to the departed spirits of friends and relatives, to the grandfathers who go to Heaven with Jesus our Father, to the grandmothers who lay in the ground until they are remarried in the future. I can communicate with spirits and can tell what they say. We may have much crying for the departed people of the family.

He also showed me a small drum about twenty inches in diameter with one head; some stones (*tunkan*), which he called "talking stones"; and a braid of dried sweetgrass to burn as incense to purify the altar and the participants. He described the binding of the *pejuta wicaša,* his fingers, hands, and body, and the covering with a blanket; the lights flickering; the gourds and drums sounding all around the room. He said that if I wished to return sometime, I should bring red, yellow, black, and white cloth, and 405 cloth-wrapped tobacco offerings, *canli wapahta*, one for each spirit. He concluded: "Try to get Horn Cloud to come as a singer, and if you could arrange that, and bring tobacco and groceries, a ceremony could be held. Perhaps."

My first scheduled *yuwipi* meeting, confirmed by several visits and many exchanges of messages, was on August 19, 1968. We arrived at Fools Crow's house at sundown and talked for three hours, but his singers, he told us, had all gone to Red Scaffold and no ceremony could be held. It was sixty miles back to camp, and no moon.

On August 21 we tried again, bringing William Horn Cloud and his wife from Pine Ridge town. We arrived at Fools Crow's on Three Mile Creek, again at sundown. His ranch swarmed with children and dogs, around a cluster of small houses. A creek runs behind his house, and beyond it, several miles away against the sunset sky, is a conical hill used for fasting and vision seeking. We sat talking through the dusk for several hours with the family. Fools Crow, sitting apart from the conversation, cut and peeled several chokecherry wands and prepared other paraphernalia for the ceremony to come. At dark, we were invited indoors for more talk, playing with the small children, looking at photo albums, discussing pictures on the walls, and drumming and singing. The women were cooking the groceries that we had brought, making stew from the pile of steaks, and preparing a large batch of fry bread.

Eventually we all removed to a large log cabin lit by one kerosene lamp placed on the floor. Twenty adults were present, with many children and infants. The door was locked and the windows were covered with canvas or blankets. The floor, of heavy planks, was cleared by pushing all furniture against the walls. In the middle Fools Crow prepared a bed of sage. At each of the four corners a tin can of dirt held a peeled wand with a cloth banner, white at the far left (east) corner, red at the far right (north) corner, yellow at near left (south) corner, black at near right (west) corner. A larger wand with three ornate eagle feathers was placed in another tin can beyond the center of the altar. Rattles were placed beside each tin can, and tobacco was sprinkled around this entire assemblage. Also at the center, a can of earth from the hill of a gopher was poured onto the floor, flattened with the side of the medicine man's small, one-headed drum, carefully smoothed, and inscribed with the symbols of *Wakinyan* (the Thunder-beings), a jagged line with forked ends, as well as dots and lines representing stars and planets. A pipe was laid down on the left of this altar, which Fools Crow referred to as "the center of the earth," and a quilt and rawhide rope were placed at the foot. The altar and sage pallet were encircled by the string of cloth-wrapped tobacco offerings that I had brought.

Fools Crow then removed his clothing, except for trousers and an undershirt, and knelt on the sage pallet. At first there had been much loud talking, laughing, and story telling, but after a while the talk died down. The children grew quiet. Everyone took seats on chairs or on bedrolls placed on the floor around the walls of the room, and in respectful silence sprigs of sage were passed around for each person to rub on his head and arms. The pipe was filled and passed to an elderly woman, who held it through the rest of the ceremony. After a long song the light was put out. In total darkness an extended prayer was given in Lakota to the pipe, the spirit of the stones, and the Grandfathers. Another long song followed, and the light was relit.

Then Fools Crow stood up, and an assistant carefully tied his fingers, hands, wrists, and arms behind him. The quilt was wrapped round him, covering and overlapping his head and feet, and this was tightly bound with the rawhide rope. When the binding was complete, two men lifted him and lowered him face down onto the pallet of sage. He moaned and struggled, and the light was put out again. The singers and drummers led a series of long songs in Lakota, the others joining in. This was accompanied by flickering blue lights (apparently caused by a cigarette lighter without fluid), vigorous hammering on the floor and walls announcing the arrival of the spirits (apparently done with a heavy stone), and loud groans. I often felt that the hammering was beneath my chair or beside my feet. Sometimes the whole house of heavy logs seemed to vibrate with it. The drum sounds seemed to move around the room and ceiling.

The *pejuta wicaša* gave forth with short cries, phrases, and muffled groans, all becoming gradually more organized until finally the chief drummer stopped suddenly and called my name loudly. He said: "I have been asked [as part of the communication between spirits and shaman] to inquire as to your intentions of having this ceremony done." Startled at being asked for a public statement of my problem, I could think of no plausible illness or complaint. With a new academic appointment in mind, I said: "I have a new and difficult job to do. I would like to know if I can do it well." He then put this conversation into a lengthy dialogue in Lakota. More singing followed, with groaning, squeaking, and unidentifiable sounds, and heavy drumming on the floor. I was struck heavily in the face by a hide. Lights crackled and flickered. There were groans and agonized bits of speech. Sudden drafts of air came— I was told later—from the wings of *Wakinyan*.

At length the translator said to me: "There is a man from where you are from who thinks he is very important. He will go on a vacation, but he will not return; he will die. Now you will have to take a personal view about the job. Make up your mind to do it and you will do it. It is up to you." He then gave comments on the illnesses of several people present, and advice about a surgical procedure which one woman was scheduled to have at the hospital. The lamp was relit to reveal Fools Crow sitting quietly on the sage bed, the ropes and quilt in a pile against the far wall. He slowly dressed and methodically put away his equipment. Then, as the principle sponsor of the ceremony, he called me aside and took me far from the house on the prairie. He prayed in Lakota over some bits of food, ending with the English words, "Have pity! Help the poor soul to live a good life." He threw the food into the darkness, and we returned to the house. The cloth and tobacco offerings were burned in the stove. A large meal was served consisting of stewed beef, soup, fry bread, and coffee. The men and women chatted loudly in Lakota; children were asleep on the floor or in their mother's laps. I went around the room, saying something to each person, and after much handshaking, the evening was over. It was long past midnight.

After this initial experience, my interest in native Lakota healing practices continued to grow. As part-time staff psychiatrist at a mental-health clinic at the Public Health Service hospital in Pine Ridge, my interest was professional. Over the years some of the healers on the reservation had approached the PHS physicians and suggested cooperative practice. That had not occurred, perhaps because some members of the community fear that the healers can exercise dangerous powers as well as curative ones, perhaps because no safe bureaucratic precedent could be found, and because there is no civil-service job description to cover "medicine men." Nonetheless, substantial numbers of reservation patients continue to consult native practitioners instead of modern clinics and hospitals.

Robert Holy Dance, another native healer, shared his knowledge of the healing arts with me over a period of years. One day I asked him about *yuwipi* spirits, and he replied:

I went to one *yuwipi* [held] for a man whose father died a year before. The *yuwipi* man said, "There is a man on the other side of the door. Shall we let him in or not?" The people said, "Yes, because we are here to be doctored of our ailments." They were singing. He said, "Shine your flashlights," and they did; and sure enough, it was his father standing there. I been thinking and thinking, and I think it was a hypnotizing deal. One brother got angry and said, "Why did you do it? You should never do that," and them womens, they began to cry when they saw them flashlights on him. He must have hypnotized us, done something to make us imagine. . . .

All these *yuwipi* have a vision first. That's where I got mine. A *yuwipi* gives a preamble about his vision. I don't do the *yuwipi*. I did it twice but found it was no good [for me]. I deal with herbs and medicine. They are two different things. They don't match. They don't work together. . . .

The *yuwipi* spirits are very small. A good medicine man will have about 500 of them. If he is not so good, he'll have less. If there is something important he'll get help. It takes about 1,000 to bring in a saddle. Once they got the guy from Slim Buttes. They told the man who was wanting the ceremony they needed more power. They had to sing about eight songs. The saddle was a long way off, I guess. They had about twenty singers and every other man had a drum. You could hear the saddle coming. They lit up the lamp and told him to see if it was his. He examined it and it was his. But they wouldn't tell him who had stolen the saddle.

The next day he wanted his horse back so they sang a lot of songs. They sang all night that time. They said, "You will go up a valley and see many birds. And under the birds you will find your horse." He went up that hill and there was his horse and it was dead, shot, and all kinds of birds over it. Ha! It was there, but it was dead and they never would tell who done it.

A good *yuwipi* man, if you go to him, them gourds would come to you and talk right in your ear.

One afternoon I was sitting with a Lakota healer whom I had known for six years, discoursing about his *yuwipi* cures and the methods of his rival practitioners, when he said: "This woman you met today, who brought the white dog. She is sick. They are going to make a feast tonight. A catch-the-stone singing. It will keep you from sickness all your life. Come and bring your children."

That evening the healer, the woman patient, and several guests gathered in his front yard, and after several hours of desultory conversation and long silences we were taken into his small house and seated on the floor against the walls. The windows and doors were covered with blankets, and a kerosene lamp was lit and placed on the floor.

The healer placed paper on the floor, then formed an altar of earth, and prepared it much as for the *yuwipi* ceremony described above. He lighted a braid of sweetgrass and waved the smoke over the altar and all the persons in the room. The lamp was extinguished by an assistant, and rattling noises began, accompanied by prayers to the Grandfathers (*Tunkanšila*) and the plea "*Wakan Tanka*, be merciful that my people may live." Songs accompanied by drumming continued for an hour

or more. The long prayers and long songs following monoto-
nously on one another, the stifling heat in the cabin, the spirit
noises that seemed to come from all directions, the sparks of
light, and the drumming all contributed to an involuntary
dimming of attention. At length the drumming stopped, and
the healer began to pound on the earth altar. His voice became shrill, the words rapid and loud. Then the lamp was lit.
He poured some water on the altar, drank some, and passed
the bowl to an assistant. Suddenly he pointed dramatically
at the altar, where a black spirit stone, called *yuwipi inyan*
("yuwipi stone") had appeared. The smooth, shiny, opaque
pebble was then wrapped in buckskin and tied to a necklace-
length cord. It was presented to me with a muttered prayer.
The woman patient was given advice from the spirits in Lakota,
and the evening ended with a ceremonial meal of dog soup,
the ritual drinking of water, and smoking of the pipe.

This ceremony is clearly related to *yuwipi*. Besides prayers,
songs, and spirit advice, it gives the participant an amulet, a
magical stone like the sacred stones of the *yuwipi* spirits, to
protect the wearer against illness and danger. He is told that if
disease or injury threatens, he will be awakened in the night
by spirits and given appropriate verbal warnings. He may
also, under the influence of the stone, have powerful protective dreams. For the Lakotas it provides a powerful preventive
approach to the serious health problems that beset the isolated rural dweller and the very poor.

The patient who seeks the services of an Oglala medicine man
inadvertently embarks on a group-therapy experience. He
encounters preliminary arrangements which seem protracted,
contradictory, vague, and unpredictable. Eventually he may
come to realize that he is involved in a long, ongoing process
which will change the rhythms of his interactions with the
healer and with others, a long process of psychological preparation for a specific night-sing ritual at some unspecified time
in the very indefinite future. To all of this the patient must
adapt his importunities and his so self-important personal
issues and schedules. The medicine man invites leisurely con-

versation about the problem, but first and later there are post-
ponements, renewed supplications, restatements of purpose,
reminders, afterthoughts, and difficulties, all in the service of
clarification of the problem and a testing of the seriousness of
the client. The long waits allow assessment of the client by
healer and healer by client. The difficulties discourage the
ambivalent client and add to the involvement of the committed one. They contribute to a growing implicit-explicit
contract and obligation of both parties. The healer has time to
select good clients and good problems, to assess the validity of
the client's desire for help or change, and to weigh the work-
ableness of the issue at hand. The client's relationship to the
community becomes clearer to the medicine man, and his
problems are seen more and more in the context of his family
and neighbors.

In an immediate, pragmatic fashion the *yuwipi* medicine
man provides advice to his rural clients. He gives primary
care for chronic and acute disease, family-practice instruction,
and referral when appropriate. He evaluates advice and care
given elsewhere and has influence in supporting or opposing
what the patient or family heard at a clinic or hospital, and in
affirming, encouraging, questioning, or particularizing a given
therapeutic regimen.

With a shrewd attentiveness to reservation news, moccasin
telegraph, history, and gossip, the *yuwipi* ritualist is a social
mediator with ability to diffuse conflicts, to dispense conven-
tional wisdom, to counsel caution, and to direct action. The
thief who cannot dispose of his loot, and the victim who wants
his property back are brought together in some semblance of
anonymity and nobody loses.

In his repetition of Lakota themes and values, the *yuwipi*
practitioner reaffirms and strengthens tribal identity. The recounting of myths and songs, the repeated testimonials, the
emphasis on the unity of the living, the departed dead, and
the historical heroes, all forge stronger links between the participants in *yuwipi* ceremonies and help them glory in their
differentiation from off-reservation culture.

The *yuwipi* ritual is reservation theatre, rural music, archaic poetry. As drama it attracts both the inhabitant and the outlander. Very few people in the vicinity of a good sing fail to sit in. The conjurer artist, the illusionist, the serious poet, and the actor find their roles. The storyteller has an opportunity and audience for variant and traditional themes. The Christian liturgist has his counterpart in the *yuwipi* singer and drummer. The variation in ritual gives scope to the creativity of the ritual leader, which is soon reflected in his fame and drawing power, and in public critiques and the carping comments of competitors.

The medicine man is careful to preserve his naming prerogatives. He explains the world in his own terms. He defines and labels problems. He gives strong testimony to the comprehensiveness of his understanding. This naming power, by musical extension, gives him power over the objects named. That he can assert this power in an ambience of drama and share it with the spirits who are his helpers, is a measure of his skill in addressing the ancient elements in human thinking, in establishing in the minds of his clients a plausible connection between object, word, and deed. As the healer names the problem, he also fixes blame and offers causal explanations which make sense in his culture. His answers to problems are at least firm. They may not always be correct answers, but they are answers, and that is organizing, reassuring, and comforting in itself.

The medicine man is formulator and teacher of the old religion and the creator of the new; his services are carefully planned and presented. He offers immediacy of experience of, and contact with, the spiritual powers of the world beyond. His symbolic representations of the universe and time emphasize their circular, ever-beginning, never-ending nature, transcending duality. He leads the thoughts of his celebrants to the ultimate and to origins, to the beginnings of knowledge and to a perspective on death. The intensity of the *yuwipi* experience develops from the long drawn-out ritual itself, but the intensity of the relationship with the leader must be examined also. He is a figure of authority and awe, beyond scepticism and criticism. He is an unfailing master of procedure and a sage omnipotent. The patient, in his surrender of autonomy and initiative, hopes that previous gratifying benefits of submission will be regained. He is introduced to the lost times of childhood when dream, fantasy, and reality intermingled. Every movement, every symbolic act, every gesture of the shaman with his sacred objects, focuses attention on his ability to evoke an extraordinary experience. His pronouncements have the ring of universal truth. The carefully nurtured concentration of his client's attention, and the evocation of dependency and regression, suggest the office techniques of twentieth-century Western medical practitioners, and their only partly cynical dictum, "It doesn't matter if you are right or wrong, just never be in doubt."

The Lakota healer pays scant attention to allopathic-homeopathic dualities, to cellular physiology, germ theory, biochemical dynamics, or other fundaments of Western medical theory. Instead he emphasizes his special status as an intermediary with the Beings Beyond Knowing. He ascribes therapeutic efficacy to his supernatural helpers, to his knowledge of legend and myth, to the strengthening of tribal identity. He participates in the ubiquitous Lakota search for personal power, the generation of which controls health, prosperity, and mastery. And he knows that this search permeates Lakota healing as well as life's other preoccupations.

The healer focuses upon the individual rather than on symptom, sign, disease, or diagnosis. He has a rich knowledge of community and family relationships and interactions. He has experimental as well as intuitive understandings of his patients' needs, and he often succeeds in recognizing unspoken wishes and expectations. The medicine man has little interest in linear or multifactorial causality in a Western sense. He is impatient with sequential certainties. He stands upon his courage to affirm that healing will occur, and he endures as an institution in a culture that still needs him.

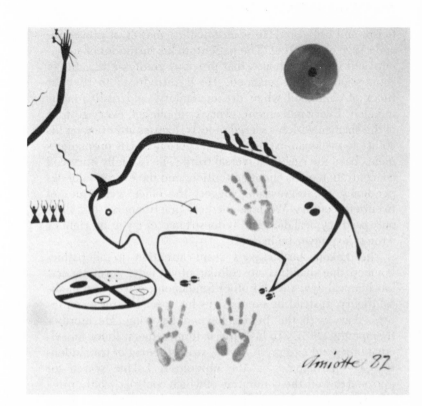

11

The Native American Church of Jesus Christ

EMERSON SPIDER, SR.

FIRST OF ALL, I'm very thankful that you boys could come to the Native American Church of Jesus Christ, which was built here at Porcupine not too long ago. I am Emerson Spider, Sr., and my title is Reverend of the Native American Church. I'm the headman of the Native American Church of Jesus Christ in the state of South Dakota.

Our church began to come into South Dakota during the early 1900s. There was a man named John Rave, a Winnebago Indian. This was before I was born. I guess this man was very smart. He was in the Catholic Church. Then he ordained another man named Henry White, also a Winnebago, as a minister in the Native American Church. That man came to the Sioux in the community of Allen, on Pine Ridge Reservation. So we got our ordination by rights.

At first we weren't organized as a church. It was a Sioux man named Jim Blue Bird who organized this peyote way of worshipping as a church and put the Bible in there to be the head instrument in our church. Then he said that we should have ministers. So in 1924 we organized as a church with ministers, like any other church. Last June we had our fifty-eighth annual convention. My grandpa on my mother's side, Reverend William Black Bear, was the first headman of the church in South Dakota. Then after he was gone, my dad took over. He was sixty-six years old when he passed away. For the past seventeen years I have been head of the church.

We started out as a traditional church. We didn't have the Bible or practice Christianity. Among the Indians, we always say that it is the oldest church in the world. Gradually we learned about the second coming of Christ, and finally we accepted the Lord as our personal savior, just as in any other church. Originally, the Native American Church followed the Half Moon way. Then the Winnebagos adopted the Cross Fire way. The fireplace on their altar looks like a half-moon, but instead of tobacco smoke they use the Bible.

The Native American Church started out with the Half Moon way of the Peyote religion. They use what they call the "Generation Fireplace." On the altar they mound the earth like a half-moon, and they put a little road on that mound which represents your life from the time you were born until you come to the center, and on to when you get old and go from there to death. They put the Generation Fireplace at the altar within the tipi, and at the center of the road they place the peyote.

We know that this Generation Fireplace pushes souls to Christ. The Cross Fire way comes in after believing on the Lord Jesus Christ. In this way we put the cross at the center to represent the place where Christ gave his life for each and every one of us. So it begins with this Half Moon way and then comes into the Cross Fire way, where you believe in Christ and pass to believing on the Lord. I'm not saying that the Cross Fire way is better, but as we come along we learn about the second coming of Christ. We put the peace pipe aside and we put the Bible in its place.

When I was becoming a Christian, I heard some people say, "I'm worshipping the same God as my forefathers." I thought that was real good, but now I think our forefathers must not have had the right kind of god. I hate to say this, but it is so. In the olden days, when people from different tribes came around, they killed them. We said they were enemies because they didn't speak our language. They had the same skin as we had, but we killed them. In those days they prayed to the Great Spirit, but I don't think that's the right god. The God we found is love. He loves us all. If in the olden days they prayed to that God, why is it they killed each other as enemies?

Also, in the olden days, one tribe believed that the souls of the departed went east, riding white horses. The Happy Hunting Grounds were supposed to be over the fourth hill to the east. Other tribes said the departed souls went south, riding sorrel horses. Every tribe had different beliefs. If they prayed to the same Great Spirit in the early days, they should all have had the same belief. Christ gave His life and made a road for us to go on. That's one way: towards heaven.

Right now some traditional Indian people say this Bible doesn't belong to the Indians because the white man made it. But I never thought of it that way. I thought this Bible belongs to any wicked man, any man with a living soul in him, so that through this Bible he would be saved. This is the way I think. It wasn't for just the white men alone but for every man, every person who has a living soul within him. It's the food for that person.

I'm not saying the traditional ways are bad, but it tells in the Bible, "Choose you this day whom you will serve, whether the gods of Amorites our forefathers served; but as for me in my house, we will serve the Lord." These are not my own words; I always like to use the words of God. Some people say they are real traditional men, but Christ is also a traditional man. He's been here almost two thousand years. That's traditional; that's a long time. I was thinking that we didn't use this peyote until after 1900, but Christ was in the world two thousand years ago. I think that's more traditional than what we have been trying to do here.

In the traditional way of worshipping in the Native American Church, the leader is called a *road man*. We still have our traditional way, especially in this area. In the traditional way we pray with the tobacco and corn-shock cigarette in place of the peace pipe. I held a service like that the other night, a back-to-school meeting. I prayed for the little ones who are going back to school. So we still have our traditional way as well. I ordained some of the traditional road men as ministers of the church. I did this because if we don't it will just be tradition, and we won't be recognized as a church.

The peyote that we use is classified as a drug by the state of South Dakota. We use it in the Native American Church as a sacrament. Because we are organized as a church, the government can't take the peyote away from us. Our church is the last thing we have among the Indian people, the peyote way of worshipping. We call it *Pejuta yuta okolakiciye*, "medicine-eating church." The Native American Church is organized among the Sioux in South Dakota on three reservations: Pine Ridge, Rosebud, and Yankton. I have some ministers working on all three of these reservations. We are supposed to keep records, but I really don't know how many members there are. The other tribes still hang onto the traditional way of worshipping. They don't want to organize as a church, but the Sioux organized as a church. I think this is good, because other churches will recognize us as a church.

My grandpa and my dad told me that when they first started using peyote in the community of Allen, the Indian police would sneak up on them and stop them. They would take away the drum and the peyote. At that time my mother was real small, and she was going to the boarding school at Pine Ridge. While she was there, they found out that she had tuberculosis. In those days it was considered incurable. They placed my mother in the hospital, in a little room all by herself. No one was supposed to go near her because the disease was contagious. So they kept her there.

One day a grandma of mine was visiting the sick ones in the hospital. The door to my mother's room was open just a little bit. Her eyes were swollen nearly closed, and her body was swollen up; she was dying. As she lay there, she was looking towards the door, and she recognized the lady who went by. Mother called her name, so that lady came into the room. Although she was my mother's aunt, she didn't recognize my mother for awhile. Pretty soon she recognized her. "Is that you?" she said.

"Yeah, that's me."

"Why are you lying here like this? Did you let your dad know that you're here?" My grandma on my mother's side passed away when my mother was real small, so she grew up with no mother, just my grandpa. I don't know what had happened, but the hospital hadn't notified my grandfather. So this grandma of mine said, "As soon as I get home I'm going to go to your dad and I'm going to tell him that you are here." I guess that made my mother feel real good. She said, "You do that."

Sure enough, in a few days my grandpa went after her. In those days there were just buggies, no cars. My grandpa really got mad because he had not been notified that my mother was sick. But the doctor told my grandpa not to take my mother because she had that contagious disease and was going to die anyway. Still, my grandpa took her home.

When they got home, my mother started taking that medicine, the peyote. They started giving her the medicine. My mother told me that it was towards springtime. All through that summer they would give her medicine, put her on a horse, and let her go out riding. She'd be on that horse most all day long. When she came back in the evening they would give her some more medicine. After a few months she was well. She was all right.

About that time they were caught while they were holding a Native American Church service. The man who ran the store at Allen at that time was against peyote, and he was the one who caught them. They called him *Nape Blaska*, "Flat-Handed," because his hands were deformed. All of them got caught, including my mother, so they took them to Deadwood for trial. The court said that peyote was a narcotic, that it was no good. The judge asked, "Why are you using that?"

My mother's dad said: "This is good. This peyote's good. It is good medicine and I can prove it."

"What have you got to prove it with?"

"This girl here." So they had my mother stand up. "This

girl had tuberculosis. The doctors gave up on her. She was placed in the sanitarium. I got her away from there. Now she's alive today."

Luckily, the doctor who had cared for my mother was in the courtroom. He asked her if she was Jessie Black Bear. "Yeah, it's me," she said.

He said, "How did you get well?"

"Through the peyote, through what we have here. I got well through that."

I guess the doctor got up and shook her hand, saying: "I thought you were gone a long time ago. I thought you were dead."

So right away the judge said, "I have nothing to do with this." "These mescal beans must be good," he said. (In those days they called peyote mescal beans.) "These mescal beans are yours; they don't belong to the white man. Give them back to them." So they gave the whole thing back, a wooden barrel full of peyote.

This is the reason that people say my mother is the one who saved the peyote. If she hadn't been there, they would have had a hard time proving that this medicine was good. After this happened, that man *Nape Blaska* went back and got into some kind of trouble. I guess he was in debt and couldn't pay, so he killed himself in the garage—committed suicide.

My dad was from Porcupine community. His family lived right across the road from here. My dad was born and raised here. He belonged to the Episcopal Church. My grandpa on my dad's side was a minister in that church. And my mother was from Allen, where the peyote church originated. They didn't tell me how they met, but anyway they got married. But my dad didn't like this medicine. He didn't believe in it. So whenever he went to Allen, and they started tying a drum for a service, he would take off. He didn't like to hear the drum or the songs. He would get on his horse and go way over the hill someplace. When they were through, he would come back. He did that for four years, I think.

My dad didn't believe in the peyote, but at the same time

he was always thinking about it. He wondered, "What does it do for these people when they eat it?" Some people told him that when you ate it you got high, just like drinking. My dad never drank and never smoked. I guess he grew up like that. So he was wondering; he had it in mind all the time. But at the same time he was scared to use it because some people said it was dope.

Finally one day, when my mother and dad were alone, he said to my mother, "Jessie, I wonder if you could give me some of that medicine you eat?"

"Sure," she said. So she picked out four dried ones. She gave them to my dad and he started to eat one. This medicine is very bitter, so as he started to chew on it, he quickly took it out of his mouth. "This is awful," he said. "I don't see how you could eat it and why you would eat it. It's no good, not fit to be eaten." Then he got up. "This is not a thing to eat," he said. He started towards the stove, and although my mother tried to stop him, she couldn't. He opened that stove, threw the peyote in there, and burned it up.

Four days later, all of a sudden my dad couldn't pass any water. It stopped completely. His kidneys were swelling up, so he came back to Porcupine. His father sent for a doctor from Rapid City. That doctor came in a hurry; the Indians called him *Wašicu Wakan Witkokola*, "Crazy Doctor." He came and got his bag out and examined my father all over. I guess he told my grandpa: "If I wanted to, I could give your boy some medicine, but I want to tell you the truth. That boy's not going to live four days. You'd better get ready for it. There's no medicine that will cure him."

So my grandfather heard that. Then he wrote out a note and gave it to my father. "You take this to your father-in-law," he said. So they got in a buggy and rushed back to Allen, about twenty miles on the cut-across. When they got there, they gave that note to my grandpa on that side. He said, "Yeah, I got good medicine for that." My dad wanted to find out what kind of medicine he had. I guess he kept asking my mother, "What kind of medicine does your father have?" Finally my mother told him. "It's the same medicine that you burned here not too long ago." My dad said: "Well, that's it. If that's the medicine they are going to give, I don't want any. I'd rather die. I'm not going to eat it." "I'm not going to take it," he said.

My dad's older brother went with them on this trip. He's still alive today, over ninety years old. My dad was real young in those days. And I guess my uncle said to my father, "Brother, you're a coward." He said: "You're a coward. I'll eat it. You're scared of it." "I'll eat it first," he said.

You know how young men are. When my dad heard that about being a coward and being scared, he got mad. "Well, bring all you got," he said. "I'll eat everything you got. Bring everything." So right away they told my grandfather. "Okay," he said. They got everything ready in no time. They boiled some of the powdered medicine in water to make tea, and they started giving my dad some of the dried medicine to eat. My dad said he didn't know how much he ate. "A lot of it," he said, "and I drank a lot of tea." His stomach and his kidneys were so swollen he could hardly walk. "I could hardly move," he said.

They were beating a drum, but it seemed to my dad that they were very slow to begin. My grandpa went after some boys, and pretty soon they came back and started their service. That morning my dad had to be excused, so he went out. There was no longer anything wrong with him. Back there about three gallons of water came out of him, I guess.

This is the way my dad told it. He said, "That's good medicine—real good medicine. It could cure anything. But the way they're praying with it, that's another thing." He grew up in the Episcopal Church, so he didn't believe in the Native American Church. "How can they pray with that peyote? How can they say that it is holy and leading a man to Christ? How could it be?" My dad kept going to church. Then one day he took some medicine, and I guess it showed him. Although he never brought out what happened, he learned that those who were weak in faith could benefit from using the peyote, that it was put here for the Indian people to lead them to Christ.

Now some of us are Christians—you might say born-again Christians. That's what we are. As we come along, we try to do whatever other churches are doing. In the past we had the Half Moon way of worshipping, and we used the peace pipe in our services, because the peace pipe is the traditional way of worshipping among our Sioux Indian people. As we came along, we put the peace pipe away, and in place of it we now use the Bible, so that we may be saved in the end. I know and believe that the Great Spirit in heaven did this for the Indian people, so that through this medicine we would find Christ.

In my own life I have experienced this, and I've told a lot of people about it. Indians from all tribes went out to hunt for roots to use as medicines, so God put this peyote here for the Indians to find. They call it peyote, but we say *pejuta*, which means "medicine" in our language. All the different tribes call it "medicine" in their own languages. Because God loves all of us he put this medicine in the world so that the Indians would find it and through it they would come to Christ.

Today I am well known among other tribes as a good person because I have the fear of the Lord and I love God and I love Jesus Christ. If you live this way you'll get somewhere. I went to school as far as the fifth grade at Holy Rosary Mission at Pine Ridge, South Dakota. Some of the teachers there talked against our church and said that I was a dope eater. The boys I played with got scared of me. They said, "Don't go close to Spider 'cause he's going to poison you. He's a dope eater. He's no good." Sometimes I cried in the classroom, or on the playground, because I wanted to have friends but the boys didn't like me. They always said things like that to me as I grew up.

About two years ago they called me to that same place where I went to school. The people there used to hate me for using this peyote, but now they wanted to find out more about it. I didn't refuse them, because I have the love of God. I went back and told them about what the peyote had done for me.

To start with, we had our services in a tipi, with a fire burning inside. Our instruments were the drum, rattle, and feather fan. And we used God's plant, the Divine Herb. Through that, some of us—not all of us, but some of us—have become Christians. We're walking hand in hand doing the Christian walk. It's pretty hard to put in words; I think it's a mystery of God and no one can bring it out in words. But I'm going to try my best to explain some of what happened to me.

One time, before I became a Christian, I was sick. At that time I used the Divine Herb and I was healed by Christ. I got hurt when I was fifteen years old. The sickness I had was osteomyelitis. The doctors told me that it's incurable. There's no medicine on earth that will cure it, they said. And sure enough, the peyote eased my pain, but it didn't kill the disease. They said it's in my bones. I got hurt when I was young, and it started from there. When I was sick, I got double pneumonia, too. I was on my deathbed. I overheard the doctor talking to my parents, and he said if I didn't make it through that night, I would die. The doctor was telling my dad and my mom to be ready.

That day a preacher came into my room, passing out tracts. He gave me one, but I couldn't read it. I had poor eyesight, so I couldn't read it. So I just put it on the table. I was lying down. I couldn't get up from bed. I couldn't sit up, and I could even hardly talk. That morning—I think it was a Sunday—it was coming daylight, and I remembered that the old people used to tell us that that's the time to talk to God. If you tell Him something, He'll hear you, they said. So that morning I was praying on my deathbed that if it's at all possible, I wanted to live longer.

God must have pitied me, because that morning He called me by my name. It was real loud. It was the first time I heard something like that, and it really hit me hard. The voice said, "Emerson!" real loud in the room. I couldn't get up from the bed but I answered that call. I said: "What? I am over here. I'm lying here." I thought it was one of the other boys in the room with me. There were about four other patients who were about to die, too, so they were placed in the room. But when I looked around they were all in bed asleep.

I just started to go back to sleep again when I heard it a second time. It got me out of bed, sitting up. I noticed I was sitting up as I said, "Hau! I'm over here. What do you want?" But there was no answer, so I lay back down again.

The third time the voice got me to my feet, standing up. I knew that I was on my feet standing up. I walked towards the aisle and looked around, and here it was, the high calling of God; and it seemed like cold water on my face that morning, like it tells in the Scriptures about spiritual baptism. And that morning Christ healed me from my sickness. So I rejoice in the Lord every day of my life. Every time in the morning, ever since then when I get up I praise the Lord. I give Him thanks every day of my life. That's the life I'm leading now.

When I came back to the bed, I noticed the tract that had been given to me. I picked it up and read it, and it said, "Come as you are." Christ was speaking. "Come as you are." I knew it meant me, because I was a real sinner. I was no good, but it said *as I am*, He wants me to come to Him. And it says in there, "If any man comes unto me, I shall in no ways cast him out." So I know Christ called me by my name to be a leader of our church. I was supposed to stop sinning and try to be a good person because I was going to be the leader of the church. I was married when I was twenty-one, and when I was twenty-three years old I stopped drinking and smoking.

While I was coming along, there were some Christians who said to me: "You should come to our church where you won't be shedding tears for your people. Although you try to tell them right from wrong, they don't listen to you." "Our church will listen to you," they said. But God wanted me to go where the church wasn't doing right, to tell them about the second coming of Christ. So actually God sent me to this Native American Church. He used me as a tool of the church to be the head man to try and guide them in the right way.

In our church we have leader helpers who can hold a service if there is no leader present. I remained a leader helper for a long time. Then I became a candidate leader. And then I became the chief leader. I gave information on how to hold a service. Gradually I became the headman of the community;

you might say a minister of the community, the headman of the local branch. Then pretty soon, when the assistant man who sat next to my dad passed away, they appointed me his assistant. So I came to it step by step, and then when my dad passed away, I became the high priest.

Before my dad passed away, he said: "This is my best. I want you to make it right for me." So that's what I'm doing now. I'm trying to make the other non-peyote people see that I can lead a Christian life in the Native American Church. I stand up for my church and say that it is a good church.

By rights we can hold our church services most any time. During the summertime we can have our services any time of the week, but during the wintertime we have to have services on Saturday because the kids have to go to school Monday. And lately some of the church members have been working, too, so we have to consider them. Also, the cost of the medicine we use is getting real high. Usually we go and harvest it ourselves, but the trip is very expensive. I know just lately there are people selling land to get the money to go and harvest peyote and bring it back.

It takes four persons to run a service: the leader, the drummer, the cedar man and the fire man. They don't pick out just anybody for these positions.

The man who takes care of the drum is supposed to be a certain kind of man who knows how to hit the drum. He can't live a wicked life and handle the drum. It's sacred to the Indians. Indians really like the drum. It is made into a great big drum which they use at powwows and things like that. We use that same drum, but we make it into a real small drum, and we use it to praise and sing unto the Lord. For that reason the drummer has to be a certain kind of person to hit that drum. He has to know how to sing, how to hit the drum, and how to live a good life. He must know how to make instruments in the church.

The man who takes care of the cedar throughout the night has to be a man who knows how to pray to the Great Creator, to the Great Spirit. He has to take care of the prayers. Every time a person prays, he burns cedar. We use the cedar smoke as incense, just like the Catholic Church. We were told that a long time ago the old people made smoke signals in order to send messages to others far away. We were told that we're doing that. That's the reason they used the peace pipe to pray to the Great Spirit, making smoke signals to pray with. During our church services in the tipi we burn that cedar whenever somebody prays, so that the smoke goes up. Our understanding is that we are making smoke signals to the Great Spirit so that He will hear our prayers. That's what we have been told.

The fire man is supposed to know how to build the fire; they don't just throw the wood into the fireplace. This man has to know how to chop and gather wood, how to build a tipi, and things like that. We have a fire going inside the tipi all the time, so this man takes care of it, he watches it. He's the only man who moves in the church, like an altar boy in the Catholic Church. He goes out, brings wood in, and keeps that fire burning. In our church building we have lights, but when we hold traditional services in the tipi, we have to keep the fire going all night.

In the traditional way our services started at sundown and continued until sunrise. That's the way it used to be. But nowadays the people come late. When the leader, drummer, cedar man, and fire man all arrive, then we start our service.

There are different instruments that we use in our services in order to praise the Lord. To start with we use this staff, which we call *sagye*. That means "cane" in our language. Each man, when he sings in the service, holds onto this cane.

We use this small drum, tied in a certain way, with water inside. Only a few men know how to tie and beat the drum. We call it a holy drum.

We use this drumstick, which can be made from all kinds of wood. One kind is called snake wood. It makes a really good-looking stick.

We use this gourd rattle, which each man holds when it is his turn to sing.

We use this sage. From the beginning of our church, the Half Moon way, we have used this sage. It was used as a traditional way of praying. They were told that they should use it to refresh themselves, to cleanse themselves, before going into a ceremonial like the Sun Dance or sweat lodge or fasting. If you wipe yourself with it there is a good fresh smell and it cleans you. That's the reason they used it all over the body in the sweat lodge. For that reason the traditional way of worship in our church uses sage. They hit themselves all over with that sage to clean themselves. Then they partake of the Divine Herb.

We use this bone whistle, made from the wing bone of an eagle. The leader blows it in a ceremonial way during the service.

We use this fan, made from different kinds of bird feathers, to perform holy orders. To start with, they used to use a feather fan made from two swift hawk tails, twelve feathers on each bird, a total of twenty-four. These feathers are arranged to form a circle. On the outside are four eagle feathers, and inside, at the center, is an eagle plume. They say this swift hawk is the swiftest bird in the world, and they say the eagle is the fiercest bird. The plume inside the fan represents the living soul that's in a person. We were told that the tail feathers are there for the swift hawks to try to catch the living soul, the spirit of a man, the soul of each person. They can surround him and catch that living soul. The eagle plume is there so that if any bad spirit comes, the eagle will fight that spirit away. This is the way we were taught by our elders. We should use this type of feather fan to come out of the traditional way into a Christian way of worship.

Today they make fans from red and blue macaw feathers, and what they call scissortails—real pretty feathers. They bring all these different feathers into the church. They're good, they're God's creation, but it didn't come to us like that from the start.

Finally, we use the Divine Herb. When a person takes the peyote in a service, if he has teeth, he usually eats it dry. When I was young, when I had teeth, I could eat it dry. Sometimes they grind it up. Then a person can put the powder in his hand and eat it like that. Or he can mix it with water and make it into a kind of gravy and eat it like that. We also make tea out of the powdered peyote, using warm water. The peyote is very bitter. If you can eat four of them it is good, and if you can eat more, it will do you a lot of good.

When peyote first started to come into our area, we used our native tongue all the time to preach the word of God. I have a Bible that's written in our language, and I can read it well. Gradually our young people have gone to school and gotten a good understanding of English. The man who had this church building built is half Sioux and half Shoshone, but he was raised in a city, so he didn't learn either the Sioux language or the Shoshone language. He speaks just this white-man language. So when we have our services and there's no person who doesn't speak our language, we usually talk in our own native tongue. But when somebody who doesn't understand our language comes into our church, we try to perform everything in English so it will be understandable. But some things we can't do in English, because we were brought up in a certain way and it has to be that way. It doesn't have to be understood by other men, just so the Great Spirit will understand us, listen to us, hear us. We believe that way.

During the service we sing songs in groups of four. Some are in Lakota and others are in English. These are the words to one set of songs. I composed the first song using words from my favorite gospel hymn, the words of the third song are in English, and the other three are in Lakota:

(1) I have decided to follow Jesus,
    No turning back.
(2) Jesus I love your words
    Because your words are eternal life.
    Give me life.
    I love your words.
(3) Praise our Lord Savior Jesus,
    Did you know that our Lord Savior Jesus died upon the cross for our sins?
    Praise our Lord Savior Jesus.
(4) God, look upon us Indians,
    We want to be saved.

After the service we eat a breakfast of four symbolic foods. They are sacred to the Indians and are eaten not for the body but for spiritual strength.

The first is water. They say everything lives by water, so in the morning we have a woman bring in water and pray over it. This is because in the beginning it was a woman who first found the peyote. Later, when the Indians learned to read the Bible, they found out about the well of Jacob, and about Christ saying "I am the living water." They found where Christ says: "The water you will give me, I'll be thirsty again, but the water I'll give you, you will never be thirsty. You will become a spring within yourself." This is what it tells in the Scripture, so they pray over the water for spiritual strength.

The second is corn. Usually at this time of year they have fresh corn on the cob, but in the wintertime they use dried corn, which they cook so it comes out just like it was fresh. We have been told that before the white men ever came across, the Indians knew how to plant corn. They already had that here and they lived by it. They use this to pray that their gardens will be good; they pray over the corn that in the summertime everything will grow real good.

The third is meat. A long time ago they used only dried meat, but today they use any kind of meat, usually beef. They boil it and serve it with soup, although some pass around just the meat itself. In the olden days the Indians used to have a lot of livestock, cattle, and wild animals like deer and buffalo. So they prayed over the meat that the hunting season would be good, that their children would have good food.

The fourth is fruit. The old people prayed over the fruit so that the wild fruits along the creeks would grow for the Indians to use. They pounded the fruit up and dried it so it would keep.

All the church services we have are not alike. We have services for birthdays, healing, marriage, baptism, prayers, funerals—anything, we have it all. Every service is different. That's the mystery of God.

One time we had a healing service here which pretty much

surprised us. We had a man who was going to have surgery for gallstones, and we had a healing service here and gave him medicine. He was seated right near the altar. A girl suffering with arthritis was seated across the room, against the east wall. We performed their healing. Lately we're trying to get the healing of Jesus Christ. We don't give sick people a whole bunch of medicine like in the olden times, but we just give them so much. One Scripture I used was, "Any man sit among you, let him call the elders of the church that they anoint him with oil, pray over him that he may get well, and if he commits any sin, it shall be forgiven." These are the Lord's words, so I used them. That man was healed right there that night. And the girl, even though she wasn't out in the center of the church, was also healed. So things like this happen. It's altogether different than the works of the peyote.

I might put it this way. When people come to a service and partake of the Divine Herb, it works on them in different ways. That's the mystery of God. Sometimes, even if a person is no good, the peyote will work for him. Through the peyote he will throw away the evil and give himself to Christ. In this way some of our church members have put away alcohol, become Christians, and gotten good jobs again. And they help other people in the church, too.

One time my dad went to a prayer ceremony. He must have eaten a lot of medicine, and the service was going on and on. And all at once he saw the door open, so he looked over there and here was a man coming in. It seemed like nobody else noticed that man coming in. But my dad kept watching him, and that man came up to him and said: "I've been looking for you all over. I couldn't find you. I heard that you were in a meeting someplace. I went to one meeting but you weren't there, so I came over here." He sat beside my dad and said, "Tonight I'm going to pray with you, sing with you." So my dad was happy. My dad wasn't a drummer, but he was a good singer, had a good voice. And my dad was a minister and a good man. The visitor had a box with him, so he took his instruments out. Everything he had was perfect. When the singing came to them, the visitor sang first. He sang good songs, real pretty songs. Then he hit the drum for my dad, but he made that drum sound different, a good sound. Then he talked and prayed, prayed real good, prayed so interestingly that the people started crying. He was really good at everything.

My dad was watching him, but he never did see the man talking. Then he saw that the man was going around to every person in there, looking at their prayer instruments, opening their boxes up and taking a good look at their instruments. Then, finally, he came to where the altar was, and he looked at everything there. They had this Divine Herb there, which they were partaking of. My dad saw him open it, and suddenly it seemed like somebody had hit the man in the face and knocked him toward the door. When he landed by the door, my dad could see his tail and horns. As he was going out, he looked back at my dad and said: "I'm going to come back and visit you again. Someday I'm going to come back again."

From this we know that the Evil One can come into any place, even a church. The Evil One can read the Bible, he can talk, he can pray, but he doesn't believe in Christ. He says he believes in Christ, that he knows Christ, but doesn't believe it. He's that powerful, fooling people all over the world. So a man should be aware that the Evil One can come anywhere.

Through my work in the church I came to know many things. One thing I wanted to find out for sure is where the souls of our departed ones are. I went around to different ministers, different churches. "I want you to tell me the truth of it," I said. "Where is paradise?" But no one could answer me. So I came back to my church and finally learned that the departed souls are here. They're not going any place. When we pray in the prayer service, and we are thinking about our departed loved ones, they come near us. They come right close to us. The only thing I found out about it in the Scriptures is that the departed souls are just like they are behind glass. They're on the other side; we're on this side. They see us, but we can't see them; they hear us, but we can't hear them. That's how it is. I found this out in our church and by reading the

Scriptures, that the departed ones are always here with us. I thought this was real nice.

We are Indian people, and we still have some of our traditional ways. One thing we have, which the Indians grew up with, is what we call the spiritual food for our departed ones. Long ago, when people were eating something good, they would think about their loved ones who had gone beyond. Then they would take a little bit of the food they were eating and throw it outside, saying, *"Wanaǧi le iyakiya,"* which means, "Spirit, find this." When my grandpa and my grandma were alive, I saw them do this, and we still have this. We couldn't part with the things that the traditionals had, so we still have them.

They prayed for these departed ones, too, and they talked to them. They grew up with that. The Bible says that when a person dies he knows nothing, he can't hear, he can't see. But the Indians say that for four days that body is holy. It can see you, it can hear you, they say. One time I went to a gospel mission. The preacher was a white man. His wife had just died, and they were having a wake service. I said: "This lady is not dead, she's sleeping, I think, resting. So she sees you." And that man started crying. He said to me, "Those are comforting words that you brought here, words we never heard before."

"That's the way I was taught," I said, "and that's the way it is." So I prayed over her, and I talked to that dead body, because that's how I was brought up.

There are some traditional things that we still have in the Cross Fire way, things we still hang onto because we grew up with them and we're Indians. But actually I don't know about the next generation, the coming generation. I notice that every generation changes. Things are changing.

I was told that God created all men equal, so this was the reason He put the peyote here for the Indians. Some of us didn't find out about it for a long time. But it is a good thing that my grandfather and my father found out about it, because it helped us to find Christ. Lately I have been going around to other churches and to schools telling about what our church is doing for us Indian people. For this reason I am happy to put my talk in a book so that people will read it and learn about our church. The days are getting short. The second coming of the Lord is at hand and we're getting ready for it. People will not be judged according to their beliefs, or according to which church they belong to. God will not say, "What kind of church do you belong to? What ways do you have?" It's not going to be that way. The bad things we've done and the good things we've done shall be weighed; and if we do good we'll be in the arms of Christ. It doesn't matter what church we belong to— the church will not save us. These are things I want to bring out to people, especially to the younger generation.

I would like you to understand that the fear of the Lord is the beginning of all knowledge. It says in the Scriptures that it doesn't matter if you gain the whole world's knowledge if you don't have the fear of the Lord. You have to be good in every way and put Christ ahead of you all the time so you won't go wrong. If you put your beliefs or anything else ahead of Christ, you'll be wrong. This world will come to an end. Everything must be stopped. So you need to have the true love of God to be saved.

Some people tell me that the knowledge of this world is the key to tomorrow. That's what they say. This earthly knowledge is good; it's necessary to get by in this world. I wish that the boys and girls will stay in school and learn—but put Christ ahead of your schooling. Read your Bible and you'll be safe in the arms of Christ. There is no other way to salvation.

If you come to the Lord, no matter what sickness you have, you can be healed. I was healed and now I'm a born-again Christian, and I'm working for my church. It used to be that when we had the traditional way of worshipping, we believed in earthly life. Now we believe in the second coming of Christ, although we still have our traditional ways. We still believe in them. I believe in the Sun Dance and fasting and all the traditional ways. I believe that they are sacred and I believe that they are good. But they are earthly, so by them alone no man will be saved.

The second coming of Christ is the only way to salvation. So I want you to know me and I want you to understand my church. There are some Christians who don't know our church, who may even think we are uncivilized. I want the Native American Church to be recognized by other churches. And I want people everywhere to pray for us, too.

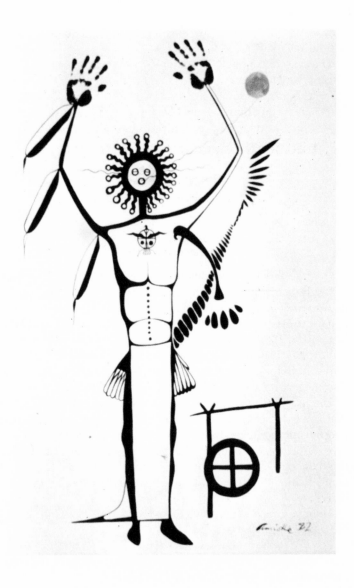

12

Traditional Lakota Religion in Modern Life

BY ROBERT STEAD

Introduction
by Kenneth Oliver

MANY people here have different ideas of what medicine men in the Indian religion are all about. In growing up around Indian medicine you realize that there is more to it than the rituals, the acts which are performed to get results. Much of it lies within the belief system, within the recognized virtues. I am a physician's assistant and feel that I am performing my duties in helping Mr. Robert Stead. Seeing Indian religion in this context brings out the virtues of the religion.

The first and main virtue is health. In many of the societies that I've come in contact with, health isn't considered a virtue; people pursue it on their own. But in the religion of the Lakota society, the people value health very highly. And within this concept of health you also have the mental aspect of health. So the Lakotas ask for *wookiye,* for health in their daily lives.

Then you have another virtue which is called *wicoicage,* or life, growth, longevity.

Then you have another virtue, *wowahwala,* peace, calmness, the ability to suppress aggression that can hurt someone else, to be able to dissolve it within yourself.

Then you have another concept, *wacantognaka,* generosity.

Then last but not least, the greatest concept is patience, the ability to be patient, to wait—wait for your children to grow, for the seasons, the years—even the ability to wait for your greatest needs.

All these are put into a prayer to the Great Spirit. The Great Spirit has chosen very few people on this earth to communicate with. Fortunately, in these times, with all the hardships, with all the disbelief, there are men who can communicate with the Great Spirit. The term Great Spirit is translated from *Wakan Tanka*, "Big Holy." We wonder what the word "big" means, what the word *wakan* means, what does "sacredness" mean?

There is a man who I have been fortunate to be with and to help who knows all this. He is willing to help anyone, at any time, with any problem. He was put on this earth to do that. He went on a vision quest, and they took him from the hill where he was standing to the place of the spirits. He describes it as being such a good place to be, such a nice place to be, to the point that he did not want to come back from there. But he has a job to do here on this earth before he leaves, to help the people to do better, to prosper, to help them get the things that they need—especially health.

He has doctored many people, and he has spoken in many places. People from many parts of the world have come to see him, to get spirituality from him, that they too can exist with these virtues and live in harmony with each other.

I think in terms of *wowahwala* a lot, the calmness and the will not to be aggressive, because there are a lot of misconceptions and exaggerations of what Indian religion is really all about. The things that happen in the ceremonies are real and true. This man can't lie to you; that is one of the rules of the pipe.

I introduce to you Mr. Robert Stead.

It's a pleasure and honor to be among you. I hope that the Great Spirit will be with you from this day on in whatever you do on this earth. May He bless you, your children, and whatever your ambitions or intentions are on this earth, as you walk on Mother Earth. I'm glad to be here.

I have had this spirituality within me since I was about eight, nine years old. Everything I do, whatever I concentrate on, whatever I attempt, it always turns out the way I want it. When I was a little boy, I abused my spiritual power in many ways, even in school. I abused what spiritual power there was within me. I was an A student without studying. I got the answers to all academic problems without work. Even though I'm small and short, I excelled in athletics—made the hundred-yard dash in nine-eight, nine-nine, because I prayed. In basketball I wanted to be on the first team, varsity team. Although I was short, I was very fast. Everything I did through spiritual power. I abused it and misused it in many ways.

But when the time came that I had to go up on the hill, I was scared. I was very scared. I didn't want to go. For some reason I just didn't want to go up on that hill to be a medicine man, but I had to, because they brought about eight medicine men to dissolve that sacredness or whatever it was that I had within me. They told me I was a chosen one, that I had to go up, I had to go up.

My path to that sacred hill was rugged. Many temptations, many earthly desires, many bad notions, many bad thoughts I had, but I still had to go up on that hill. I prepared for one whole month through the sweat lodge, praying, fasting, and in many other ways. A voice kept telling me to go on, to go on. "Your people will need you. Your red people will need you." And to this day sometimes I just don't believe it myself. Sometimes I'm amazed. Why is it me who was chosen? Why is it that it's me when many, many young people want to be medicine men?

I spent four days, four nights, on that hill without drinking, without sleep, without eating, and it was a very torturous four days and four nights. Many things came to me during the nights. They asked me to leave because I wasn't ready to help the red people on this earth. But I held on to the pipe for four days, four nights. My mouth was so parched, my throat was so swollen from not drinking I couldn't breathe for a while.

But in the meantime I prayed to the Great Spirit, *Wakan Tanka,* because He's the creator of you and me. Everything that grows on Mother Earth, that He put on this earth, our lives revolve around it. We cannot live without air, we cannot live without water, we cannot live without food. We have to take care of ourselves, our bodies. He only gave us one—no spare. Our body is a sacred thing that He gave us. What we consume is what we are going to live on. If it's something bad, not good for our body, we're going to have a slow death. Alcohol, drugs, these are not fit for human consumption. It's up to us. We all want to live longer. We all want to see our children grow up, and our grandchildren. It's up to us through the Great Spirit's guidance to live a longer life. He gave us skill, talent, knowledge, wisdom. We have to utilize them, because these are His gifts to us. The grass He put on this earth, we live by it. The animals eat the grass to make their flesh, and we eat the animals' flesh to make our flesh. From our flesh come our children. We have to realize what the Great Spirit has done for us on this earth.

In many ways we have to pray. The most powerful thing in your body is your prayers. If you know how to pray, go out on a hill by yourself and pray with an open mind. You will cry because it's the truth. I couldn't concentrate on prayers through a book, because it wasn't I who wrote that book. The words were written for somebody else. It isn't my prayers. I couldn't pray with it. People call me sacred, people call me many things which I'm not. But through the Great Spirit's guidance, counseling, strength, I'm able to help my red people.

But through all this, I'm humble. I humble myself before all men. I don't talk big, I don't brag about myself, I don't try to influence anyone. I'm not trying to influence anybody to join my Indian religion. Up on that hill they showed me where our red people are after their death. They're on this earth. Our body returns to the ground, but our spirit lives on. Many of these spirits that I use are medicine men from many, many years ago who were powerful on this earth with their medicine. I have eight medicines that they have shown me, and now I'm the only one who knows these medicine roots and herbs. I'm the only one who can help my people by using these roots and herbs. It's the Great Spirit's work that He put these on earth for the use of mankind. He made many things that are mysteries to us yet.

Today money is our god. That's what we want. We want more money. What about your spirituality? What about your family? These we have to consider before money. Most of all, the Great Spirit who helped us on this earth, who put us on this earth. Many people come to me for advice from far away—they invite me to many reservations. I've been to thirty-three reservations. I've been from one coast to the other, from Canada as far south as New Mexico.

I help many people to get back on their feet again. My speciality is strokes, paralyzation. I made people who were paralyzed walk. I made people who had strokes use their arms and legs again. And it's not me—it's through the Great Spirit's ways. There are many people who were possessed. The night before I left home, they brought a boy from Kansas who was possessed: "Mr. Stead, there's something within me that tells me to do something dirty, stab, beat. Something within me that tells me to hit him, hit him. I can't help it but I have to hit." There are some people who are mentally ill; physically, they're disturbed. Through my spiritual ways I help these people.

But all in all, I think the Great Spirit is with me, and the spirits that I have are with me. I cannot go and drink, I cannot do anything bad, I cannot say anything to hurt people. The Great Spirit gave me a mind, a good mind. He doesn't want me to discriminate, to be prejudiced, to spread vicious gossip. I've learned all of this, and I'm quite sure you people can follow the good ways on this earth instead of the bad. The sacred that is in me, it hurts, it hurts. But I have to abide by what they have shown me, what they have taught me, what I have learned. On this earth we have only one life. And as I keep telling you, in good ways we can do a lot of good things. We can have a lot of good ways on this earth.

Perhaps I shouldn't be saying these things. Maybe some of the people will not utilize what I've been saying. Maybe, you might say, this is my business, this is my life but it's not yours. He who made you can dissolve you, take you away. It's up to us. Nobody's sacred on this earth. No one is sacred. It's only the Great Spirit who is sacred. Through Him all things are possible. My walk on this earth is very short. I make the best use of it by helping my people, and I also help many people of other nationalities.

Today I'm very happy to be with you people, and I'm quite sure the Great Spirit will guide you, strengthen you, encourage you, bless your little ones, bless your fathers and mothers, your grandmothers, and all your relatives so that you may lead a good life on this earth. I want to conclude by asking the Great Spirit to guide you, to bless your homes, that you might walk hand in hand with your children on Mother Earth, that you will be blessed as you walk through life in good ways.

Suggestions For Further Reading

THERE is a wealth of published material that records the development of Sioux religious traditions during the past century and a half. The suggestions that follow do not constitute a complete bibliography on the subject, but they will lead the reader to many of the high spots of this literature. The topical arrangement allows readers with specific interests to follow one or another aspect of Sioux religious history; however, real understanding of any aspect depends on broad knowledge of the full context of Sioux religious traditions over time. Thus the body of literature presented here comprises a unified whole, any part of which informs all the others.

Syntheses of traditional Sioux religion.

The earliest syntheses of traditional Sioux religion relate to the Santees (Eastern Dakotas) of Minnesota. Mary Eastman, *Dacotah; or, Life and Legends of the Sioux Around Fort Snelling* (1849); James W. Lynd, "The Religion of the Dakotas" (1869); and Stephen R. Riggs, *Tah-koo Wah-kań; or, The Gospel Among the Dakotas* (1869), are all reliable and informative sources. The first overall synthesis that includes the Teton (Western) Sioux as well as the Santees is James Owen Dorsey, *A Study of Siouan Cults* (1894). Dorsey's study is particularly valuable because it includes important material originally written in Lakota by George Bushotter, an educated Sioux. The first extended account of Sioux religion written by a Sioux is Charles A. Eastman, *The Soul of the Indian* (1911), a somewhat romanticized but very readable and informative overview of Santee religion.

The summary of Oglala religious beliefs and rituals by James R. Walker, "The Sun Dance and Other Ceremonies of the Oglala Division of the Teton Dakota" (1917), remains a classic reference based on almost twenty years of study on Pine Ridge Reservation. A popular account of Yankton Sioux religion is included in Sarah Emilia Olden, *The People of Tipi Sapa* (1918). Her book is valuable for the information dictated by Tipi Sapa (Rev. Philip Deloria), an Episcopal priest who was the son of a Yankton chief and medicine man. An excellent and readable introduction to Sioux religion (and to traditional and reservation Sioux culture in general) was written by Tipi Sapa's daughter, Ella Deloria, *Speaking of Indians* (1944). It contains much valuable information on traditional religion taken from the unpublished manuscripts written in Lakota by George Sword, an Oglala medicine man and a later deacon in the Episcopal Church. Royal B. Hassrick, *The Sioux: Life and Customs of a Warrior Society* (1964), gives a popular overview of traditional Lakota religion based largely on James R. Walker's material.

A good, brief summary of Oglala religion and the changes in religious practices that developed during the reservation period is included in Gordon Macgregor, *Warriors Without Weapons: A Study of the Society and Personality Development of the Pine Ridge Sioux* (1946). An excellent systematic survey of all types of reservation religious practices on Pine Ridge is Stephen E. Feraca, *Wakinyan: Contemporary Teton Dakota Religion* (1963). The most recent overview of both traditional religion and its development during the reservation era at Pine Ridge is William K. Powers, *Oglala Religion* (1977). Although complicated by a pervasive analysis from the perspective of structural anthropology, the book nevertheless is an attempt to synthesize a large body of literature on Sioux religion.

Documents for the study of traditional religion

Many of the basic documents written or dictated by Sioux people that are the basis for detailed study of Sioux religion were collected by James R. Walker: "The Sun Dance" (1917); *Lakota Belief and Ritual,* edited by Raymond J. DeMallie and Elaine A. Jahner (1980); *Lakota Society,* edited by Raymond J. DeMallie (1982); and *Lakota Myth,* edited by Elaine A. Jahner (1983). Natalie Curtis, editor, *The Indians' Book* (1907); Edward S. Curtis, *The North American Indian,* vol. 3 (1908); and Frances Densmore, *Teton Sioux Music* (1918), present additional documentary collections.

Autobiographical accounts by Sioux medicine men also are valuable documents for the study of religion. Most important are the teachings dictated by Black Elk, the Ogalala holy man, to John G. Neihardt, originally published as *Black Elk Speaks: Being the Life Story of a Holy Man of the Ogalala Sioux* (1932) and *When the Tree Flowered* (1951). The entirety of the original interviews with Black Elk from which these books were written has been published as *The Sixth Grandfather: Black Elk's Teachings Given to John G. Neihardt,* edited by Raymond J. DeMallie (1984); it forms the primary source for understanding Black Elk's religious life. Black Elk's detailed presentation of the sacred rituals of the Oglalas, dictated to Joseph Epes Brown, is published as *The Sacred Pipe: Black Elk's Account of the Seven Rites of the Oglala Sioux* (1953); it is essential for understanding Lakota ritual. More recent works, *Lame Deer, Seeker of Visions,* by John (Fire) Lame Deer and Richard Erdoes (1972), and *Fools Crow,* by Thomas E. Mails and Dallas Chief Eagle (1979), record the life stories of two prominent contemporary medicine men. A personal account by Arthur Amiotte, "Eagles Fly Over"

(1976), provides an insightful glimpse into the revitalization of traditional religion in recent years.

Finally, Eugene Buechel, S.J., *Lakota Tales and Texts* (1978), published in the Lakota language only, includes a large number of important documents on most aspects of traditional Sioux religion, written or dictated by Oglala and Brule people during the early part of this century.

Mythology

The sacred stories of the Sioux have been recorded in a variety of sources. Basic myths appear in Mary Eastman, *Dacotah* (1849); Stephen R. Riggs, *Dakota Grammar, Texts, and Ethnography*, edited by James Owen Dorsey (1893); James Owen Dorsey, *A Study of Siouan Cults* (1894); Clark Wissler, "Some Dakota Myths" (1907); and Marie L. McLaughlin, *Myths and Legends of the Sioux* (1916). Good modern collections of Sioux myths include Wilson D. Wallis, "Beliefs and Tales of the Canadian Dakota" (1923); Martha Warren Beckwith, "Mythology of the Oglala Dakota" (1930); and Ella C. Deloria, *Dakota Texts* (1932). Basic to an understanding of the religious dimensions of mythology, however, are the works of James R. Walker. "The Sun Dance" (1917) includes a considerable body of important myths not available elsewhere, and *Lakota Myth* (1983) presents Walker's own synthesis of these myths, as well as additional material. William K. Powers, *Oglala Religion* (1977), and Michael Edward Melody, "Maka's Story: A Study of Lakota Cosmogony" (1978), present speculative analyses of the Lakota origin story as retold by Walker, but do not adequately evaluate the extent to which Walker, a non-Indian, reworked the mythic material in his writings.

The Sacred Pipe

The first published version of the story of the bringing of the Sacred Pipe to the Sioux is George A. Dorsey, "Legend of the Teton Sioux Medicine Pipe" (1906). Edward S. Curtis, *The*

North American Indian, vol. 3 (1908), and Frances Densmore, *Teton Sioux Music* (1918), also include long versions of the story. Important retellings appear in James R. Walker's "The Sun Dance" (1917) and *Lakota Belief and Ritual* (1980). Black Elk's version of the story is printed in full in *The Sixth Grandfather* (1984) and is retold in *The Sacred Pipe* (1953).

An account of the Sacred Pipe with photographs of the Pipe bundle is given in Sidney J. Thomas, "A Sioux Medicine Bundle" (1941). J. L. Smith collected material relating to the Pipe in "A Short History of the Sacred Calf Pipe of the Teton Sioux" (1967) and "The Sacred Calf Pipe Bundle: Its Effect on the Present Teton Dakota" (1970).

The Sun Dance

One of the best early accounts of the Sun Dance was written in Lakota by George Bushotter in 1887 and is published in James Owen Dorsey, *A Study of Siouan Cults* (1894). The same work includes an excellent eyewitness description of a Sun Dance by John G. Bourke. Alice C. Fletcher, "The Sun Dance of the Ogalalla Sioux" (1882), and Frederick Schwatka, "The Sun-Dance of the Sioux" (1889–90; reprinted in Franks, ed. [1976], with the author misidentified as Remington) are also eyewitness accounts. George Sword's detailed description of the Sun Dance ritual, published in Ella C. Deloria, "The Sun Dance of the Oglala Sioux" (1929), is a valuable source originally written in Lakota by an Oglala medicine man.

The best extended description of the Oglala Sun Dance and its meaning is given in J. R. Walker, "The Sun Dance" (1917). Also see the valuable account by Black Elk in *The Sacred Pipe* (1953). For comparative purposes, Alanson Skinner, "Notes on the Sun Dance of the Sisseton Dakota" (1919), and Wilson D. Wallis, "The Sun Dance of the Canadian Dakota" (1921), provide a good basis for understanding variations in the Sioux Sun Dance ritual.

A synthetic description of the Sun Dance, based on published accounts, is presented in Michael E. Melody, "The

Lakota Sun Dance: A Composite View and Analysis" (1976).
Åke Hultkrantz, "The Development of the Plains Indian Sun
Dance" (1980), is an historical reconstruction of the develop-
ment of the Sun Dance ritual among the Sioux and other
Plains peoples.

For the revitalized Sun Dance on the Sioux reservations,
Stephen E. Feraca, *Wakinyan* (1963), is a basic source. Ethel
Nurge, "The Sioux Sun Dance in 1962" (1966), is also a valuable description. Thomas H. Lewis, "The Oglala (Teton Dakota) Sun Dance: Vicissitudes of Its Structure and Function"
(1975), summarizes changes and continuities in the ceremony
during recent years. Beatrice Medicine, "Native American
Resistance to Integration: Contemporary Confrontations and
Religious Revitalization" (1981), discusses the political rami-
fications of the Sun Dance today. Thomas E. Mails, *Sundancing at Rosebud and Pine Ridge* (1978), presents very detailed photodocumentaries of the contemporary Sun Dance.

Yuwipi

The *yuwipi* and related healing and conjuring ceremonies are
well described in the literature. Frances Densmore, *Teton
Sioux Music* (1918), and James R. Walker, *Lakota Belief and
Ritual* (1980), present the historical foundations of *yuwipi* in
the ceremonies of Stone Dreamers. Gordon Macgregor, *War-
riors Without Weapons* (1946), discusses the historical devel-
opment of *yuwipi* in the reservation context. Robert H. Ruby,
The Oglala Sioux (1955); Stephen E. Feraca, *Wakinyan* (1963);
Wesley R. Hurt and James H. Howard, "A Dakota Conjuring
Ceremony" (1952); Wesley R. Hurt, "A Yuwipi Ceremony at
Pine Ridge" (1960); Stephen E. Feraca, "The Yuwipi Cult
of the Oglala and Sicangu Teton Sioux" (1961); Eugene Fugle,
"The Nature and Function of the Lakota Night Cults" (1966);
and Luis S. Kemnitzer, "Structure, Content and Cultural
Meaning of Yuwipi" (1976), all provide richly detailed descrip-
tions of particular *yuwipi* ceremonies. Two essays by Luis S.
Kemnitzer, "Cultural Provenience of Objects Used in Yuwipi"

(1970) and "A 'Grammar Discovery Procedure' for the Study of a Dakota Healing Ritual" (1975), and Elizabeth S. Grobsmith, "Wakinza: Uses of Yuwipi Medicine Power in Contemporary Teton Dakota Culture" (1974), give valuable sidelights on the significance of the *yuwipi* ritual in reservation life. The fullest discussion of *yuwipi* and its associated beliefs and rituals is William K. Powers, *Yuwipi: Vision and Experience in Oglala Ritual* (1982), a very readable introduction to this aspect of contemporary reservation religious life.

Ghost Dance

James Mooney, *The Ghost-Dance Religion and the Sioux Outbreak of 1890* (1896), remains the standard study of the Ghost Dance among the Sioux. Valuable supplementary accounts by Short Bull appear in Natalie Curtis, editor, *The Indians' Book* (1907), and in James R. Walker, *Lakota Belief and Ritual* (1980). Raymond J. DeMallie, "The Lakota Ghost Dance: An Ethnohistorical Account" (1982), attempts to situate the movement in cultural context. James H. Howard, *The Canadian Sioux* (1984), discusses the diffusion of the Ghost Dance religion to the Sioux in Canada.

Native American Church

Weston LaBarre, *The Peyote Cult* (4th ed., 1975), is the basic introduction to the historical development of the Native American Church. Stephen E. Feraca, *Wakinyan* (1963), provides a good description of both the Half Moon and Cross Fire rites at Pine Ridge Reservation. Paul Steinmetz, S.J., *Pipe, Bible and Peyote Among the Oglala Lakota* (1980), gives detailed information on the history of the Native American Church at Pine Ridge, a presentation of beliefs associated with the peyote religion, and transcriptions of both a Cross Fire and Half Moon meeting. Michael F. Steltenkamp, *The Sacred Vision* (1982), also describes a Half Moon meeting at Pine Ridge.

Christianity

The acceptance by the Sioux of Christianity, a long historical process, is well documented by an extensive literature. The work of the American Board of Commissioners for Foreign Missions in laying the foundations for Congregational and Presbyterian missions among the Santees is presented in Stephen R. Riggs, *Tah-koo Wah-kan* (1869) and *Mary and I* (1887). John Willand, *Lac Qui Parle and the Dakota Mission* (1964), is a detailed study of the mission at Lac Qui Parle, Minnesota, from 1835 to 1854. Winnifred W. Barton, *John P. Williamson* (1919), is a biographical study of the son of Thomas S. Williamson, one of the first ABCFM missionaries among the Dakotas (John P. Williamson devoted his life to mission work with the Santees, 1860 to 1869, and Yanktons, 1869 to 1917). A convenient summary of Congregational and Presbyterian mission work is found in Dakota Presbytery Council, *The First 50 Years: Dakota Presbytery to 1890, with, Dakota Mission Past and Present A.D. 1886* (reprint, 1984).

A history of Episcopal mission work among the Sioux is presented in Church Missions, *A Handbook of the Church's Missions to the Indians* (1914), and in Virginia Driving Hawk Sneve, *That They May Have Life: The Episcopal Church in South Dakota 1859–1976* (New York: Seabury Press, 1977). M. A. DeWolfe Howe, *Life and Labors of Bishop Hare* (1911), is a biographical account of William Hobart Hare, founder of the Episcopal missions among the Sioux. Sarah Emilia Olden, *The People of Tipi Sapa* (1918), includes a biography of Philip Deloria, one of the first Sioux men to be ordained an Episcopal priest by Bishop Hare.

A detailed history of Roman Catholic missionization in South Dakota is given in Claudia Duratschek, O.S.B., *Crusading Along Sioux Trails: A History of the Catholic Indian Missions of South Dakota* (1947). Recent movements in Catholicism to incorporate Lakota concepts of prayer into church ritual are documented in Paul Steinmetz, S.J., "Explanation of the Sacred Pipe as a Prayer Instrument" (1969) and "The Relationship Between Plains Indian Religion and Christianity: A Priest's Viewpoint" (1970). The same author's *Pipe, Bible and Peyote Among the Oglala Lakota* (1980) examines traditional Lakota religion, the Native American Church, and the Body of Christ Independent Church in the context of life on Pine Ridge Reservation and from the perspective of a theory of religious acculturation. It serves as a good introduction to the diversity of religious beliefs and practices that characterizes the Sioux reservations today. Michael F. Steltenkamp, *The Sacred Vision* (1982), is an evocative discussion of modern Sioux religion from the perspective of a Jesuit missionary.

Bibliography

Albers, Patricia and Beatrice Medicine
1983   *The Hidden Half: Studies of Plains Indian Women.* Washington, D.C.: University Press of America.
Amiotte, Arthur
1976   Eagles Fly Over. *Parabola: Myth and the Quest for Meaning* 1, no. 3:28–41.
1982   Our Other Selves: The Lakota Dream Experience. *Parabola: Myth and the Quest for Meaning* 7, no. 2:26–32.
Barton, Winifred W.
1919   *John P. Williamson: A Brother to the Sioux.* New York: Fleming H. Revell.
Beckwith, Martha Warren
1930   Mythology of the Oglala Dakota. *Journal of American Folk-Lore* 43:339–442.
Beede, Aaron McGaffey
1912–20   Journals and letters. Orin G. Libby Manuscript Collection, University of North Dakota, Grand Forks.
Berkhofer, Robert F., Jr.
1978   *The White Man's Indian: Images of the American Indian From Columbus to the Present.* New York: Alfred A. Knopf.
Bidney, David
1953   *Theoretical Anthropology.* New York: Columbia University Press.
Black Elk, Nicholas
       See Neihardt (1932, 1951); Brown (1953); and DeMallie, ed. (1984).

227

Board of Commissioners
1865   *Proceedings of a Board of Commissioners to Negotiate a Treaty or Treaties with the Hostile Indians of the Upper Missouri*. Washington, D.C.: Government Printing Office.

Boller, Paul E., Jr.
1969   *American Thought in Transition: The Impact of Evolutionary Naturalism, 1865 to 1900*. Chicago: Rand McNally College Publishing.

Bosch, Aloysius, S.J.
1898   Letter to Fr. J. A. Stephan, Sept. 21. Bureau of Catholic Indian Mission Papers, Marquette University Archives, Milwaukee, Wisc.

Brown, Joseph Epes, recorder and trans.
1953   *The Sacred Pipe: Black Elk's Account of the Seven Rites of the Oglala Sioux*. Norman: University of Oklahoma Press. Reprint ed., New York: Penguin Books, 1971.

Buechel, Eugene, S.J.
1913   Letter to Fr. William Ketcham. Bureau of Catholic Indian Missions Papers, Marquette University Archives, Milwaukee, Wisc.

[Ca.
1930s] "Give Him Time." Printed document in Archives of St. Francis Mission, St. Francis, S. Dak.

1978   *Lakota Tales and Texts*. Edited by Paul Manhart, S.J. Pine Ridge, S. Dak.: Red Cloud Indian School.

Bushotter, George
1887–88 Lakota texts with interlinear English translations by James Owen Dorsey. Manuscript in National Anthropological Archives, Smithsonian Institution, Washington, D.C.

Church Missions
1914   *A Handbook of the Church's Missions to the Indians*. Hartford, Conn.: Church Mission Publishing.

Commissioner of Indian Affairs
1866   *Annual Report of the Commissioner of Indian Affairs For 1866*. Washington, D.C.: Government Printing Office.

Costo, Rupert, and Jeannette Henry
1977   *Indian Treaties: Two Centuries of Dishonor*. San Francisco: Indian Historian Press.

Curtis, Edward S.
1908   *The North American Indian*. Vol. 3. Reprint ed., New York: Johnson Reprint Corporation, 1970.

Curtis, Natalie, ed.
1907   *The Indians' Book*. Reprint ed., New York: Harper and Brothers, 1935.
Dakota Presbytery Council
1984   *The First 50 Years: Dakota Presbytery to 1890, with, Dakota Mission Past and Present A.D. 1886*. Reprint ed., Freeman, S.D., Pine Hill Press.
Deloria, Ella Cara
1929   The Sun Dance of the Oglala Sioux. *Journal of American Folk-Lore* 42:354–413.
1932   *Dakota Texts*. Publications of the American Ethnological Society, vol. 14. New York: G. E. Stechert.
1944   *Speaking of Indians*. New York: Friendship Press.
Ca.
1929–38   Manuscript writings in English and Lakota. American Philosophical Society Library, Philadelphia, Pa.
Deloria, Vine, Jr.
1974   *Behind the Trail of Broken Treaties: An Indian Declaration of Independence*. New York: Delacorte Press.
DeMallie, Raymond J.
1982   The Lakota Ghose Dance: An Ethnohistorical Account. *Pacific Historical Review* 51:385–405.
———, ed.
1984   *The Sixth Grandfather: Black Elk's Teachings Given to John G. Neihardt*. Lincoln: University of Nebraska Press.
——— and Robert H. Lavenda
1977   Wakan: Plains Siouan Concepts of Power. In *The Anthropology of Power: Ethnographic Studies from Asia, Oceania and the New World*, edited by Richard Adams and Raymond D. Fogelson, pp. 154–66. New York: Academic Press.
Densmore, Frances
1918   *Teton Sioux Music*. Smithsonian Institution, Bureau of American Ethnology, Bulletin 61. Washington, D.C.: Government Printing Office.
Digmann, P. Florentine, S.J.
1886–
1922   "History of St. Francis Mission, 1886–1922." Manuscript in Archives of Saint Francis Mission, Saint Francis, S.D.
1887   Letter to Fr. George L. Willard, July 20. Bureau of Catholic Indian Missions Papers, Marquette University Archives, Milwaukee, Wisc.
1889   Letter to Fr. George L. Willard, Oct. 7. Bureau of Catholic

Indian Missions Papers, Marquette University Archives, Milwaukee, Wisc.

Dorsey, George A.
1906   Legend of the Teton Sioux Medicine Pipe. *Journal of American Folk-Lore* 19:326–29.

Dorsey, James Owen
1894   A Study of Siouan Cults. *Eleventh Annual Report of the Bureau of American Ethnology*, pp. 351–544. Washington, D.C.: Government Printing Office.

Duratschek, Claudia, O.S.B.
1947   *Crusading Along Sioux Trails: A History of the Catholic Indian Missions of South Dakota*. Yankton, S. Dak.: Grail.

Eastman, Charles Alexander
1911   *The Soul of the Indian*. Boston: Houghton Mifflin.

Eastman, Mary
1849   *Dacotah; or, Life and Legends of the Sioux around Fort Snelling*. New York: John Wiley.

Eliade, Mircea
1959   *The Sacred and The Profane*. New York: Harcourt Brace and World.

Feraca, Stephen E.
1961   The Yuwipi Cult of the Oglala and Sicangu Teton Sioux. *Plains Anthropologist* 6:155–63.
1963   *Wakinyan: Contemporary Teton Dakota Religion*. Studies in Plains Anthropology and History, no. 2. Browning, Mont.: Museum of the Plains Indian.

Fletcher, Alice C.
1883   The Sun Dance of the Ogalalla Sioux. *Proceedings of the American Association for the Advancement of Science* 31 (1882):580–84.
1884   Indian Ceremonies. *Report of the Peabody Museum of American Archaeology and Ethnology* 16:260–333.

Franks, Kenny A., ed.
1976   "The Sun-Dance of the Sioux." Written and illustrated by Frederic Remington. *South Dakota History* 6:421–32. Reprint of Schwatka (1889–90).

Fritz, Henry E.
1959–60 The Making of Grant's Peace Policy. *Chronicles of Oklahoma* 37, no. 4:411–32.
1963   *The Movement for Indian Assimilation, 1860–1890*. Philadelphia: University of Pennsylvania Press.

Fugle, Eugene

1966   The Nature and Function of the Lakota Night Cults. *Museum News* (W. H. Over Museum, University of South Dakota) 27, nos. 3 and 4.

Geertz, Clifford
1973   *The Interpretation of Cultures.* New York: Basic Books.

Goll, Louis, S.J.
1919   Holy Rosary School. *The Indian Sentinel* 1, no. 12:24–26.

Grobsmith, Elizabeth S.
1974   Wakinza: Uses of Yuwipi Medicine Power in Contemporary Teton Dakota Culture. *Plains Anthropologist* 19:129–33.

Hassrick, Royal B.
1964   *The Sioux: Life and Customs of a Warrior Society.* Norman: University of Oklahoma Press.

Howard, James H.
1984   *The Canadian Sioux.* Lincoln: University of Nebraska Press.

Howe, M. A. DeWolfe
1911   *The Life and Labors of Bishop Hare: Apostle to the Sioux.* New York: Sturgis & Walton.

Hultkrantz, Åke
1979   *The Religions of the American Indians.* Trans. by Monica Setterwall. Berkeley: University of California Press.
1980   The Development of the Plains Indian Sun Dance. In *Perennitas: Studi in Onore di Angelo Brelich,* pp. 223–43. Roma: Edizioni dell'Ateneo.

Hurt, Wesley R.
1960   A Yuwipi Ceremony at Pine Ridge. *Plains Anthropologist* 5:48–52.
———— and James H. Howard
1952   A Dakota Conjuring Ceremony. *Southwestern Journal of Anthropology* 8:286–96.

The Indian Sentinel
1919   Editorial. *The Indian Sentinel* 1, no. 12:4.

Kemnitzer, Luis S.
1970   Cultural Provenience of Artifacts Used in *Yuwipi,* A Modern Teton Dakota Healing Ritual. *Ethnos* 35:40–75.
1975   A 'Grammar Discovery Procedure' for the Study of a Dakota Healing Ritual. In *Linguistics and Anthropology: In Honor of C. F. Voegelin,* edited by M. Dale Kinkade, Kenneth L. Hale, and Oswald Werner, pp. 405–422. Lisse, Netherlands: Peter de Ridder Press.
1976   Structure, Content and Cultural Meaning of Yuwipi: A Modern Lakota Healing Ritual. *American Ethnologist* 3:261–80.

LaBarre, Weston
1975   *The Peyote Cult.* 4th ed. New York: Schocken Books.
Lame Deer, John (Fire), and Richard Erdoes
1972   *Lame Deer, Seeker of Visions.* New York: Simon and Schuster.
Lewis, Thomas H.
1972   The Oglala (Teton Dakota) Sun Dance: Vicissitudes of Its
       Structure and Function. *Plains Anthropologist* 17:44–49.
Lynd, James W.
1864   The Religion of the Dakotas. *Minnesota Historical Collec-
       tions* 2:150–74. 2d ed., 1881.
Macgregor, Gordon
1946   *Warriors Without Weapons: A Study of the Society and Per-
       sonality Development of the Pine Ridge Sioux.* Chicago: Uni-
       versity of Chicago Press.
McLaughlin, Marie L.
1916   *Myths and Legends of the Sioux.* Bismarck, N. Dak.: Bismarck
       Tribune Co.
Mails, Thomas E.
1978   *Sundancing at Rosebud and Pine Ridge.* Sioux Falls, S. Dak.:
       Augustana College.
———— and Dallas Chief Eagle
1979   *Fools Crow.* New York: Doubleday.
Malan, Vernon D., and R. Clyde McCone
1960   The Time Concept, Perspective, and Premise in the Socio-
       cultural Order of the Dakota Indians. *Plains Anthropologist*
       5:12–15.
Medicine, Beatrice
1979   *Newsletter,* National Indian Education Association.
1981   Native American Resistance to Integration: Contemporary
       Confrontations and Religious Revitalization. *Plains Anthro-
       pologist* 26:277–86.
Mekeel, H. Scudder
1931   "Field notes Summer of 1931, White Clay District, Pine
       Ridge Reservation, South Dakota." Archives of the Depart-
       ment of Anthropology, American Museum of Natural History,
       New York.
Melody, Michael Edward
1976   The Lakota Sun Dance: A Composite View and Analysis.
       South Dakota History 6:433–55.
1978   Maka's Story: A Study of Lakota Cosmogony. *Journal of Ameri-
       can Folklore* 91:149–67.
Mooney, James

1896   The Ghost-Dance Religion and the Sioux Outbreak of 1890. *Fourteenth Annual Report of the Bureau of American Ethnology*, pt. 2.

Neihardt, John G.
1932   *Black Elk Speaks: Being the Life Story of a Holy Man of the Ogalala Sioux*. New York: William Morrow. New ed., Lincoln: University of Nebraska Press, 1961, 1979.
1951   *When the Tree Flowered: An Authentic Tale of the Old Sioux World*. New York: Macmillan.

Nurge, Ethel
1966   The Sioux Sun Dance in 1962. *Proceedings of the XXXVI International Congress of Americanists*, pp. 102–114.
————, ed.
1970   *The Modern Sioux: Social Systems and Reservation Culture*. Lincoln: University of Nebraska Press.

Olden, Sarah Emilia
1918   *The People of Tipi Sapa*. Milwaukee: Morehouse Publishing Co.

Pearce, Roy H.
1971   *Savagism and Civilization*. Baltimore: Johns Hopkins University Press.

Pommersheim, Frank
1976   *Broken Ground and Flowing Water*. Aberdeen, S. Dak.: Northern Plains Press.

Powers, William K.
1977   *Oglala Religion*. Lincoln: University of Nebraska Press.
1982   *Yuwipi: Vision and Experience in Oglala Ritual*. Lincoln: University of Nebraska Press.

Priest, Loring Benson
1942   *Uncle Sam's Stepchildren: The Reformation of United States Indian Policy, 1865–1887*. New Brunswick, N.J.: Rutgers University Press.

Prucha, Francis Paul, S.J.
1976   *American Indian Policy In Crisis: Christian Reformers and the Indian, 1865–1900*. Norman: University of Oklahoma Press.
1979   *The Churches and the Indian Schools, 1888–1912*. Lincoln: University of Nebraska Press.
1984   *The Great Father: The United States Government and the American Indian*. 2 vols. Lincoln: University of Nebraska Press.

Rahill, Peter

1953   *Catholic Indian Missions and Grant's Peace Policy*. Washington, D.C.: Catholic University Press.

Riggs, Stephen R.
1869   *Tah-koo Wah-kań; or, The Gospel Among the Dakotas*. Boston: Congregational Publishing Society.
1887   *Mary and I: Forty Years with the Sioux*. Enlarged ed., Boston: Congregational Sunday-School and Publishing Society.
1893   *Dakota Grammar, Texts, and Ethnography*. Edited by James Owen Dorsey. Contributions to North American Ethnology, vol. 9. Washington, D.C.: Government Printing Office.

Ruby, Robert H.
1955   *The Oglala Sioux*. New York: Vantage Press.

Schwatka, Frederick
1889–90 The Sun-Dance of the Sioux. Illustrated by Frederic Remington. *Century Magazine* 39:753–59.

Sisters of Saint Francis
1886–   "Notes from Saint Francis Mission, 1886–." Saint Francis Mission Papers, Marquette University Archives, Milwaukee, Wis.

Skinner, Alanson
1919   Notes on the Sun Dance of the Sisseton Dakota. *Anthropological Papers* (American Museum of Natural History), 16:381–85.

Smith, J. L.
1967   A Short History of the Sacred Calf Pipe of the Teton Dakota. *Museum News*, W. H. Over Museum, University of South Dakota, 28:1–37.
1970   The Sacred Calf Bundle: Its Effect on the Present Teton Dakota. *Plains Anthropologist* 15:87–93.

Sneve, Virginia Driving Hawk
1977   *That They May Have Life: The Episcopal Church in South Dakota 1859–1976*. New York: Seabury Press.

Society for the Preservation of the Faith Among Indian Children
[Ca. 1911]   "Appeal." Printed document in Archives of Saint Francis Mission, Saint Francis, S. Dak.

Spicer, Edward
1969   *A Short History of the Indians of the United States*. New York: D. Van Nostrand.

Stanley, Manfred, ed.
1972   *Social Development*. New York: Basic Books.

Stars, Ivan
Ca. 1915–20   Lakota texts. Manuscript. Saint Francis Mission

Papers, Marquette University Archives, Milwaukee, Wisc. Printed in Buechel (1978).

Steinmetz, Paul, S.J.

1969   Explanation of the Sacred Pipe as a Prayer Instrument. *Pine Ridge Research Bulletin* 10:20–25.

1970   The Relationship Between Plains Indian Religion and Christianity: A Priest's Viewpoint. *Plains Anthropologist* 15:83–86.

1980   *Pipe, Bible and Peyote Among the Oglala Lakota.* Stockholm Studies in Comparative Religion, vol. 19. Motala, Sweden: University of Stockholm.

Steltenkamp, Michael F.

1982   *The Sacred Vision: Native American Religion and Its Practice Today.* New York: Paulist Press.

Stephan, J. A.

1895   *The Bureau of Catholic Indian Missions, 1874 to 1895.* Washington, D.C.: Church News Publishing.

Stocking, George W., Jr.

1968   *Race, Culture and Evolution: Essays in the History of Anthropology.* New York: Free Press.

Stoltzman, William, S.J.

1986   *The Pipe and Christ.* Pine Ridge: Red Cloud Indian School.

Sword, George

Ca. 1909   Lakota texts. Manuscript. Archives of the Department of Anthropology, American Museum of Natural History, New York, and Colorado Historical Society, Denver. These manuscripts are currently being translated and edited for publication by Raymond J. DeMallie.

Thomas, Sidney J.

1941   A Sioux Medicine Bundle. *American Anthropologist* 43:605–609.

Trimble, Joseph E. and Susan S. Richardson

1983   Perceived personal and societal forms of locus of control measures among American Indians. *White Cloud Journal* 3:3–14.

Tyler, S. Lyman

1963   *A History of Indian Policy.* Washington, D.C.: U.S. Department of the Interior.

Tyon, Thomas

Ca. 1911   Lakota texts. Manuscript. Colorado Historical Society, Denver. Printed in Walker (1980):147–71.

Utley, Robert

1953   The Celebrated Peace Policy of General Grant. *North Dakota History* 20, no. 3:121–42.

Walker, James R.
1917   The Sun Dance and Other Ceremonies of the Oglala Division
       of the Teton Dakota. *Anthropological Papers* (American Mu-
       seum of Natural History), 16:50–221.
1980   *Lakota Belief and Ritual.* Edited by Raymond J. DeMallie
       and Elaine A. Jahner. Lincoln: University of Nebraska Press.
1982   *Lakota Society.* Edited by Raymond J. DeMallie. Lincoln:
       University of Nebraska Press.
1983   *Lakota Myth.* Edited by Elaine A. Jahner. Lincoln: Univer-
       sity of Nebraska Press.
Wallis, Wilson D.
1921   The Sun Dance of the Canadian Dakota. *Anthropological
       Papers* (American Museum of Natural History), 16:317–80.
1923   Beliefs and Tales of the Canadian Dakota. *Journal of Ameri-
       can Folk-Lore* 36:36–101.
Westropp, Henry, S.J.
1908   Catechist Among the Sioux. *Catholic Missions* 2:113–15.
[Ca. 1911]   *A Bit of Missionary Life.* St. Francis, S. Dak.: St. Francis
             Mission.
Willand, John
1964   *Lac Qui Parle and the Dakota Mission.* Madison, Minn.: Lac
       Qui Parle County Historical Society.
Wissler, Clark
1907   Some Dakota Myths. *Journal of American Folk-Lore* 20:
       121–31, 195–206.

Index

THE LIBRARY
ST. MARY'S COLLEGE OF MARYLAND
ST. MARY'S CITY, MARYLAND 20686